Advance Praise for AN IMPO:

"On the surface, AN IMPOSSIBLE DREAM STORY and the successful cross-country bike ride to benefit AIDS was Vince's personal proof point that he could overcome adversity and defy the odds. But for the reader, the true interest lies in peeling back the layers and discovering the vulnerability and core values that ultimately resulted in triumph and self-actualization. Why was Vince successful in the military? Why did he succeed in business leadership? Why did he succeed in his early family life and ultimately in his current intended life? Why did he fall and how did he pick himself back up again? Vince calls her Grace, but success comes from core values and serving others which will always lead him back to his intended life and make ours better."

~Ben Gibson~

Ben Gibson is VP of Business Development for Blue Heron Consulting and has over 25 years executive experience in Engineering, Marketing, and Business leadership.

~

"He fought an inner struggle for accepting himself. He fought a struggle to survive his youth. He fought as a soldier for his country abroad. He fought against an aggressive virus. He fought to make his dream come true. He fought against the elements of nature during his bike tour through the country. And in all these fights he became the winner, but the nation let him fall because he was gay and HIV-positive. This is an amazing story which shows us all the dark side of tolerance and freedom in the USA!"

~Lt. Johan Heine, Retired~

Johan Heine is a retired lieutenant in the Dutch army and is a Mental Health Care Nurse, specializing in PTSD. He is openly gay and former member of the board of the "SHK" (foundation for homosexuality and equal LGBT rights in the Dutch armed forces).

~

"An inspiring odyssey of self-discovery, AN IMPOSSIBLE DREAM STORY is starkly honest with poignant descriptions of love and loss. The story evokes real pathos as it portrays the bitter disappointments and jubilant triumphs of the main character—a gay man who suffers the prejudice of school kids, his parents, the wife he loves, the homophobic army he joins and the businesses he works for but still comes out a victorious. This book is a winner!"

~Kathryn Shay~ ~Author of THE PERFECT FAMILY~

Kathryn Shay has been a lifelong writer and teacher. She has published 42 novels from the Berkley Publishing Group, Harlequin Enterprises and Bold Strokes Books, and she has several online works featured. There are over 5 million copies of her books in print with an international distribution. Best known for her emotional and poignant stories, Kathryn has won five RT Book Reviews awards, four Golden Quills, four Holt Medallions, the

Foreword Book of the Year and the Bookseller's Best Award and several "Starred Reviews." Her work has been serialized in COSMOPOLITAN magazine and featured in THE WALL STREET JOURNAL and PEOPLE magazine. She lives in upstate New York with her husband and children.

~

"Part of AN IMPOSSIBLE DREAM STORY focuses on a bicycle tour. This tour is a metaphor for a journey all of us take in some form. Like a grand bicycle tour with its ups and downs, twists and turns, glorious sun and raging storms, we are taken on a journey of the author's life, and we are given insights into our own. A bike ride can be both trying and exhilarating, but somehow at the end something worthwhile is added to our life's experience. The same may be said after the reading of a good book such as this one."

~Reverend Neal Rzepkowski, MD~

Dr. Neal Rzepkowski earned a MD from SUNY Upstate Med University and SUNY Health Sciences Center, Syracuse, 1978. He also became an ordained Spiritualist minister, and is a registered medium in Lily Dale. As a certified and licensed medical doctor, his specialties include HIV Medicine and Family Practice with a holistic approach. As a spiritual leader, he began conducting sweat lodges in Lily Dale 15 years ago. He continues both practices today.

~

"AN IMPOSSIBLE DREAM STORY is just that –a gritty, heart-wrenching, no-holds-barred story of one remarkable, resilient life. Throughout the ups and downs of his life, Vinny Pirelli's courage, vulnerability, and strength come through loud and clear. If you're seeking to learn more about one gay male's journey, the beautiful and the painful experiences alike put AN IMPOSSIBLE DREAM STORY on your list. J.V. Petretta's well-written, gripping narrative reminds us that our stories are never finished. There is always grace and redemption ahead."

~Reverend Lee Ann Bryce~

Rev. Lee Ann Bryce is an ordained United Church of Christ minister. She is married and lives in Western New York.

~

"Vinny tells his rollercoaster story with passion and humor, inviting all of us to join his bicycle ride through the many winding paths of his life. Coming out, growing up, serving his country and fighting for others against all odds: This journey gives hope to anyone on the frontline of our equality struggle."

~Lt. Dan Choi~

Lt. Dan Choi is a West Point Graduate, Iraq War Veteran and Infantry Officer, honorably discharged for telling the truth and starting a group of West Point LGBT Graduates.

~

An Impossible Dream Story

J.V. Petretta

J.V. Petretta © February 15, 2011
West Henrietta, New York
Archismo1@yahoo.com

First published by Dog Ear Publishing
4010 W. 86th Street, Ste H
Indianapolis, IN 46268
www.dogearpublishing.net

ISBN: 978-145750-680-2

This book is printed on acid-free paper.

Printed in the United States of America

Dedication

For bicyclists, dog-lovers, dreamers, and angels in our midst: I love you all.

Foreword

He learned early on that life without a dream is not worth living, so Vinny dreamed big time, striving to live his life to the fullest. Pursuing that dream would take him on a raging whirlpool of life, slamming him often to the extreme outward fringes to be bashed and broken, only to be sucked back for more. You will follow his adventures from the humble beginnings of a three-room school house, to surviving childhood abuse, to tuberculosis, and through the perils of war—to become a leader and successful business and family man. You will meet the many loves of his life, one of which is peddling his bicycle to anywhere his mind and tired legs will take him. Then, you will witness his self-destruction, his fall to that lowly humble place called grace—to a point where there was nothing left but an impossible dream. All he wanted was to be somebody's hero.

~

This is *An Impossible Dream Story*, a work of fiction, songs, and poems inspired by many true events in my life. All portions of this story have been fictionalized, some to enhance understanding, some to lessen my own embarrassment, a few embellished to dramatize situations and a couple came out of thin air. As was true with the story line, so is it with characters, companies, and companions. Some public identities were fictitiously used in a clearly historical context. All other names have been changed, some intended to protect the innocent, a few altered to protect the guilty, a couple created from scratch, and the balance reinvented to be more interesting. In other words, this is a product of my imagination. By disclaimer, any resemblance of actual persons, living or dead, business establishments, events, or locales used in this book is purely coincidental.

Table of Contents:

Introduction

I t snowed last night, on Halloween. Although an early snowfall is hardly a phenomenon in Western New York, seeing snow almost two months before winter officially begins is not particularly welcomed. Though a treat to watch, the pups found the flurry of flakes a bit freaky, and Button, our Cavalier King Charles Spaniel, kept barking at the snow falling as if it were some ghastly trick. Trying his best to catch the falling stars, he seemed spooked by the flecks disappearing as they melted on the pavement or turned into tiny droplets upon his nose. He was named for the preferred button spot atop his head, noticed only after I said while holding him, "I don't know what to call you, but you're as cute as a button." Chouchou is our newest addition to the family, a Chihuahua-terrier mix, beautifully blessed with a colorful coat in perfect symmetry of caramel and coffee with an espresso streak down her back and bang-like tassels from the tips of her ears. With her raccoon eyes, grin-like jaw line and fox-like tail, she is one foxy gal. "Chou" (*Xiao/Qiao* in some Chinese dialects) can mean both dainty and smart, and possessing both physical traits, it is only appropriate that she be called Chouchou. Snow is anything but a treat for our delicate lady, already shivering inside her sweater.

~

As much as I love New York, I'm really not a snowbird. I've never once been snowboarding or skiing, haven't ice skated since my adult children were kids, and on my measly budget I can barely keep all-weather tires on the gramps-mobile, let alone afford a snowmobile. Though I appreciate four distinct seasons and adore the coming holidays, especially Thanksgiving, snow simply puts the kibosh on my sport of choice—bicycling. I planted roots here many years ago, however, and without sufficient means to travel to moderate climates during snow season (November through March), I reluctantly suspend my bike from rafter-hooks mounted in the garage two levels below

1

this apartment, as well as my warmest passion, for the long, cold winter ahead. Putting the bicycle up is a real challenge, and not just because I've aged well beyond my sixty-plus years. Yes, it is a struggle to dead-lift forty pounds of steel and rubber above my head, but I was referring to the difficult task of occupying my hours constructively without losing what little cycling stamina these tired, old legs defy.

Placing the bicycle in storage is, to me, tantamount to putting my dreams on hold. Neither does me much good during the dark, slumbering days of winter. These two things are so ingrained in me, *dreaming* and *biking*; it's as if there was a genetic imprint woven into this mystical, mad, mess of a man who goes by the name of Vinny. Bicycling and dreaming are as much a part of me as my family heritage, brownish-green eyes, balding head, pasta belly, and sexuality. Vincent Pirelli may as well have been bicycle bred with handle bars and ball bearings, nurtured by faith, and maintained with prayer.

There was never a time when I was not at least infatuated or outright in love with pumping peddles. My first vivid memory is of a TV character called Spanky on a tricycle of sorts. All the boys on television had bikes, including the boys on *Leave It to Beaver*, Jeff on *Lassie*, and *Dennis the Menace*. Hell, even Popeye once peddled his way to Olive Oyl's house and heart, and he was a sailor man. After all these years, I still mount the bicycle saddle with the same seriousness and splendid silliness I recall feeling the very first time my little-boy butt was hoisted upon a beautiful bike. I still eye my wheels with the same lust for life that I've always held; I still daydream the miles away.

There's something innocent and adventurous about cycling, getting to see and be part of nature as I cruise down the road avoiding gravel and stones, potholes (some filled with leaves), limbs, and road-kill blocking the path. A good body stretch to limber the legs helps reduce the early burn, but burn they will until the brain starts releasing endorphins about 15 minutes into the ride. By then, the saddle is at one with my backend as I lean forward, glancing through the upper lens. Euphoria takes hold as I click into high gears on a straightaway, always keeping a cadence of 60-70 peddle revolutions per minute until reaching a cruising speed of twenty-plus miles per hour, depending on wind direction and body-to-air resistance (and, in my case, age).

That's when the art of cycling slips from the conscious to subconscious state and daydreams are free to flourish. Every beam of light filtering through clouds and flickering through towering trees flashes new thoughts. Every scent, no matter how subtle, is breathed in to mesh with the thought process. Each wisp of air brings a new fragrance and climatic feel. Even beads of salty sweat bring a taste of life to the lips.

Instantly, I am six again, losing training wheels to know precious freedom for the first time. I become ten again, driving a pretend school bus, or showing off in a mustang at age twelve. I remember bicycle-cruising the girls at age fifteen or drift to a thought of teaching my own son the first joys of biking. I dream all the "what ifs" life has to offer, each with a lust and grandeur greater than the last.

I relive the hurts of long past as they mix with hopes of the future. I dredge up the losses in life, the times when my bicycles were left behind during yet another move. I recall working hard to replace those wheels with my own money, all while pledging to myself that *nobody* will ever again take them away. Then all the people I loved come to mind, all who loved me back, and all who didn't. I pine for the rabbits and dogs still missed after all these years. Tears form when I invoke thoughts of my son first tugging at my pant leg, wanting his daddy, or when my two-day-old daughter slept contently on my belly while her mom lay near death in the hospital. I smile when thinking of the times I bicycled with my grandchildren, proving we had something more than blood in common. I remember how I was thrilled when grandchild number nine let me hold her for the very first time without a fuss.

I am reminded of all my heroes growing up: Superman, Popeye, Ritchie Rich, Mom, Aunt Ruthe, David, "Pete the Bartender," and "Joe the Pharmacist." I hark back to schools and childhood buddies, college days and late-night bull sessions that were surely going to fix the entire world's ills; then a bomb explodes in my head and I find myself in Vietnam again. I mentally memorialize with gratitude the boy soldier who made it possible for me to still be biking this very day. I am overcome with rapture when I think of my most sacred of loves, of those which came to pass, and those that might have been, *if only*. In that mix is a never-ending love for cycling. There is no doubt in my mind that constant desire came from God. I am a daydream believer, but more than that, an unconventional achiever.

~

Suddenly, I find myself racking the bike for yet another season. I wonder how many people are joking about my stated plans to bicycle 2,500 miles when I reach the retirement age of 65. I am accustomed to contempt, emboldened by abuse, strengthened by others' insecurities; I know, just as sure as I feel the stabbing pain in my right knee each time I climb the 36 steps to this apartment that, if there is a way, I (Vinny) will indeed succeed! *An Impossible Dream Story* 2,500 will be the first known "bicycle-book tour" where I will be peddling miles, books, hope, and love.

As seasons turn into years, and years point to a lifetime, I have to wonder if, when, and where my own dream dies. Until then, I need to whip my ass back into shape, because I have forty pounds of early retirement to shuck, medical challenges to conquer, a book to finish and edit, a publisher to secure, and a whole lot of sponsors to convince. Even I admit that's a lot for a sixty-something-old man, who feels like he's going on a hundred.

Wait a minute! The sun is peeking through the snow clouds. It's going to be near fifty degrees today. Gee, that's almost summer—way too early to say so long to my newest two-wheeled "Dream Machine." If I hurry, I can get another thirty-five miles in, but I better consider long underwear. "God, please let me have some more biking days this year. Amen!" Oh, it feels like being six all over again. Look out world, Vinny's on a bike.

Vinny's Got a Bike

One of the expressions I learned early on that stuck with me habitually is *big time*, admitting that I use it more often than not when trying to describe, in adolescent terms, anything that exceeds normal expectations. "We got in trouble, *big time*" and "I was in love, *big time*" are two examples. It may have come from my cousin Clarence (Clip for short), a boy only a year older than me who possessed all the traits I wanted. He was never sick, never missed a day of school, always got straight *A*s, shined in every sport, had tons of brothers, and was a blue-eyed towhead with a smile that made him friend to everyone, even me. Clip was short on words: He'd give only the instruction "Do it this way," then he'd show me how the task was accomplished. So, if *big time* was okay with Clip, it was just fine with me.

Naturally, I can remember incidents prior to the first grade, but that is when life started coming together for me. Love at age six is a warm, fuzzy feeling of belonging, of being the focus of gleeful attention, of being happily surprised with that special something, and of eagerly looking forward to the future (which at that age is the very next morning). With no other delineation understood for love, it's probably what I felt for Clip. He certainly acted like my big brother whenever I was around, and I loved the thought of having one. Because he was the youngest of seven boys, I'm certain Clip enjoyed being a big brother, too, and teaching me to tie my laces, float in water, blow farts in the tub, and all those fun boy things. One time, Clip bicycled to my house on a Saturday. Oh, did he get in trouble; it was over a mile. Cousin Clip (at the age of seven) became my very first hero, Superman in the flesh.

Life for me was so full in the first grade. It was all I could do to stay out of trouble with my lifelong buddy, Jeff Borkman, "Mr. Late from recess" himself. My lateness once cost me a devastating trip to the corner. The shame of having to put one's nose in that ninety-degree angle for ten minutes is hell, almost beyond recovery. How could I ever live this one down in a community of first-graders, once friends, but now enemies, whose stares pierced both body and soul with daggers of hate, disgust, and invective?

Oh, the pain of it all! Then after lunch Jeff got caught slurping bubble gum, big time. At least I got to hide in the corner! Jeff's punishment paralleled the *Scarlet Letter* as the merciless Mrs. Adams made him stand at attention in front of the world's future rulers with pink bubble gum adhered to his nose. I chuckled as my friends taunted the pitiful, outcast "Bazooka Bandit." They'd already forgotten about my minor infraction with such a grand criminal among us. Oh, the pain of it all, yet it couldn't happen to a better guy!

I was sworn to secrecy, but after so many decades I cannot harbor it any longer. During our final recess that day, Jeff dared utter the foulest words against Mrs. Adams my virgin ears had ever heard: "God damn her!"

I loved the first grade. Life was so good; it was a happy time. We lived on Huffman Street in the prettiest old house. My best friend in the world, next to Jeff that is, was my Dad, and even though I wasn't a Jr. technically, I was Vinny Jr. for a long while. It's all in focus now, but how could I have known then that those were Dad's heydays (in other words, AA days)? Nobody ever told me that; I overheard it discussed between Dad and Uncle Bob Murray, whom Dad never really liked, but tolerated for the sake of Aunt Ruthe (Mom's sister) and peace in the family. Dad saw Uncle Bob as a swishy, wishy-washy pushover who pushed a broom at the Rambler Dealership while claiming to be a mechanic. On the other hand, Uncle Bob did operate his own lawn mower and bicycle repair shop as a sideline.

~

Fifty-one Huffman Street was quite an upgrade, having just moved from Liberty Park subdivision (you know, the WWII stick homes specifically built for the American Dream). In comparison, Huffman Street flaunted old oak trees, grass-trimmed sidewalks, Victorian-style lamp posts, and houses—big houses with big rooms, tall ceilings, fun bath tubs with legs, and brass-knobbed doors. It was the carved woodwork which spoke of the character and quality of this glorious home, in the historic town of Crown Point.

The bright sun was shining. It was always shining, even in winter. It meant nothing to me that our Huffman Street home was just a rental. It was *our* house for all I knew or cared; repossession of the Liberty "Park Place" had no significance in my mind. I didn't understand that Dad had drunk and gambled the house payments away, forcing foreclosure. All I knew was that this guy (a fearful monster at times) was really the best Dad any boy could hope for. He was my pal, my hero, and my life. No man could have loved a son more and no boy could have been more proud to be a junior. During that year Dad painted my room blue and put up a shelf for my "Wooden Man" (a handmade figure Dad cut out from hardened redwood). He took me to buy my first pair of blue jeans, enrolled and coached me in Little League, and built my most prized possession of all, a meticulously hand-crafted wooden toy box all my own.

Nobody had a greater box. It was Dad. It housed his love. It took weeks to build. Dad ventured to the cellar each night after work to continue his greatest creation yet. There was to be no skimping. It had to be perfect from hasp to hinges, from casters to countless coats of stain and varnish. It was presented in grand style, right down to my very first padlock and key. My sisters tattled each time I would sneak downstairs to spy on recent construction progress. Dad was teaching me patience, persistence, and pride. He knew I was sneaking glances, but I was convinced Dad knew everything. Instinctively he knew that every boy needs an element of privacy, ownership, and control. We needed our own rooms, soft balls, bats, gloves, electric trains, and lockable toy boxes to secure it all forever. Yes, I had it all—everything, including a Dad second to none. Everything, that is, except a bike.

Okay, I admit it! When you're the only son, you're supposed to be spoiled—not totally rotten, just pampered a bit. Dad wants it that way, and Mom—she can't help it! I was never a mama's boy per se, but I was her little man. No, I was Dad's boy, his biggest dream of all, and boys are supposed to have dream bikes. I had a trike as a kid, but now that I was big and six-years-old I needed my own two-wheeler. Unable to quite fit into the turtle races at Community Center, I had a better chance of ruling the pack on a bike, and it couldn't be just any bike. It had to be fire-engine red with clickers on the spokes and streamers from the handle grips—a boy's dream.

Then, one afternoon in April, it happened. It was Friday and sunny. It wasn't even my birthday when Uncle Bob arrived in his truck. What was on that truck? A bicycle, just exactly the way I dreamed of it—but wait! *Ohhh-hhh*, it had a kick stand and a bell. It had a real bell! I didn't know about those training wheels, but seemed to me I could lose them easy enough. Uncle Bob (who obviously had some mechanical ability) built this wonder at his repair shop in Hebron and sold it to Dad for ten bucks, supposedly the cost of parts. In 1958, that couldn't have been cheap.

"Thanks Mom. Thanks Dad. Thanks Uncle Bob. Thanks Sun." Look out world, the boy's mobile now, training wheels and all. It was freedom at its finest, no more walking to school. Would I be popular? Wow, I could ride to Little League. I couldn't wait to show Jeff. I could see it all. I felt special; I felt loved. I felt cocky and superior. I felt eager, motivated, and free to conquer the world. I felt all boy, worthy to be Dad's one-and-only junior—Mr. Hell on Wheels. Move over toy box, Vinny's got a bike!

Mama and Papa
(Melody and Lyrics: 1972)

V.1   Mama, Mama
The years are hinting gray
But may those precious years ahead
Be more fruitful everyday
And let there be no tears
To fall with bitter pain
But tears of happiness
Sweetly flow time and again

Chorus   Sunrise, make happiness
Every new day a pleasure
Bring not a day's distress
But memories to treasure

V.2   Papa, Papa
Your youthful days have gone
But as each sunset passes by
A better man lives on
A man with many a dream
A man of truth and pride
A complicated, simple man
With mountains of love hidden inside

V.3   Mama and Papa
Hard times have been around
But with strength and faith untold
Happiness, we've found
A loving, helping hand
Whenever I need call
Though Mama and Papa, you're parents good
You are my friends most of all

Repeat Chorus Twice

Racing for Roots

The year 1960 was one of mixed blessings for a boy already learning to mistrust home roots. Our family began preparation for yet another move, making Grandpa's house to be my fifth home in as many years. On one hand, life sported great hope for the future, yet the other was teaching me brutal lessons of losing friends and possessions. If I were forced to leave my buddies and bike behind, I would take with me the satisfaction of winning the race of my life.

~

Wagons come to mind when I think back to that time, all kinds and sizes of wagons. I daydream of the huge tractor-drawn wagon literally pulling tons of our town's people during my first ever hayride through the country roads of Leroy, Indiana. Not that Crown Point is any major metropolis, but Leroy (though only five miles in distance), by contrast, was a world away with population still under 200, counting us. While Kenny Foster (the local lover boy) strummed his guitar, nearly a quarter of the town harmonized "Daisy, Daisy," enjoying together the wagon sway while tossing hay in horse play. The thrilling ride ended at Verona's Dinette, which had become the town hub. In today's terms, it's where it was happenin'. Verona is my mother, hub of our family, a hard-working woman who never failed to open the grille by 0700 seven days a week. Juggling her many hats, she could be found still plugging away, keeping books, as late as midnight. We had moved to Leroy to fulfill Mom's dream of prosperity and independence. Always scraping to make ends meet, Verona's generosity showed no limits. She fed the poor (as if we weren't), contributed to all local events, and hand-dipped free ice-cream cones for Leroy's hay-riders.

Although the sign stated "Verona's Dinette," it was really the Pirelli Place, in that each of us children had part-time jobs. The girls did everything from waitressing to washing the floors the old-fashioned way, on hands and knees (no mops in Mom's place). I kept busy washing dishes, peeling potatoes, cleaning the tiny bathroom, or sorting pop bottles. Imagine what a task that was before the soda machine was invented. Each heavy wooden crate held 24 glass bottles; each bottle was designated exclusively for its own type of soda pop: Coca-Cola, Pepsi, Orange Crush, 7-Up, Squirt, and both Dad's Root Beer and Cream Soda. Bottle mixing was prohibited, and mixed crates would not get credit. It was before states charged bottle deposits (which Indiana still has yet to implement some 50+ years later), but stores and restaurants got 25-cents credit off their bill for each full, sorted case of empties, which bottlers then sterilized and re-used (hmm, sounds like an energy-saving possibility now). Since I didn't make tips like the girls, Mom usually gave me a nickel for each case I filled and hauled to a storage spot out back. I'd almost always get 50 cents or more, but on occasion, I could earn a whole dollar in a week. When I saved up enough nickels, dimes, and quarters, Mom would cash them for me. I would have spending money to buy a Cubs baseball cap or caps for my toy gun at *Bargain Town*, a discount store. Speaking of caps, I also salvaged bottle-caps and shared them with my buddies to toss, hit with our baseball bats, or use as wagers for dare and double-dare contests. Climbing trees, eating bugs, or exposing privates, what won't boys do on a dare?

~

Old wagon wheels propped together supported the mailbox of our three-classroom, red-brick schoolhouse. Mrs. "Educated" Edgingstone served both as the junior high teacher and principal. Mrs. Washburn ruled the first and second grades with outlandish, backward ways. Poor, cross-eyed, "four-eyed" Patty Strickland got held back a grade level because "Wicked" Washburn viewed her as slow. Why? Even after having her left hand tied down, she was unable to write with the *right* hand, her right hand.

My memories, however, revolve mostly around Mrs. "Headless" Header, nicknamed after the headless horseman of "The Legend of Sleepy Hollow," a story we first heard from her. I now appreciate her vast tutorial skills, ranging from art to music. This lady taught four grade levels in a single classroom, separating each by facing the desks in four directions. Every grade had distinct expectations, assignments, and blackboards, keeping us all occupied. Mrs. Header rotated around the room in wheel fashion, providing tasks and attention to all. It was Mrs. Header that brought adventure to learning, exposing this now third-grader to new experiences while internalizing a lasting competitive drive.

Dress-down Fridays were especially fun when all grade levels participated in combined projects, like playing my favorite spelling game called Hangman's Noose. (Each student making a spelling error had to place a line or circle on the chalkboard to fashion a stick-man being hung, then take a seat. When the man was fully hung, the last standing student was the winner.) My tomboy sister, Marci, just one year and rotation ahead of me, and I gained local fame by always being the last standing competitors in the big spelling bees. Marci invariably prevailed, never missing an opportunity to taunt me about it. Generally, class was released early on Fridays to support the softball team, prepare for family bingo night, practice for the Christmas concert, or rehearse our first stage play. I chuckle at the appropriateness of me being cast in the whimsical title role of Peter Pan. Gee, what did Mrs. Header know that I didn't? She certainly was adamant that boys be *boys*, right down to teaching us the *art* of boxing. I liked, no, loved being pitted against Tom "Pansy" Morgan, just as I disliked, no, despised getting knocked on my ass by Bobby Ross. Speaking of asses, mine belonged to Mrs. Header when I earned shame and three swats of the infamous paddle for cheating on the multiplication tables, but I learned! Everyone in the school, at one time or another, memorized her words: "This is going to hurt me more than you." How little did this educated wonder know?

Science, history, and geography captured my interests as "Headless" told stories of small pox, President Eisenhower, and a tremendous redwood tree in California that was so big that cars could actually drive through it. While daydreaming, I must have bicycled through that tree a thousand times then, and countless times over the years. If only I could see that redwood in my pretend car . . .

Like most boys, I also loved cars, except Station wagons, which still leave an eerie feeling in my gut from two experiences. First, there was the Ross Family Ford Wagon. It was being fueled up at our local Mobil dealer, a dilapidated, roof-extended, two-pump gas station that showed age even in 1959. Crammed with kids' faces to the windows, seven in all, the small box in back made eight. It held the dead body of the eldest, but infant-like son, who was twenty-one. The Ross family was departing for Kentucky to bury their boy in the family cemetery. I heard it said, "This passing is a blessing in disguise." It was my first close-up acquaintance with death. I peered quietly from the dinette window across the street, sad and sorry, but haunted none the less. The jukebox blared out "Yellow Polka Dot Bikini" while truckers sang along. The aroma of coffee and chocolate-covered doughnuts sweetened the room, but nothing could divert my attention from that box.

My second visualization of death came from another station wagon parked a block away at Cole's Union 76 Filling Station and General Store. It was an abandoned antique ambulance that Tom Cole (one of three sons) scrounged up for conversion into a stock car. Our house was one of Cole's rental properties; the backyard meshed with their junkyard. Tom had wrecked his Hudson, race car #11, and needed this replacement to compete with his kid brother Larry, who raced #2, a Ford Model-T, on the dirt track at Broadway Speedway, a racetrack often dominated by four baby-blue coupes representing father & sons. Every day became Saturday night to this boy as Tom allowed me to grasp the wheel, playing "pretend driver" in his prized junk. My mind raced through time, hitting the pedals, shifting the gears, and honking the horn, all while leading the pack, of course. The keys remained dangling from the ignition. Easily fascinated, I liked keys, too. They were mystical and magical to me.

Always inquisitive, I investigated the ambulance tailgate. Sure enough, it unlocked and opened, but what's this—compartments? Yes, they extended from the protruding wheel wells on both sides all the way to the rear hatch door. They were locked, but wow, what a great find. I continued exploring, trying each key. "Success" was often followed by "Shit!" (This expression I learned from Tom Cole, no doubt.) The first bin was empty. I couldn't be disappointed. "Please oh please God, let there be something in the other," I prayed. "Finders Keepers" ran through my mind when I found a black metal first-aid kit, complete with all the essentials for playing Doctor—even "*blooooood!*" "*Oooie!*" There was splattered old blood all over the case and compartment. With vivid imagination, I could see the entire scenario . . . *Squeal! Smack! Splat!* . . . Sudden and sure death! From horror to hallucination, I panicked—big time. I fled the scary scene, but I couldn't manage to run from those images in my mind of countless, broken, bleeding bodies, of seeing death first hand, and of the boy in a box. That mental fixation kept me sleepless many nights.

Other nights lying awake were spent missing my little sister Sandi. Though she was four years younger, we had grown close during my visits to Hebron where Sandi lived with Aunt Ruthe and Uncle Bob until school age. During the daytime, we played our live version of Clue on the upper abandoned floor of their green, three-story house. The seldom-used top level, complete with a rickety, narrow, and steep staircase, housed secret trap doors and tunnels linking closets of one bedroom to another. It was also Uncle Bob's secret weapon to quiet little brats at night: "I'm telling you one last time to be still, or you can sleep in the attic with the bats that come out at midnight!"

~

Independence Day had always been a major hometown celebration in Hebron, complete with an all-day picnic and carnival and the annual parade, second only to the "biggies" on TV. This was a time of grand parades, when pomp and spirits flourished. There were marching bands, old cars, scout troops, Legionnaires, teams of bicyclists (my favorite), fire trucks afire with lights and sirens, horse riders, and wagons—many wagons, big and small, each tossing coins, balloons, and bubble gum. Great floats danced atop huge wagons while Sandi and I rode on a smaller version produced by the American Legion Ladies Auxiliary. We must have been cute, depicting the story riddle-rhyme "Peter, Peter, Pumpkin Eater" as we waved proudly from our bigger-than-life papier-mâché' pumpkin that was hollowed to house "sickening-sweet" Sandi. I recall being mildly, no, horribly jealous when Sandi got the recognition and ribbon, but even I realized what a cutie-pie she was, so perfectly perched from the pumpkin's port hole.

Oh, how I missed my baby sister. I didn't understand why she had to be so far away, six whole miles. I cried, oh so softly—something I knew boys shouldn't do. In time, I would drift off to sleep, thinking about my next visit, or next year's parade of wagons.

~

The one wagon which enraged me was the High Flier red wagon Doug Morgan tried to disguise as a soapbox during our Spring Derby. Here, the rest of the town's boys worked diligently for days, each building competitive creations. My pal Jeff Borkman (whose family also moved to Leroy) and his older brother teamed up to build a long, sleek, red box they appropriately labeled "Hot Dog." Doug, that ruddy, red-headed, freckled boy, and his little brother naturally had a devilish black box. We all believed they were devils, because they were from the only Christian Science family around (a religion the town found freakish) and we all believed the boys to be nothing less than "Satan's Sons." Yes, black was necessary (at least back in the day, when black and white still represented evil and good). Bobby, the best looking of the Ross boys, whom my sister Marci had a crush on, arrived with his slick blue soapbox, a vortex version which pushed its way through the group. I didn't have a brother, but tried with all my might to build a functional machine pieced together from old two-by-fours and buggy wheels donated by Marci. After completion, I held a trial run down the big hill of our front yard. It ended halfway down in a jackknife, ripping off the wooden front axle, warping both spikes holding on the rear wheels, and putting a rusty nail into my kneecap. This time, I had an excuse to cry, only more from frustration and shame than injury.

David Wade, a big high schooler, witnessed the devastation as he walked toward Cole's Store. Unlike the other townsfolk, David seemed to be mature and educated, definitely among Leroy's "upper crust." Genuinely friendly and helpful, and being the only boy in his family, David knew my predicament. Without hesitation, he patched things up—first me, then my mess.

Revisions to Vinny's Junk included two metal axles, yet it was this boy's confidence which David strengthened even harder than steel. I was ready and eager!

On race day, all the boys showed up at Cole's Hill (my front yard) eager to take the prizes, a used ball & bat donated by Larry Cole, who was still acting like one of the boys, never wanting to grow up. Even before it occurred, I predicted Jeff would pounce on Doug Morgan. Tom, too chicken to fight, ran "*wee, wee, wee* all the way home," pulling their wimpy wagon. Doug soon followed with a bloody nose. Guess that meant they were disqualified. I never liked the Morgan Boys, those big fat cheaters. We always called them "queers," even though I didn't know what queer meant. I don't recall the method used in determining the winners, only that we took several individual turns rolling down the soapbox slope. It was an all-Saturday-morning affair, yielding several winners for sure. The Morgan boys got what they deserved. Jeff walked away with his "new" old bat. I walked away head high because my silly soapbox made it down the hill in one piece, earning me the ball. David, my hero, won the admiration and respect of a boy who tried to believe he now had a brother.

~

There was another wagon to agonize over, the biggest of all—the one my dad fell off. It came with the same crashing force as the new green (and now totaled) Edsel had when the tree jumped in Dad's way. Though he always managed to escape harm, we family members were never as lucky. When Dad slipped, we went off balance. When Dad fell, we went down. When Dad hit bottom, we were hurt—literally. He was two separate men in one body, as good and bad as the black and white tiles he carefully checkered the diner floor with. On the upside, Dad could be as warm as Sniffles and Wiggles, the white angora and brown spotted rabbits he gave me; as strong as the two-storied cage he built for them; as patriotic as JFK's "Ask Not" speech; as mellow as George, our German Shepherd; as complex as my first Erector Set; as phenomenal as our first transistor radio; as full of promise as the song "Telstar"; and as humorous as the jukebox playing "They're Coming to Take Me Away, Ha, Ha."

On his downside, even filthy jokes couldn't ease the terror of four kids knowing Dad would be home soon, but not knowing which of us would be on his "shit list." Dad sought out infractions to vent his fury upon: a dirty dish, a wrinkled bedspread or perhaps a trace of dust on the TV. We had become Dad's animals, in his own wild kingdom, often demanding that we crawl and beg for mercy. What was his idea of mercy? That meant getting belt welts, hair holds, cruel kicks or nasty names like "Sissy," "Pissy," "Piggy" or "Ubangi Lips," but just getting it over with. More severe punishments took the form of things which are the lowest: eating dinner without utensils from a bowl on the floor, scrubbing floors with our own toothbrushes, scraping black tar (which oozed from Dad's rotten tile job in the diner), or sitting for hours kneeled on broken linoleum, knees over knuckles, until they, too, were black and oozing—but always, always on the floor.

Mom didn't escape Dad's wrath, either. Just off the kitchen was a tiny walk-in closet with curtains for a door. From this, my converted bedroom, I often woke up overhearing Mom slave at the ironing board. Frequently, Dad would come in from his drunken poker parties he held in the diner after closing to harass Mom one last time for the day. It was *her* fault the diner was losing money, or he saw her smile while serving pie and coffee to some trucker. At any rate, "You make me drink," was always Dad's excuse for smacking her hard a couple of times.

"Please Vince, you'll wake the kids," Mom pleaded through her tired tears. Shaking and needing to pee, I pulled the blankets over my head to muffle Mom's misery. I knew better than get up. In time, it would be dark, quiet, and safe enough for me to sneak to the toilet; I just couldn't make noise flushing.

~

Overhearing those late night episodes, I may have been the first sibling to know the one element of truth exposed: Verona's Dinette was doomed to die. It came as no great surprise to me that Mom would soon announce the sale of our diner, her new job at the Merrillville Wagon Wheel Restaurant, and our pending move back to Crown Point to live with Grandpa. Divorce of my parents seemed inevitable, but Sharon's dramatics (typical of the eldest) of blaming herself kept our splintered family together—all except Sandi, the lucky one.

"Cool," was Jeff Borkman's response when I informed him of my move, and for good reason. His dad had purchased the house across from Small's Dairy in Crown Point, a move upward for Jeff. We would be only blocks apart, but, unfortunately, in different school districts. However, unlike Jeff, I was being asked to leave my bike behind. Mom said I had outgrown it, and could get another next spring. But of all people to inherit my red roller, why did it have to be the red-headed devil worshiper? My fluffy friends, Sniffles and Wiggles, were also promised away by Dad, citing some arbitrary law which didn't permit wild animals in the city. My rabbits weren't wild! They were trained to walk with me on a leash, to play ball in the yard, and pray before supper—even if I had to help them. I knew they understood, just as I'm absolutely certain they talked with me. They cried when I told them; they would miss me. Still, how could I have expected to keep these newest additions to the family? After all, Sandi was given away, and everyone could hear her talk.

[In a conversation with Sharon some fifty years later, I learned my rabbits were never given away, but slaughtered for dinner. Sharon asked in disbelief "Don't you remember asking Dad what kind of chicken this was and him replying, 'the four-legged kind?'" Strangely, I did recall the incident. Now I wonder if I didn't fully understand, or if I mentally blocked out the obvious. Either way, I needed that truth to wait.]

As David Wade pitched hay for the horses in his barn, he listened to my sobs and troubles. Trying to cheer me up, we mounted a single horse to stroll a one-eighth mile dirt track surrounded by a white picket corral fence. (A white picket fence was Mom's certainty of their upper-class situation.) I straddled the saddle post end, crunching my baby balls, but that didn't matter. Secretly, I felt secure and comforted as David's strong arms wrapped around me to rule the reigns. Why couldn't I have a big brother? At that moment, I felt loved—and in love with my idol.

"Vinny, I have an idea," David said with an air of confidence in his voice. "Let's hold a bicycle race on this track."

"Wow," I returned. "What a great idea!" I didn't know what *sex* was, but I knew this had to be better. Perhaps I was "Sissy" to Dad, but David knew me better than anyone, except for Jeff and the rabbits, of course. I was "wheel wise," a bad-assed, ball bustin' brutal boy on a bike! We would prove who the *real* mud master is! Temporarily at least, my troubles of tomorrow were overcast by thunderous thoughts of greatness and glory. This would be my last chance to leave Leroy with a legacy.

David planned an after-school race, and the weather couldn't have cooperated more. Although pits of mud were present from previous rain, most of the track was dry and dusty. All the boys were permitted three trial laps to acquaint themselves with the rugged road. They were all there—even "Red from Hell", who could hardly wait to inherit my bike. Too bad he couldn't race, but it was still *my* bike until I moved. David officiated, having borrowed genuine flags from the biggest boy of all, Larry Cole. Tom Morgan wouldn't risk scratching his girlish-green bike, or his knees for that matter, opting to sit his fat butt out. Sam Peron, a fifth grader, borrowed his sister's rusty road hog to make sure we had enough racers. Peer pressure prevented anyone else from precluding participation.

Rules were read. Riders were ready. Forty laps, a total of five miles, and the winner would take home a lucky horseshoe. "Gentlemen, start your engines," David shouted from his school bull horn, and we boys instinctively made rumble sounds in unison, revving our engines. Time trials had placed me in row three, outside, being one of the fastest. Opposite from authentic races, David's rules fairly granted the disadvantaged a leading edge and placement on the track. Down came the green flag.

As we simultaneously peeled out, dust formed a choking cloud aimed for the tail-end bikers. With only one lap complete, already the caution flag flew. Two riders lost vision from dirt in their eyes. I was one. In fairness, David started lap two from initial placement, imposing a rule disqualifying any biker who initially dug dirt, because that was playing dirty. With a second, but successful start, it didn't take long to reveal the leader of the pack. I couldn't believe it—Doug Morgan of all butt holes. *Thump! Crash! Ouch!* "Yes," I thought as Doug "the Dud" dumped his bike *big time*. He was out. There was no way that pansy would regain competitive confidence. Spectators were comprised of our sisters, who not only cheered us on, but counted laps for each of the bikers.

Battling to be boss, my primary focus was to outmaneuver Jeff and Sam. The rest of the miserable lot lagged behind. With ruthless ambition, one by one I passed the pack by high-banking turns while leaning dangerously left, using centrifugal force in my favor. There was no pavement, just pitfalls, potholes and mud-sli-*i-i-des*. *Screech! Clink! Clank! Crumble! Unh!* Red flag!

Someone announced, "Wow, there goes Vinny, flipping the fence."

"He's okay," another squealed, "but oh my God, look at his bike!"

"Shit!" I screamed when witnessing a warped wheel. Now what? My bubble had just busted with seven laps to go. Devastated, I yelled while kicking dirt at my broken bike, "I'm alright, David!" But David knew the situation was anything but right.

Then, in a just ruling (slanted in my favor), my hero said it wasn't the bike but the biker who could win the race. He then suckered my second sister, Paula, also known as "Piggy" to let me use her ugly gray bicycle to reenter the race. Thank God there was no upper bar, because my little legs permitted no such provision. As it was, the seat poked into my spine about midway, making no means for momentarily resting on my rear. Barely seeing over the mammoth basket in front of me, I clung to the broad handlebars for dear life as the race resumed. Having achieved front position before the accident, I held front spot at restart.

I don't know if it was my damned determination, or perhaps the weird way I wobbled Paula's two-wheeled wagon, but no one dared devour my lead. *White* was waving, signaling one lap to go. Gone were my wrecked red bike, and rabbits, but Dad couldn't take away this moment. I had survived the checkered floor to gain this gut-wrenching checkered-flagged glory. Victory was even sweeter than the lime Kool-Aid Mrs. Wade served. I smiled, holding my horseshoe, leaving everyone else green with envy.

~

How can such a little town make such a big impact on one's life? Leaving Leroy meant leaving the brotherhood of friends. Little could be worse, except that I would also be leaving behind David, my "make-believe" big brother. When the last box was loaded onto one of Cole's trucks for our move to Crown Point, Dad's work animals (us kids) were loaded like cattle onto the open back of the pickup truck as well.

I don't recall the town's women folk coming out to say goodbye, but by golly, the boys were all there, lined up, linking arms in protest of losing one of their own. Then I heard the leader, David Wade, shout, "Vinny Pirelli, you remember us, you hear?"

Yes David, I heard you; I will never forget my big brother. I will forever long to be back in Leroy, racing for my rugged roots.

Memories of Home
(Melody & Lyrics: 1971)

V.1   In the morning of the day
     A pleasant thought passes my way
     A thought that carries me back home
     To a life from which I've come

Chorus   Memories of home
     The only place where I belong
     All the joy, all the life that I have known
     Memories of home
     Dance to the tune of a magical song
     In my mind, when I find I'm all alone
     With memories of home

V.2   And in the evening of the day
     Again, my mind begins to stray
     Thinking not of what's to come
     But memories of where I'm from

Repeat Chorus Twice

Lonely Roads

Autumn of 1961 was particularly bitter as seen from the eyes of a nine-year-old boy growing up among seven girls on an Indiana Farm. Granted, Mom plus four sisters does not total seven, however Robyn and Sheila are included. They were two of the countless Fox children from the shack a half mile down Old U.S. Route 30 in Merrillville, Indiana. Dad had rescued them from a pot-bellied shanty comprised of three walls and a Pepsi-Cola sign. The girl's parents were dad's fellow alcoholics from the local watering hole. Unlike my sisters, I resented taking them in, not from childhood greed, but strictly from a fairness point of view. With my sister Sandi back home, why did we need more girls? What could females offer the family that boys couldn't? Not that being an only boy didn't have its advantages—it did. Regardless of the number of girls, my status warranted a private room—a place to shelter myself from the torment of more "Sissy" jeers by everyone except Mom. Though I was seldom pampered, Mom did devote more than equal time to my development. It was exclusive time where I learned both useful skills and a sense of responsibility that is still with me today.

Our three acres of farm/playground hosted barns, coops, and a variety of gardens. During the summer, my tiny hands grew green thumbs as I helped plant, prune, weed, and harvest, then can and freeze an endless array of fruits and vegetables. Beyond gardens, there were several varieties of fruit and nut trees, strawberry patches, and Concord grape vines. Surrounding them all was a mass of grass the boy of the house assumed independent responsibility for. Bruised, blistered, and bleeding hands gave way to calluses in time as I force-pushed the manual reel mower almost daily to keep up with this never-ending chore. To gain Dad's acceptance and Mom's praise, I practiced attention to detail by hand trimming the stone sidewalks, trees, fences, and foundations of every structure. Hard to believe today, but we rented all of this and more from Old Man Phillips of Crown Point for a mere fifty dollars per month. However, with so many mouths to feed and girls to groom, that amount must have seemed a fortune to Mom.

I didn't require much, having learned to pay my own way. Mom helped me set up a small road-side stand to peddle some of our bounty, including corn, tomatoes, onions, peppers, melons and, of course, Kool-Aid. She always paid me ten percent of gross and taught me to spend it wisely. In time, I had earned fifteen dollars for another used bicycle from Uncle Bob. This one, though perfect in size, arrived without a spruce up. Carefully, I painted it black with some old paint found in the washhouse. Three years had passed since the promise of getting another bike "next spring" was made. Relying on *me* was the greatest lesson I could learn. From bee stings while picking strawberries to the burning sting of raw palms, I learned indeed to count on me. This time I bought my own bike, and *nobody* would ever take it from me!

~

With no heart to replace the rabbits, our folks permitted an accumulation of pets including countless cats, several dogs, four pigeons, three hamsters, two chickens, and one each lamb and goat. (Were you singing ". . . and a Partridge in a pear tree"?) Marci and I took turns caring for them, making homes for all in barns, chicken coops, and the old milk house, complete with wind mill. I recall using many of the food staples provided by Welfare to nourish the lot, reserving powdered milk for the cats, oatmeal for the dogs, cooked rice and cornmeal for the remaining creatures. The lamb ate fresh grass until its belly exploded; the goat ate everything else in sight, including toys left unattended. I haven't mentioned the pig because it lasted only one day. Instead of being fed, it became part of the food chain for our Labor Day pig roast and family reunion. I will never forget that pig. My friend Wally (son of another of Dad's drinking buddies) and I were responsible for keeping the fire burning overnight to ensure the pig was completely roasted by the time company arrived for our picnic. The tiny bag of charcoal Dad bought didn't last long.

"I know, Wally; I'll get a bucket of coal from the washhouse."

"It doesn't look the same. Are you sure it will work?"

"Wally, coal is coal; it's black and it burns."

I ignored Wally's reply, that this coal had a different smell, like kerosene. It was a very dark night; as the sun began to rise, I noticed that this pig was not golden brown, the way Dad had explained. It was *coal* black! Never was there a better way to be on Dad's black list. Well, at least Dad had a good drunken story to tell.

~

Prior to Welfare, Vincenzo Pirelli (Dad) was employed by EJ&E Railroad in Gary and Mom had trained to become a union meat cutter for a large supermarket in Highland, Indiana. As luck would have it, Dad worked nights, coming home just after Mom departed for work in the morning. We kids didn't care during school season, but summer was hell. Always brutal, Dad made his daily marks on us physically and mentally until Mom returned near dinner time. Our saving grace was when Dad went off to the tavern to escape his hell: us, the bigger animals that ate spam and potato pancakes.

Things changed one morning when instead of coming home from work, Dad drove to the hospital, believing he was having a heart attack. An Emergency Room physician determined he suffered from an advanced case of tuberculosis. It didn't take long for financially tough times to become unbearable. With Dad now unable to work, Welfare took the Fox girls just before the Board of Health took Mom's job. Creditors took the car and almost everyone in the relation, except Aunt Ruthe, took a hike. We had become "untouchable" due to the stigma of this contagious disease. Everyone treated us like outcasts, with the exception of deliberate displays of charity by "do-gooders" intended more to humiliate than help, a lesson I wouldn't learn until Christmas.

Already intimidated by the opposite sex, I grew more introverted from the invisible "untouchable" label branded upon my brow. I needed someone to talk to—a brother, a pal. I missed my old friends from Leroy, especially David Wade, and I frequently daydreamed about the times he would hold and hug me. I loved Tina and Trixy, my two mutts, but they didn't seem to communicate like the rabbits. The one and only time I spoke of my loneliness with Mom, she quickly dismissed the subject by reminding me that my cousin Clarence (Clip) had to grow up without a father, who was killed cleaning a rifle. I thought about Clip's situation in depth and quickly became jealous of him. Poor Clip had several big brothers and a couple of uncles, who all focused on providing him with proper male supervision. Nobody except me recognized that I, too, was growing up without a father. Mom, instead, got me enrolled in the local Boy Scout troop, which I wholly enjoyed. I grew; I was accepted. Yet the two-hour weekly meetings and periodic jamborees didn't adequately supplement the void of boyhood left behind in Leroy. If I wanted playmates, I had to choose among "jacks" with "Big Lips" Sharon, "skip rope" with "Piggy" Paula, "artsy" things with "Pissy" Marci, or playing "house" with "Sissy." Oh, that's right, "Sickening Sweet" Sandi was perfect; I was "Sissy"! If I needed to talk, it waited until laundry day when Mom and I orchestrated the massive washhouse operation. We pretended it was a boy's job to help, and in fact it required both skill and muscle to handle the antique manual wringer-roller-type washer with separate galvanized rinse tubs. During fair weather, we hauled our loads to dry on lines strung across the yard. Inclement weather necessitated organizing the washhouse to dry clothes by means of a coal-operated stove—yes, the same coal used for the pig. One big laundry day, the temperature dropped below freezing and all the wet ware froze on the line. I was flabbergasted, unsure what action to take. Mom wasn't, she knew what to do. "Just leave 'em Butch, they'll freeze-dry overnight. We'll pull 'em off in the morning." I beamed when Mom called me "Butch"; it bolstered my ego beyond anything else. I would carry that masculine feeling to bed at night, and I would fall asleep with a smile. I wasn't a "Sissy"; I was Mom's "Butch" boy, yeah!

Looking back, perhaps Mom did recognize my need for male companionship when she recommended that I tag along with Sharon. She babysat for the Sims' children in Highland, a lady friend of Mom's that still worked as a butcher. Stanley was two years my senior, and made no bones about being the boss. Grateful for a new pal, I presented myself as a most compatible friend. I didn't learn much from him, except what he called "Special Boy Games" which took place only in locked bathrooms, barns (when he visited me) or in bed. Viewing Stanley as wise, I naturally followed his lead.

From my only father-son outing, a fishing experience at Willow Slough, I thought Stan's games might be taboo. Most of Dad's repeated lecture during that trip focused on what men cannot do. But Stan's games didn't seem to fall into the *sex* category as explained by Dad, so I was safe. Sex was something one did with girls, and I wasn't about to have sex with Stanley; only "beat the meat." But in case I was wrong, I thought it best not to mention those times to Dad. I giggled from a ticklish "winky" as we took turns tying each other up, then playing until we couldn't take any more. Always promising not to pee, I was certain Stanley did anyway. I would get mad and quit—just take my balls and run.

~

Dad had been gone two months already to Paramore, a sanitarium for tuberculosis victims, when Mom became a full-time mother, striving to feed the masses of anxious young faces all at the dinner table. I don't think we lacked enough food to go around, but I recall the last piece of Spam, the last pancake, or the last helping of potatoes which no one dared to take, pretending they were all full. Often times, Sharon would say, "Give it to Vinny. After all, he's a growing boy." Always hungry, always guilty, I ate the last.

Dad cultivated a new craft while recuperating. Carefully and skillfully bending coat hangers into skeletal shapes of animals, he later tied on dozens of yarn pompoms to create toy dogs that truly resembled poodles. With black button eyes and red felt tongues, he dressed them as clowns, horses, and ballerinas. As his first and only handicraft other than crude carpentry, Dad was rightfully proud to the point that one could visualize a sense of new life emitting from this healing soul. He often boasted that there could be a market for such talent. Viewing his now sober smile, I believed him, and soon in mass production, Dad's creations became a menagerie of poodles in every color and dress combination imaginable. I chose to make his marketing idea real, something nobody expected from "Sissy."

I cannot forget the cold—so much that my ears burned on an uncommonly early frigid day. Unable to afford gloves, I removed the stockings from my hands just inside Mrs. Evans's door in an effort to open the beat-up, black briefcase which housed two of Dad's prized dogs. While bicycling there, I rehearsed my lines like a fervent prayer, one that God perhaps heard? I recited the plight of my family and desire to help by selling poodle pups, "each made from streams of yarn and love." Promising to have one delivered within two weeks, I wanted to cry, to run, or to do anything except ask for the ten bucks it would cost to purchase one. Then as my young heart raced to a stop, I heard Mrs. Evans say "Yes, I would love to buy one—in green." That was the beginning of many successful sales, all because I believed: in Dad again, in God, in our family, and in Mrs. Evans. For the first time in a very long time, I believed in myself.

Upon returning home, I found the girls already seated around the red enamel table eager to learn of my adventures. Mom was sniffling over the hot stove as I pulled the crunched up ten-dollar bill from my jeans pocket. She didn't talk much, and supper was unusually quiet that night. I guiltlessly ate the last helping of potatoes, which filled not only my belly, but Mom's heart.

Several months after Dad's hospitalization, Marci was admitted to the hospital for tubercular pneumonia. A month later, it was my turn with a TB form of pleurisy. Confined to the hospital for months, Marci and I became ever so close. Her room was one over and one up from mine. I was fortunate to become among the first ever to attend school by telephonic means called "Intercom" to Merrillville Junior High where students carried the plug-in amplifier to each of my classes. Marci, on the other hand, barely had the strength to communicate with me and missed a year of school. Risking her health, she devised a message system by dangling bags tied to yarn, then swinging it to my window. Frequently getting caught, we passed notes, candy, toys or *Superman, Archie* and *Little Lulu* comic books, always ignoring our scolding. Knowing we would soon be in the same grade, Marci and I, by choice, become fraternal twins, a natural bond for two middle kids who even looked alike—one a Tomboy, the other a Sissy. This bond only strengthened as we grew older.

Peter, a bartender from Hammond, was a fellow "inmate" of Paramore and precious friend of the family. Always wanting a son, Pete and I grew into hospital chums. He spoiled me rotten with model cars, candy, and immense attention. Within weeks, I had learned every poker game there was, including "how to bluff the old buggers," and how to master thousand-piece puzzles in a hurry. During periods of isolation, I remained in tune with the world thanks to a special gift from Pete—my own transistor radio. I often listened through a neat device they called an "earphone" so that my class did not hear the radio blasting *Deep Purple (Dreams)* by Nino Tempo and April Stevens and other favorites on WLS Radio from Chicago.

~

Then, on November 22, I heard an announcement, "This is a Special Report from ABC Radio News: President Kennedy has been shot. I repeat President Kennedy has been shot in Dallas, Texas." I unplugged the earphone and let the AM radio blast into the intercom. At first, kids giggled at my naughtiness, followed by a warning from Mrs. Neilson. Before long, I heard shouting and crying, "Oh my God, President Kennedy has been shot. Class, let's bow our heads and pray for our President." Then, except for sobs and sniffs, the room fell quiet; I let the radio continue the announcements that President John Fitzgerald Kennedy was declared dead. Not just the music, but the world stopped.

Like everyone else, I wept and mourned through the loss of President Kennedy, a genuine shock to America, only to soon be over-shadowed by even bigger news: "The Beatles are coming!" Caught up in Beatle-mania, I forced Pete to listen to my one-strum version of *I Want to Hold Your Hand* on a country guitar, my newest hobby thanks to the instrument Pete picked up from Woolworths at Christmas. I also "ooed" and "ahed" each time a Mustang (the hottest car ever to cause a craze) would drive by the hospital, and told Pete of my bicycle fantasies—that I was cruising in my black Mustang convertible. I told him how I pretended to drive through this tree in California, big as a house. Pete would laugh. Pete, the bartender (whom I never saw take a drink) might well have been the kindest man I ever knew, with never a smidgeon of "want" for himself, except perhaps to have had a son of his own. I loved my adopted dad fiercely.

The four of us were permitted to go home for Christmas week (Marci, me, Dad & Pete). Two of the church ladies stopped by with a plate of cookies, telling Mom to "keep the plate, you understand." Even though we all wore protective masks, the women kept to the opposite end of the room and wouldn't even sit down. After about ten visibly uncomfortable minutes, they wished the family a Merry Christmas and promised to pray for us. I could see

Dad's phony smile, even behind his mask, as he also wished them a Happy New Year. The very second the door shut, Dad spouted a truth that sticks with me yet today, "In other words, you won't do a Goddamn thing to help! Kids," and now mocking, "anybody can say 'we'll pray for you', but prayers, with maybe a five-dollar bill, might do somebody some Goddamn good. Like *Hell*, you'll pray for me!"

~

Getting to go home in May of 1964 was a spectacular twelfth birthday gift. With Marci still in the hospital and the other girls all in school, I dug out my old bike, pumped the tires, and off I rode, enjoying splendid freedom again. I could feel bright life shining down to warm my face. In my black pretend Mustang, I traced the school bus route, rode by what became known as "The Fox Mansion," then religiously ended each journey at my private hideaway, the rock (my rock). About a quarter mile down the road stood a grand old boulder at least six feet tall. Jumping the shallow gully, I parked my bike and butt against the rock, facing the field of corn. It wasn't tall yet, but soon stalks would tassel and cascade over my spot, a solemn refuge. Soon, I would be sheltered again from the world. Yes, in time I could drench the soil without being seen and drench my loneliness with daydreams: of my first bike, my brother David, Jeff, and, of course, Pete.

My final ride to the rock remains part of my soul. It was August that same year. We were anticipating another big move, this time to Hot Springs, Arkansas. The climate and warm natural springs offered health and hope for a recovering family trying to lose their past. There was no room in the 1959 silver-gray Pontiac Wagon for my toy box or bike.

I slumped upon the rock, scanning my brain for all I had lost. This time, hugging my bike, I drenched my sleeves. This time, there was no promise to replace it. I would leave my wheels and learn to walk again—like a man. Trusting only in myself, and perhaps God, I would someday bike again, I believed—at least in my dreams. As I daydreamed, I further pondered, "Are all of life's roads so lonely?"

Daydreams
(Melody & Lyrics: 1968)

V.1   Minutes go flying by
      Hours so quickly die
      When daydreams capture your mind
      Let your mind go wandering
      No worries, no pondering
      Follow your daydreams to find

Chorus   In your dreams, in your daydreams you can see
      How meaningful life can be
      Life is just a merry-go-round
      But you can whistle to the sound
      Of daydreams—daydreams—daydreams

V.2   Mend all your sorrows
      By dreaming of tomorrows
      And all good things the future may bring
      If you keep your heart gleaming
      With all of your dreaming
      Then, you can do most anything

V.3   Though dreams won't assure
      You'll be wealthy, not poor
      They'll give you the strength deep inside
      To hope, care and strive
      To build up your life
      You'll meet that merry-go-round with pride

Repeat Chorus

Hearts on the Line

Shortly after securing a rental house in Hot Springs, Dad was medically released to return to his switchman's job at the railroad in Gary. Having just settled us kids into new schools, Mom agreed that it would be in the best interest of the children for Dad to return to Indiana, alone, by bus. He was to visit every couple of months; however, Dad's re-employment made our solitary year in Arkansas a foregone conclusion. Still, we absorbed all the glitter and gusto this Hollywood-style city had to offer for a full school year.

My twin Marci and I all but linked ourselves together as we explored this virtually crime-free environment. Each evening and weekend, we toured Gothic hotels, gilded auction houses, grand theatres, and the famous Promenade Walk, interweaving the baths of natural hot springs with glorious magnolia trees. We shared private thoughts between us. While strolling along the winding walkway, we embraced this dreamlike beauty. We also wondered why colored people stepped off the curb when whites approached. *Integration* was a term being kicked around on the evening news with speculation that segregated schools would cease within a few years. Having met our first colored person, an honest-to-God Aunt Jemima look alike and cook (meant as a compliment) from the Majestic Hotel where Mom waitressed, we were sensitized to apparent inequities. Unjust as it may be, I'll never forget visiting Thelma's apartment one evening, only to learn firsthand that a lower lifestyle and strata did exist, solely as a matter of color. To think this lady slaved twelve hours, six days per week for such a bleak existence burdened my pubescent heart with mixed feelings of guilt and gratitude. I felt ashamed that Dad had referred to all blacks as "Niggers," yet thankful somehow their plight was not my fight. Marci and I really liked Thelma. She couldn't be a "Nigger!"

On the old gray front porch of our Oak Street house, Marci and I hammered out our first genuinely catchy tune with less than creative lyrics:

"You're Not Away From My Heart." In time we would forget this song, but it served as an impetus to continue our adolescent and amateur singing careers. A hit at all family affairs and teen parties, this love relic in simple harmony propelled our mutual drive for greater acceptance and recognition. Never fully developed and frequently off key, my voice took a back seat to Marci's. Instead, I was devoted to learning new rhythms, chords and lyric structures. Conversely, Marci possessed an incredible, yet unique voice and style which caught the attention of all who heard. With a slight tinge of Southern nasal tones typical of the era, my partner in rhyme blended our sound with guitar octaves, controlled pitch and vocals, which fortunately drowned out much of this boy's squealing. Always on beat, my black-haired angel carried each performance to an exhausting, yet grand conclusion.

Grasping for all it was worth, our music filled us with false stability. In less than a year we fled the farm, said adios to Oak Street, tread a Third Street rental and crowded a motel cottage, all prior to packing our parcels without a plan—except to head home to Indiana. Masquerading homelessness, we pitched an olive, drab, canvas tent at Indiana Dunes State Park, on the shores of Lake Michigan, while our parents pursued some form of permanence. With my eldest sister now married and two others pawned off to relatives for the summer, Marci and I frolicked through the forest, hiked the sandy hills, waded in the blue-green waves, and sang tirelessly to the seagulls. For a generous moment, we breathed the crisp, morning air, crackling pine on the evening fire, and freedom, sweet freedom, that peaceful, playful commodity always in short supply.

~

Half the distance from Gary to Chesterton on U.S. Highway 20 lays the Indiana port town of Portage, where Dad spotted a trailer park unlike any other we had seen. Richly landscaped with the greenest of grass, superb sycamores and flurries of flowers, Ted's Lake Town featured double-wide trailers fashioned in the form of real houses. Ted was a wheeling, dealing self-made millionaire whose intentions proved never as pure as his all-white suits, hats and Cadillac. Yet he probably surprised even his seedy, greedy self by making it possible for Dad to purchase what was to be our first owned home in over a decade. Soon struggles succumbed to a likable life. Our near-normal neighbors, comprised mostly of Senior Citizens, were determined not to be deemed as trailer trash. Our family flourished, as did the modest music of two teens that long learned to turn turmoil into triumph.

~

The late 1960s represented a splendid time for growing up. Mass media reported rapidly changing cultures, while the emergence of a new generation forced out many traditions. New objects and groups blossomed: flower children, bell-bottoms, Nehru collars, afros, McDonalds, marijuana, civil rights, *Laugh In*, Tom Jones, divorce, remote controls, *The Brady Bunch*, "hangin' out," miniskirts, Aerospace, credit cards, K-Mart, smog, Speedos, stereo, banana-seated bicycles, three-piece sectionals, Motown, Beach Boys, Chicago Transit Authority (the musical group), The Beatles, The Monkeys and a host of other British musical wild life. Things filing their place in history included reel mowers, dial telephones, Ramblers, *Three Stooges*, manual typewriters, the Twist, modesty, AM Radio, Lawrence Welk, innocence and trust in government.

Beyond changes attributed to progress, colliding emotions from events challenged, shaped, and rocked the United States and the Portage High School Class of 1969. Memories have been indelibly marked in this man's mind: the assassinations of Bobby Kennedy and Martin Luther King, Jr., the Presidential Candidacy of George Wallace, the Stonewall Riots (although much of this was kept from our TVs), the 1968 Democratic Convention (and the associated Black Panther Party followed by the Chicago Seven Trials), the 1968 Riots (Chicago, D.C., Baltimore, and Louisville), Woodstock, and the escalation of the Vietnam War. The Kent State Shootings were considered to be part of the era (actually taking place in May of 1970). Combined, they marked the beginning of a decade of rebellion. Life continuously volleyed in equal impact between those worldly problems and the major problems of my world, such as having to decide between Latin and Spanish next semester, how my hair should be cut or who I was taking to the sock hop.

An array of paradoxes molded my life. While pledging certain loyalty to Pastor Abrams and the youth group at our Lutheran Church, I simultaneously pinched Marlboros, slurped down Budweiser, and talked trash to pass time with my best bud, Scott Silvestre. Scotty exhibited all the desirable characteristics of that perfect "All-American" boy. Slightly envious of him, I clung tightly like a shadow, knowing his friendship unlocked cliques, thereby lifting me into the "in crowd." Though a year younger, Scotty kicked around with an air of subtle arrogance and confidence. His blondish curly locks, fair build, athletic prowess, unblemished skin, quick wit and dimpled smile gained him assurance of winning over all whom he met, especially the cutest girls. I marveled at his command of skateboards and watched in awe as he "popped wheelies" on his gold BMX dirt bike. Without wheels of my own, Scotty allowed me to double up behind him or straddle the handle bars. We bike-cruised the giggling trailer park girls, showing off for all it was worth. At that age, it was worth a lot!

Invariably, we shared Friday nights, hoofing the two miles each direction to Portage Commons where we meshed into the black lights and strobes of our first teen night club, the Hullabaloo. It sponsored mostly local groups and new talent, like the unheard of Moody Blues from Britain, but it was a "cool" place to spend money and expend energy. Contrasting darkened skin with the purple glow of our white shirts, we portrayed our favorite Rock stars while the deejays blasted away ear drums with endless decibels of the Hollies, the Doors, and especially Iron Butterfly. We lived "In-a-godda-da-vida," pounding floors and tapping walls, tables—anything solid—losing ourselves in Ron Bushy's drum solo. Closing my eyes, I pretended I was there in person. If only I could see Ron playing those drums . . .

~

More frequently than not, Scotty and I exchanged turns sleeping over at the other's house. On occasion, we managed to convince our parents (who never took the time to know each other) that their wonderful son was safe spending the night with his buddy, freeing us up to party hearty. Always more courageous than I, Scotty found and suckered some old "wino" into purchasing us a six-pack for the additional cost of a half-pint of cheap Red Rose Wine. Sitting along the railroad tracks sheltered from view by Ted's huge garbage incinerator (his trash burning, cash earning economizer) we slowly sucked beers through straws, believing the practice induced a greater, more rapid high. Sooner or later, usually sooner, conversation flowed to the "tell all" of our individual experiments with sex. I sat almost breathless, inhaling both the vocal etchings of every dirty detail of Scotty's trashy affair with Linda and the pungent stench of burning rubbish. More inquisitive than outspoken, I usually dug for deeper dirt rather than resort to lascivious lies of my own. I dared not share my lackluster life or latent longings to tenderly touch and seduce Scott. Fearful of my feelings, I cautiously kept them on reserve for the nights when we shared the sofa-bed in his living room. Always patient and prudent, always back to back, I waited for signs of Scotty snoozing to shamelessly scoot backward until we were butt to butt. Like David Wade, Scotty had become my brother, and I needed to feel my brother's body, to draw from him comfort and confidence, strength and support, passion and peace. Then, and only then, could I rest, reassured that I lived with love. Soon, I could doze and dream.

Early on, Scotty and I cultivated enterprising skills by competing for grass cutting jobs in the trailer park. Being both shrewd and farm-experienced in lawn care, I quickly wormed my way into the grass game, bagging the bulk of our trade through trailer trimming, weed whacking (with a manual sickle), and undercutting prices. Before long, I hired the help of other boys just to keep pace with "growing" demand. Cleverly, I committed to verbal agreements with Lot renters to guarantee weekly work. Reluctant to be bossed by his buddy, Scotty traded grass cutting for box cutting as L-Mar Pharmacy's newest stock boy. As I sweated the soil, yielding a dollar a yard, Scotty earned as much per hour pushing dollies and picking up living dolls in air conditioning. It didn't take long for this boy to see Scotty's grass was definitely greener.

~

By the end of my sophomore year, I too, whittled my way into the retail racket, sweet talking Gracie, manager of the Short Stop (convenience) Store, into placing her product into my humble hands. I loved Gracie for giving me a chance, and for not letting Scotty best this boy for another miserable minute! Our friendship continued to mature as we expanded our circle of friends to include Doug Crossman and Terry Jerboas. With a few weeks left in the school year, spring fever fell upon us one sunny Saturday in May, waking up our dormant "bad" streaks. Doug had just gotten his driver's license and a '57 Chevy, and Terry was in charge of beer money. Scotty and I already switched stories of who was staying with whom with our unsuspecting parents to prevent their knowledge of our promiscuous plans. Both of us worked afternoon shifts, and were scheduled off before dark. I had just stepped into the fading sun, headed two doors down to meet Scotty at L-Mar when I heard an attention-getting whistle and looked around.

Not seeing movement, I continued a few more steps before hearing, "Vinny, over here!" It was some fellow calling from the coolest red Firebird parked in the lot near the highway. I thought I recognized his face, so I curiously ventured over to the driver's opened window. He seemed so familiar, but I couldn't quite place him. Tom? Danny? I just wasn't sure of the name, but I was sure I had met him somewhere. I couldn't mistake the stocky build of this man, several years older than me, nor his round, slightly chubby, but clean-shaven face. His dirty-blonde flat top neatly brushed upward registered in my mind, but I couldn't help but think his hair style and short-sleeved light blue shirt were both clean and safe. Yet, somehow he looked out of style.

"Feel like going bowling?" he asked.

I returned with a fair, "Do I know you?"

"Don't you remember me? I'm Dan. We met at a wrestling meet last winter. So what about bowling?" Declining his offer, I told him of my plans for the evening, but he pressed on. "Come on; I'll get you back early. I promise."

Scanning my brain, I felt both stupid and confused. How could I know this man, name and all, yet not trigger a thought of how we met? Slightly intimidated, I rejected his offer again, only to be sharply shut down. "Go tell your friend I'm taking you for a ride in my new car and that we might go bowling."

For the life of me, I don't know why, but I followed his instructions exactly as directed. Still confused, I opened the passenger door, not getting in, hesitating and staring at this somehow scary mystery man. In a mild but decisive pitch of voice, he spoke, looking dead through my eyes into my soul. "Vincent, get in! We're going for a ride, or I'll have to tell your friends and family all about you."

Just as certain that I knew him without knowing where, my heart and head leaped in a rush of knowledge that without knowing how, he knew I was queer. Fearful as I was of getting in the car, I was more afraid that someone might know my hidden shame. Without another word, I slowly slid into the black leather bucket seat, closing the door of his Firebird. In the same instant, I panicked to close the closet door he pried open. I decisively closed my mind to all that would transpire in the next 24 hours, slammed shut so tight nothing could penetrate the cracks. My secret was sealed and filed away forever. It had to be—forever . . .

~

. . . It was after dark on Sunday when I broke through the fog, finding my way to the front door of our trailer. Still dazed and immensely fatigued, I somehow managed to rotate the front door knob enough to open reality. Oblivious to my entry, Dad was hovered over the Sunday Post Tribune in the dining room. He would be leaving for work soon. Slightly interrupting her TV program, Marci looked up to ask, "Where have *you* been?" Ignoring her question, I headed right to bed, clothes and all. I felt sick to my belly. I heard Mom come in from Bingo, justifying her night out to Dad: "Vince, you wouldn't believe how close I was to the $500 jackpot. Just one number and I waited and waited. That dirty dog called out 0-75, and I needed 0-72 for at least five balls."

Massive abdominal cramping kept me from falling asleep until a trip to the bathroom seemed logical. I felt a strong case of diarrhea coming on, intense enough to trigger nausea as well. *What had I eaten to cause this?* I wondered. Even more curious a thought was trying to figure out where my underpants had gone. I just needed to go, big time. *Oh God, what's wrong with me?* Relief was moments away, until . . . *Jesus*, the toilet was full of blood. I started shaking, feeling light headed, crying, just wanting my mom! Pulling my pants up, I unlocked the bathroom door and cried out to her. Momentarily shielded from embarrassment by her concern, she called for my dad. A flurry of questions quickly lashed me, but I didn't know what happened. Mom said I looked "peaked" as she sent me to bed with a promise that I would see Dr. Baker first thing in the morning. Dad went on to work. With continued moderate bleeding, I lay awake for hours praying for my life.

Still fatigued, but comforted in the hands of Dr. Baker at our Michigan City Hospital, I wasn't alarmed by his insistence that I be admitted for full examination, which took three days. There were enemas, tubes, dyes, proctors, scopes, fingers, and eyeballs up this boy's ass before Doc diagnosed colitis, inflammation and a tear in the colon lining. "These things just happen sometimes, but keep him off roughage for a while," were his instructions. A simple prescription followed by three days at home was good enough for me. Lord knows I wasn't ready for finals, anyway!

~

"Time heals all wounds," they say. Time and music healed mine, especially after learning that Gracie gave my job to her nephew while I was hospitalized, that bitch! Playing sour grapes, I recall shouting, "Fine with me, Gracie; Bud and Al have been after me to run Burger Boss next door, anyway!" It wasn't the truth; I knew it. Pretending it was all planned, I marched next door to the car-hop diner called Burger Boss, begging for a buck-fifty an hour to Band-Aid my big-mouthed blunder. Imagine my surprise when they hired me on the spot to be cook and night manager. It was a perfect "I told you so." Everyone knew Bud and Al were petty criminals that met in Indiana State Prison who were likely using the drive-in as a front for some illicit activity. But absolute knowledge of impropriety or illegal dealings, even my understanding of what all that might be, eluded this innocent teen. What didn't escape me was an opportunity to roll in the green, and I don't mean just from stained jeans. With a lawn care business by day and playing "Burger Boss" by night, all my pals, especially Scotty, were green with envy.

~

Progressively, I plummeted into my music with all the ambition, zest, and devotion I could muster up. Transcending my own abilities, I learned to extract emotion from scattered cultural events, placing them in a more organized fashion. My songs of the era included both patriotic and rebellious views of the Vietnam War. One was written in response to the news of North Vietnam's 1968 Tet Offensive. (It should be noted that there were no women in combat roles in Vietnam.) During the early stages of U.S. involvement in that civil war, most Americans believed our purpose was to thwart off the advancement of communism and their goal of conquering the world. Our history and tradition is to promote world-wide freedom while protecting our precious freedoms at home. I believed in that tireless cause; one song was specifically intended to promote patriotism in supporting our troops.

As it turned out, we as a nation *did not* support the war efforts. The nobility and honor of our entire endeavor still stands in question. Barriers placed by our military's civilian leaders deliberately prevented our battle superiority, yet Americans blindly blamed the soldiers, whose lives were being sacrificed, for "losing the war." With months turning into years and continuous expansion of monetary and military investments, dissension grew into civil unrest in our own land. Demonstrations and riots were the order of the day. Like many of my peers, I fell into the proverbial rock and hard place with split loyalties of love and compassion for my fallen soldiers and of love and concern for my country as a proud citizen. Go and fight, or fight not to go; either way, I would be wrong. In time, my songs would change to match the division within me. That conflict continues yet today, both in my mind and in the history books.

Other rebelling subjects encompassed sit-ins, dropouts, suck-ups, put-downs, and pushovers. Cautiously realistic, but frequently idealistic, the melodies and lyrics flowed through me to create the full spectrum of life's expectations, regardless of their antagonistic diversity. Mine were songs from the heart; it only mattered to me if Marci thought they were good or bad. I knew she could vocally dramatize any song she identified with. The twins, locally popularized as "Gladd & Happi," grew in demand within Lake and Porter Counties. Clad in a number of look-alike costumes that Marci designed, we two frequently found our way on stage and into the hearts of church-goers, diet clubs, and coffee house groupies. We even landed a big gig at Hotel Gary for the EJ&E Railroad and U.S. Steel Safety Award Celebration in 1967, where we filled in during breaks for another act that won the primary entertainment slot. Some group called "The Jackson Brothers," a group that was also born in Gary with a dad employed by the cooperative industries was, like us, relatively unknown, wanna-be big-time recording artists. (Hmm, I wonder what ever became of them.) Meanwhile, every student at Portage High knew our names by the time we auditioned for the 1968 Spring Convocation. Being selected was a "gimmie," but our merit rested on the approval of an all-school audience. How would we rate?

We matched from head to toe, green-and-white checkered shirts, white Levi's, tennis shoes, and black hair pitched against contrasting scared, pale faces. With a cold sweat dripping from brows and hands, we nervously warmed up to the crowd of two-thousand with an old favorite from Peter, Paul and Mary. Having survived the ice breaker, we whisked into "Day-dreams," a song finished only hours earlier and specifically written for the occasion. The auditorium acoustics generously blended our brisk harmonies, surprising not only the student body, but Mr. Lyndhurst, our Music Instructor. Nobody could have predicted the surprise and jubilation of two battered kids who honestly brought down the house, *big time*. It was our first standing ovation—and encore! Then during my first-ever hug with Marci, my star, we instinctively knew the timing was right to sing *our* favorite: "I Will Be Free." Any other time, we might not have pulled it off, but the audience and moment was ours alone. Having pumped them up, having won their attention, could we now steal their hearts and the show? By the second verse, we could have heard a pin drop, barring our voices. By the crescendo of our final chorus, tears freely flowed among the bleachered masses. It was done, and there was that long-awaited split-second of silence before the crowd erupted into the most exhilarating and thunderous roars of standing applause we had ever achieved.

Having put our hearts on the line, I recaptured that moment in my mind's eye many times over. If only it could make a difference to some soldier whose heart and heartbeat were both on the line!

I Will Be Free
(Melody & Lyrics: 1968)

V.1   Battle grounds in a foreign land
Where our soldiers go to fight
A rifle sounds from a trembling hand
It may go on all through the night
He fights this war for me—so that

Chorus   I will be free; I will be free
Thank God for men like you; so I will be free

V.2   A soldier delays to shoot his gun
As he looks up to the sky
For courage, he prays "Please don't let me run"
Although he does not want to die
He'll pretend to be brave for me—so that

Repeat Chorus

V.3   (Spoken while humming in background)
A soldier, though brave and strong, is often filled with fears.
He doesn't know what the next step might uncover.
And as he struggles right along, only God can see his tears.
But he must hang on until his job is over.
This he will do for me—so that I will always be free!

Repeat Chorus Twice

Everlasting War
(Melody & Lyrics: 1971)

V.1   War is an everlasting sore
           That'll never heal, causing pain that we feel
           Deep down inside for the brave who have died
           Whose blood was shed for the many who've said:

Chorus   "I want no war; I need no war
           I can live without war
           Why must it be; can't they see
           War is hurting you and me
           Why have they fought; what have they sought
           That can't be bought
           With a peaceful end to everlasting war"

V.2   Peace is a dream that'll never cease
           For those who bear the pain of war, and want to share
           Their hopes of love and belief in a Power Above
           Who sees them fall, yet ignores to hear their call . . .

V.3   Time is an everlasting rhyme
           For those who try to live in peace, before they die
           And so they fight for everlasting truth and right
           And as time dies, I hear their everlasting cries:

Chorus   "I want no war; I need no war
           I can live without war
           Why must it be; can't they see
           War is hurting you and me
           Why have they fought; what have they sought
           That can't be bought
           With a peaceful end to everlasting war"

Repeat Chorus (Add heavy drum-beat)

For the Love of Dad

Dad knew! I was certain of it. He didn't talk to me very much, and hadn't for years. How do I go about winning the love and respect of the one man most dominant in my life? I smartly feared his volcanic physical and mental brutality. Yet, I was a determined young man who longed to conquer his own timorousness by first suppressing any visible hint of homosexuality, then magnifying whatever masculine traits he possessed that might prove manhood to Dad. Strength in any form was revered by my senior. *Power! Control!* These are man's necessities to thrive; it didn't matter how they were achieved. There was no way this scrawny, 130-pound weakling with a concave chest and biceps smaller than his earlobes would ever confirm masculinity through physical strength, so I had long since abandoned any hope of athletic superiority. I still shudder from thoughts of those forced little league days of early childhood. How was it possible to be the only kid in town who's every contact with the ball came from blows to the body? I wonder why Dad stopped going to my games...*NOT!* Though I feared embarrassment even more than the ball, I clearly acknowledge self-admiration in the mirror as I donned that neat ball cap and uniform. An even greater thrill electrified my brain each time I slithered into my first athletic supporter. How could it be that an eight-year-old lad without knowledge of sexuality, let alone homosexuality, who hadn't yet sprouted a single pubic hair, could self-ignite from the slightest odor of his own sweat-soaked jock strap? At that point in time, morality issues didn't exist, but for me, the natural inclination to sniff, stimulate, and venerate did. That same spontaneous reaction dwelled within me throughout my high school years.

The one sport I gravitated toward, other than cycling, was wrestling, but social pressures thwarted all interest there. How could I explain a condition induced by the sights, sounds, and smells of the locker room and shower? Fear of injury on the mat greatly paled to that of exposing the torturous,

uncontrollable beast each time my opponent or I handled the other's eroge-
nous zones. In my case, that meant anything below the head! I resolved to
remain a spectator, where, from a safe distance in the bleachers, I could cam-
ouflage the beast within me. All the while, in my mind I was the one tumbling with and touching my idol, my newest pretend brother, Lenny
Trumpet as he pawed, pushed, and pinned me down triumphantly, thereby
making me the rock-solid victor.

Lenny was the most popular jock in school, lettering in several sports
while maintaining scholastic excellence. To me, he was "God like," never too
good to spare a kind word of encouragement to those of us struggling in gym
class. I remember that after one frustrating session of basketball blunders,
Lenny kiddingly whipped his towel at my butt, saying, "Well Vinny, you're
better at hoops than I am on the guitar!" Though I continued adoring him
from afar, I don't believe we ever spoke after that. Then, during a wrestling
match over Christmas Break, Lenny snapped his neck from an up-side-down
slam by his opponent. Several days later he died from pneumatic complications. Part of Portage High School Class of 1969 died with him. As we dedicated Trumpet Field in honor of Lenny the following year, the PHS
Marching Band silenced the crowd with royal trumpets before the loud-
speaker bellowed a recent Hollies' pop hit *He Ain't Heavy, He's My Brother*.
Slapped by reality, I woke from a tearful dream with the truthful knowledge
that he wasn't my brother, but a heavy burden lay to rest! With Lenny, I
buried all aspirations of becoming a wrestler, illusions of having a brother,
and visions of being embraced by a man who cared.

Words from another song of the era (transcribed from the book of Eccle-
siastes and made famous by Pete Seeger) reflect life as I saw it then:

> To everything/Turn, turn, turn
> There is a season/Turn, turn, turn
> And a time to every purpose under heaven

Always changing, yet leaving behind an unfulfilled need to make the
grade in Dad's eyes, my burden represented the only constant in this boy's
life.

~

Unlike me, my buddy Scotty found his love, moving away to share a life
with our friend Lorraine from L-Mar Pharmacy. Then, shortly after graduation, Marci married her high-school dream boy. I fumbled my way through
several teen crushes involving Wanda, her sister Rita, and at least three girls
named Debbie, the last of which I was engaged to for a day. Never did I generate the kind of passion required for a serious two-way relationship. One by
one, each of my girlfriends split to find boys who could love them in all ways.

Aimlessly, I stumbled through two difficult years following my seventeenth birthday, not knowing what I desired from life—only what I couldn't accept. I did, however, take on a stock-boy job with Pratt Drugs in east Gary during my senior year, which qualified for the PHS Business Department Work-Study Program. Joe, the entrepreneurial Pharmacist, picked me as his personal project and decided he would teach me everything he could about retail. I slyly pretended to fight joining the Retail Clerk's Union to stay on the pampering-management side of Joe the Pharmacist. Joe taught me display with his own "you really wanna buy me" clever approach, turning shelf stocking into projects far greater than mundane labor. He supplemented my knowledge with invoice checks, markup procedures vs. profit percentage add-ons, FIFO (first in, first out) pricing and inventory rotation. He also risked his own career to teach me store budget and payroll. By reducing waste we could gain discretionary spending, ultimately the key to my own pay increases. By graduation, I had earned a reputation for strength in display and product organization, strong enough to land a mobile marketing and summertime promotions job for all six Pratt Drug Stores. Never a pretend brother, Joe the Pharmacist rightfully won the title "substitute dad."

While working in Pratt's Hobart store, I began dating Gloria Gianetti, a cosmetic clerk and beautiful lady of genuine Italian origin. She neared twice my age, yet treated me with the respect and friendship of an equal. Recently divorced, Gloria shared accounts of her husband's neglect, abuse, and infidelity as we split a pizza or sipped wine in one of several lounges we frequented. In time, Gloria took me home to meet her two sons, Timmy, the youngest at two years my junior, and Tommy, my own age. Timmy had a cute personality; Tommy had a cute face and ass. After a few visits, I was invited to spend the night. I had fallen in love with Gloria, always basking in the warm glow of her perky smile, energized by those blue-rimmed, dark, sparkling eyes, and massaged by her words of comfort and kindness. It was my turn to take the lead, but I sat clueless.

Even with the chill of an overpowered air conditioner, I sweated from both embarrassment and confusion. I had already noticed the boys' behavior, but Gloria still blurted out, "Listen, the boys like running around in underwear, and I tell their friends and mine, 'When in Rome, do as the Romans do.' It's okay! You can put your clothes in my room."

Oh my God, is all I could think. Trembling from a combination of excitement and shyness, I nearly choked chugging my Heineken. Instinctively following Gloria's instructions, I undressed deliberately slowly, taking time to neatly fold each item of clothing removed, while retaining the tee-shirt to help cover my briefs and electro-charged condition. Popcorn, Oreos, and several more beers couldn't ease the scrambled mess in my head. I was most definitely in love, even more in lust, but why couldn't I experience both emotions simultaneously for the same person? I needed Gloria to embrace me; I wanted so badly to hold her eighteen-year-old Tommy.

In time the boys went off to bed, kissing their mom and bidding us goodnight. Without awkwardness in their actions, I concluded this was a repeat performance. Didn't they think it odd that I was about to sleep with their mother, or did they actually see me as another visiting authority figure? *God, what am I supposed to do?* Then, in a stroke of intuitive understanding, Gloria tossed me a pillow and blanket saying, "I think we'll all be more comfortable if you sleep on the couch." Humbled, yet relieved, I smiled in embarrassment as Gloria patted my knee while pecking my cheek. Guessing my way to sleep, I questioned myself: *Did I misinterpret her invitation? Did she accidentally see, and then reject my predicament? Had I sucked down too many brews? Do I have bad breath or BO? Did her eyes catch my eyes taking in Tom's jockeys one too many times tonight?* Then, I slept. Though we remained friends, I never learned the answer. This was partly because we stopped dating, but also because I never received a second invitation to spend the night. Instead, I spent the balance of summer working hard, saving money and gearing up for Dad's dream of his son going off to college.

~

What a disaster! Indiana State University and "Skinny" Vinny mixed like raw eggs and vinegar the morning after the night before. Faster than the belly can eject those pleasantries, the Academic Dean threatened to expel my fuzzy ass. I was out of control, having been whisked into a cyclone of activities having nothing to do with my curriculum. Amassing a wealth of extraneous knowledge, I occupied my days with political rallies, retreats, folk concerts, student government, and WRIM Amateur Broadcast Radio (*Revolution in Music*). I also kibitzed around with Jeff Borkman, my early childhood buddy, who quite coincidentally ended up in my dorm. Unlike Jeff, I couldn't manage to fit classes and homework assignments into my already rushed schedule.

Nor could I fit in sleep! Nights were reserved for enjoying the wit, humor, and talent of a few select new friends who introduced me to the world of theatre. I felt comfortable and accepted in their exclusive club. This brilliant crowd dissected every Beatles song and world issue, intent on solving many complex problems of the day, but their passion was for theatre, impressing me with awe-inspiring acting, which included a creative, silent skit set to George Harrison's *Here Comes the Sun*. An underlying terror built as I confronted the realization they had more plays in mind than scripts on the table! *What am I, a queer magnet?*

That was it for me! Before semester finals, the Dean and I cordially agreed withdrawal would be far less painful than trying to recover from a point-five average. Ashamed, yet relieved, I quit and went home.

~

Having failed in Dad's eyes, I struggled to regain some sense of dignity. At the time, a job, *any job*, seemed a more suitable choice than the military. Fortunately I landed a good one. Trendstyle Department Stores, a division of Emerald Foods, planned to open their newest outlet in Gary. Standing in line for hours with hundreds of applicants, it hadn't dawned on me for a moment that I might not get hired. Perhaps my confidence alone snagged Werner Gladstone's attention. Whatever it was, I walked out as the newest member of Trendstyle's display team. That position necessitated my relocation to Illinois for training. With the help of my sister Paula (now married and living in Chicago), I tentatively bounced from hotel room to her sofa, then ultimately to a house share in Skokie, a North Suburb. This time, I just had to succeed!

Almost immediately I sensed a special bond among the highly skilled window trimming squad similar to that of the Terre Haute theatre group. Unfamiliar with stereotypes, I found the display team's antics, though crude, to be friendly and funny. By summer, during our team barbecue, I witnessed overly-friendly funny business transpiring among many of the crew. *How on earth do I keep getting myself caught up in this? Is everybody queer? That's it!* Ashamed, yet relieved, I quit and went home. Now, what do I tell the old man?

Over a chess game, Dad and I really talked for the first time in years. I risked a new lottery draw for the Army, which could sweep me into the next round of draft. Accepting Dad's guidance, he accompanied me to the Gary Recruitment Center to investigate enlistment options. Dad convinced me that enlistment might offer better opportunities than receiving the dreaded "Greetings. You have been selected" letter. What do you know? He was actually and factually right!

After two full days of brain and body examinations in Gary and Chicago, exposing every square inch of my puny bones and inflated mind, and swearing before God and the world that I had no homosexual tendencies, I explored potential possibilities. It seemed the Army segregated a small group of elite men in a Signal Branch known as the Army Security Agency, for which the recruiter quickly highlighted the *privilege* of my meeting entrance qualifications. The lengthy schools for Morse code and Military Intelligence, along with the high cost of obtaining a Top Secret background check, warranted the required four– versus three-year enlistment or two-year draft.

Though interested in VA education benefits, it was the "You are one of the chosen few" line (complete with bait and sinker) that caught this sucker. The words of Joe the Pharmacist came back: "Vinny, if you want to be a leader in this world, first learn well by being the best follower there is." Dad believed the Army would make a man out of me; I hoped he was right.

~

By September 1970, fishing for focus in my life became a foe of the past. Drill Sergeants have an uncanny way of obtaining desirable results, and they brag that, "wimps and queers don't make it through this Man's Basic Training." What do you know? Dad was actually and factually right! I'm not a wimp, and I'm *not* a queer! I made it, damn it, just like the others! Yes, yes, *yes*! "Here's to you, Dad," I shouted to myself as I smartly whipped him a salute. Secretly, I knew the pleading boy inside this man would endure any amount of pain to gain Dad's love. Not yet legal age, I was about to step into a life-changing stage called "manhood." It should be a marker of progress in one's life, but to me, graduation day from boot camp etched a permanent reminder that true personal growth comes with understanding the price we must pay to follow—to learn, live, believe, and dream—to walk tall in a world belonging to straight men. Perhaps the Army would teach me how to be a hero, but Lord knows I'd gladly settle for an "Atta-boy" in the absence of a hug or love from Dad.

Come another Day
(Melody & Lyrics: 1972)

V.1   Searching for a smile of sunshine
Find a tear of rain
Climbing to the heights of freedom
Come tumbling down again
Gaining from what I've been giving
Losing all the life I'm living
Watching time just toss my dreams away
Come another day

V.2   Whistle tunes of peace, only to
Hear the sound of war
Light a fire of hope to find
It's darker than before
Knowing that the cost of learning
Creates a pit of greater yearning
Voices shout; but silence leads the way
Come another day

V.3   Walking straight and then discover
The crooked road ahead
Sound expressions, thoughts and reasons
Are better off unsaid
People join to secure perfection
Watch them pass in their own direction
Though I'm drifting, here is where I must stay
Come another day

Brothers in Arms

Not really seeing myself as rough and tough, I tackled life with a bolstered ego from boot camp at Ft. Leonard Wood. That almost invincible feeling embraced the existence of this newly promoted private first class now stationed at Bravo Company, 1st Signal Battalion, at the Army Security Agency Training Center and School in Ft. Devens, Massachusetts for AIT (Advanced Individual Training).

Having arrived before Thanksgiving and the first snow, our first sergeant (often called Top) asked for three volunteers to operate his new snowplow, a mini John Deer, sized perfectly to clean the sidewalks. Only three of us stepped up; the others avoided a ton of extra work. But I liked tractors and this baby looked like pure fun! Winning the coin-toss and the early shift, it was my job to get up at 0400 hours each snowy morning (every Massachusetts day) to clear the sidewalks before hungry troops headed to the mess hall. A competing Morse code student named Robert took the noon shift, leaving the night work for Phillip. All three of us earned placement on Top's *Super-Numero* list. That meant getting out of KP duty (kitchen police, which had nothing to do with security, but everything to do with the nastiest jobs in the slop hall). We still fulfilled our share of guard duty at secure facilities; we invariably won the label of *Super-Numero* for our guard shifts also, awarding us extra privileges and three-day weekends. We believed Top pulled all the strings. We three were the first new troops in Bravo Company to get promoted to PFC (private first class). We were Top's favorite hot stuff. Everyone knew it.

One Saturday morning, on my way back from plowing snow, I heard singing over machine noise coming from a room down the hall. The singer, Neil Anderson, would become my first black friend; the machine turned out to be a Singer Sewing Machine. (Today's politically correct description of African-Americans had not yet caught on. In 1971, "black" was still beautiful and the preferred description, generated by the Black Panther movement.) So, Neil was a singing, black seamster.

Lightly rapping on his door, I announced, "Are you kidding me? You can't have that in here."

"Of course I can," the worker pronounced with a wrist-snap that I found only *too* funny.

"Aren't you afraid the guys will think you're queer?"

"They can *think* what they like. I get called faggot all the time, but honey, not a Goddamn one of them can dress worth a shit on weekends. Friend, Neil is gonna be wearing the best looking outfit you've seen in a while, so they can all go fuck themselves!" With that, he did another wrist-snap, forcing a chuckle from me.

"And you've got a pretty good voice, too—Neil, you said, right?"

"Neil Anderson, at your service, honey, and sir, you are?"

"Anything but sir," I replied, and after our laughter, "I'm Vinny, Vinny Pirelli, but my roomies call me *Viper*, you know short for—" my words got cut with his reply.

"I'm guessing short for *Vinny Pirelli*; my Nana will shit when I tell her I have a friend named Viper!" And with a "La, la, la," Neil started sewing away in double time.

"And, pray tell, who is Nana, your girlfriend?"

"Honey, that's my Auntie in Cleveland; she raised me after Mama died with breast cancer."

"Oh man, I'm sorry, I didn't mean to—" again I got cut off.

"You didn't mean to bring up bad shit. I know; I can tell. Vinny Pirelli, I like you, and we are going to be great friends."

"Hey, I strum a guitar and dabble with writing songs from time to time. Would you like to hang out this afternoon to see if we can get some tunes going?"

"Nothing I would love more, Viper. Now *come here*, let me measure you for size." With that, Neil whipped out a measuring tape and began jotting down numbers. "Aren't you one of Top's *Super-Numeros*? I've seen you on his snow machine; everybody says you guys are Top's *boy toys*. Are you Top's boy toy? Do you like blue? What do you think of this collar? I know; can I make you something, Viper boy?"

"You sure ask a lot of questions, Neil. I'm down in 208; how about getting together after lunch? And exactly what is a boy toy?"

"Honey, you've got a lot to learn. I'm not eating that shit in the mess hall, but I'll come 'round 'bout Noonish. See ya Viper boy; excuse me— *Vinny Pirelli*." Before I had a chance to depart, Neil grabbed my belt buckle while holding one end of the tape measure. He pulled the other end out about eighteen inches, comically suggesting the size of my penis. *"My, my, my*, no wonder you're Top's boy toy," he said while placing his right fingertips on his chest, making a smiling sigh.

With that, I had a genuine friend, unlike any I had ever known. And, oh, could that kid sing! I talked him into vocalizing Marci's parts of our two-part harmonies; within one afternoon, we had nailed down a small repertoire. Within two weeks, we were calling ourselves, "Dr. Neil and the Viper" and singing for open-microphone night at the Coffee Plantation (a business name earning a host of flippant remarks from my pal). By spring, we landed our only paid gig at the USO in Boston—a smash hit.

Neil was a brilliant man, beyond-intense Morse operator, sewing expert, and singing sensation. He applied for, and was transferred to, Armed Forces Language School in Monterrey, California. He would learn Vietnamese; leaving no doubt about Neil's following assignment.

I still have Neil's voice on a cassette tape in a box I labeled "Keep Sakes," but they are so old and muffled that you can barely make out the lyrics. I always knew Neil was gay, but we never discussed sex or sexuality, only singing and songs. It wouldn't be long before we lost contact. There was a special song I wrote later that I wanted so much for Dr. Neil to sing. I wonder if he ever had the chance to hear it.

~

On a sunny spring day after Neil's departure, I sat on the parade field surrounded by the fresh, sweet scent of thousands of Massachusetts flowers and lilac bushes, centered among four barracks, picture-framed by the sidewalk I knew so well, oblivious to the hustle of dozens of troops all enjoying that gorgeous Saturday afternoon. Amidst the baseball and football games, I sat remarkably alone with my guitar, pen, paper, and a melody in my head. Little did I know at the time, but my scribble and hums depicting feelings for the Army Security Agency ultimately found their way into the ASA Hall of Fame as the official "ASA Theme Song." Even further from my mind was that our Commandant, Colonel McPherson, would offer to waive my military orders for Vietnam if I would promote and present our latest piece of pride with the ASA Regional Choir. What was it I had done to earn this pardon, to boast of glory to our flag, our Branch, our might, our will, and our minds? Dare I accept such an honor, and then run? How genuine were the beliefs that threaded the notes and lyrics of a passionate pen?

I found the answer in Phu Bai, Vietnam some ten months later. Robert and I were transferred together through the Orientation Center at Oakland Army Base to Saigon to be processed further to our unit assignments. We were transported by chopper, first to Nha Trang for about a week, then Chu

Lai where we almost got settled in. Instead our 328th Radio Research Detachment was being uprooted to support the 196th Infantry Brigade, Americal Division, in Da Nang. That would be home until phase-down caused our consolidation with the 509th Radio Research Group in Phu Bai, Northern South Vietnam. It wasn't until our last assignment that Robert and I would become close friends and be housed together in some slum-trailers set up years earlier as temporary housing by Philco Ford, a company that Ladybird Johnson was purportedly majority shareholder in, though that detail would never be confirmed. All we knew was that a lot of money was changing hands; we pawns were never the recipients.

Though I still believed in the tireless cause of freedom, the war raged on without a certain end. Ending, however, was the combat support of the Americal Division in a withdrawal phase during the 1972 Tet Offensive. We, the elite, were being asked to assume armed defenses with M-105 mortars, untrained. Monitoring Viet Cong communications proved critical as we also became enemy targets. Reciprocating mortar rounds terrorized our compound nightly as bewildered and mortified troops intimately acquainted themselves with the unfamiliar trenches. In the operations bunker, the radios had to be manned continuously. Four teams were necessary to cross-intercept enemy code. Always working in pairs, my partner Robert and I were one of only a few teams of highest-speed Morse Interceptors pounding away on the antiquated typewriters called mills.

In hopes of long-term evacuation plans, all four teams were split, selecting half of us for temporary duty to Udorn, Thailand. Our mission was to seek the remote possibility of monitoring the same North Vietnamese Army (NVA) air waves from the world's second largest rhombic antenna from hundreds of safe miles away. Who was to be bunkered? Who was to be transferred? Recognized for achieving the distinction of excellence in Morse code, Robert and I always copied duplicate transmissions for mutual verification and readability. When one screwed up, the other filled in the blanks. How fitting it was that we were selected to continue our assignments, but from two locations—being that of heaven and hell (Vietnam & Thailand). By luck of the draw, Robert received verbal orders for Udorn Air Base.

Moments later it was just Robert and me in the shack, scrambling to toss his things in a duffel bag. Then, out of the blue, he stopped cold, looked at me as if I were his only living brother, and said, "Viper, you've got to do this for me."

"Do what?"

"Switch places, and go to Thailand."

"Oh no, you fool."

"Shut up and listen to me. I believe in you, man, because you believe in us. It's about your song—our song? I'll help you pack. Go now; get out of here! Promise me you'll go for us! I'll be okay here, and I'll see ya in a few weeks, Scout's honor." With that, we clasped hands and hugged (a practice rarely done by Army dudes).

The Colonel didn't give a damn, providing one of us jerks was on the T-10 jet in twenty minutes. The T-10 was like no other jet I'd ever been on. It holds a pilot, co-pilot, and up to four passengers. That mini-jet elevates so fast that the cabin cannot pressurize rapidly enough to keep humans conscious. Instead, we wore pressurized helmets with oxygen and audio controls. We heard detailed pilot communications; however, we were restricted from pressing our "Talk" buttons unless directly asked a question. The flight was straight up and down, not more than thirty incredible minutes from Phu Bai air strip in Vietnam to Udorn Air Base in Thailand.

~

It wasn't until after America's withdrawal and subsequent relocation of the 328th Radio Research Detachment from Da Nang to Phu Bai that we experienced much war-like activity, excepting a rare NVA mortar shell to let us know they were near. The DMZ (demilitarized zone) had just moved south of Phu Bai, thereby placing our sensitive, secretive, subversive operations in jeopardy. Now integrated with the larger 509th Radio Research Group, we began losing our independence, identity, and confidence. We longed to be back in Da Nang where our greatest perils were the elements of nature, like the devastation of Typhoon Hester, which wiped out our entire compound, or the time when Skully burned down the shithouse after everyone acquired crabs.

Though Robert and I had been work partners in Da Nang, we only grew closer after the move, mostly because our billet assignments kept us together and separated from our other buddies. Prior to the change in DMZ, we spent evenings sharing tales of good times past, a cool six-pack, music by the Grass Roots blasting from his new-fangled cassette player and a *big time* case of giggles or munchies after a fat joint.

Secretly, Robert was as much fun for me to look at as joke around with. Somewhat scrawny, this boy-man had not developed his muscles enough to be noticeable with his shirt off. In fact, he looked delicate, though flawless, in my eyes. His creamy skin never tanned from the beating sun like my own. His sandy hair and military-cut mustache bleached out to appear almost white, as did his blonde eyelashes, highlighting bright green eyes. His mind was brighter still. I've always envied those with quick wit, but hated becoming the butt of Robert's teasing. Fortunately, my wrestling days permitted quick counter offensive techniques of tackling, tickling, and tying down my partner until he screamed "uncle" or "pretty please with sugar on top." Robert said I pounced on him like his older brother always did. I told him he was too puny to be my brother—"*so there.*" I had no illusions of Robert being my brother, having outgrown those days. I also knew that, given a chance, I would find a reason to jump his bones—to momentarily hold him in my arms.

We each had other good buddies, but ours was a unique friendship based as much on competition as it was on trust and reliance on the other. On the job, we always ribbed each other over print error and challenged one another's copy speed. Sometimes our mental signals (or brain waves) meshed so closely that we caused each other momentary mental blocks or jams. That's when I learned that ESP (Extra Sensory Perception) also took the form of BWC (Brain Wave Collisions). Off the job, we tested each other in gross-out contests (the likes of which I dare not gag you with here) or bested our partner's last raunchy story. We laughed about having to rebuild our eight-man hooches (huts) following the wrath of *Typhoon Hester* back in Da Nang; then, with water lines disrupted, how we shivered under ice-cold showers outdoors, in the open, by diverting mountainside spring water over corrugated steel, propped up on one end by bamboo sticks. Mama-sans pointed from the lower rice paddies while we flaunted our flesh. We reminisced about borrowing ration cards to stock our private club with Budweiser, sharing Viet whores (and usually a case of clap) with our roomies, singing the "ASA Theme Song" or some Christmas Carol while in drunken stupors or swiping food from the cafeteria to feed Peace, our detachment hooch pooch named after Cat Stevens' "Peace Train." Our paranoid tales revolved around the latest war conspiracies, always referring to ourselves as "pee-ons" instead of pawns. Robert added fascinating conspiracy theories involving the JFK assassination; he believed several families in New Orleans were wiped out for knowing the real truth of "who did it."

We pee-ons believed America's stand-down was a deliberate political stunt to remove that unit from further public scrutiny back home. The entire Americal Division had become tarnished and nicknamed "Baby Killers" after the infamous My Lai Massacre. That dastardly deed will forever mar the good name of thousands of troops when Charlie Company (to be more specific, one company of one battalion of one regiment of one brigade of Americal Division) tortured, raped, and slaughtered the helpless My Lai village inhabitants, mostly elders, women, and children, before reducing it to burning cinders. Whatever the cause, Americal was pulling out; we were left holding our bags. Knowing we couldn't hold out long, the Udorn, Thailand mission *had* to be a success.

~

51

I was certainly aware of bombardments and skirmishes at Phu Bai during the next few weeks; rumors claimed that a few soldiers were hit during night fire. Eagle Mountain had been overrun, as were several other once-prominent American strongholds. It was, according to "old-timers," reminiscent of the 1968 Tet Offensive. On a sunny afternoon, the chopper hovered over Phu Bai Air Strip with our returning test team. All looked quiet; once disembarked, I could only hear the faint cries of a few Vietnamese women. Near the only Quonset hut hanger were rows of pallets, each supporting 16 wooden crates: four across, four high, in crisscross fashion. Half were covered with South Vietnamese flags; half were draped with haunting red, white, and blue. A few minutes ride by jeep to the compound allowed me to see some destruction, but, surprising enough, most of the buildings remained standing. The bulk of my fellow soldiers had already been evacuated, but a skeleton crew (sick pun intended) stayed on to destroy the balance of sensitive materials, equipment, and information.

I reported to Pops (our crew leader), instantly noticing he had lost his eternal smile. Without talking, he led me to his billet, which then housed only a few cots and personal belongings. Reaching into his foot locker, he removed a boonie cap and handed it to me, saying, "Robert would have wanted you to have this." I instinctively knew, but choking on my words, I managed to ask, "Got his early out?"

"Viper, he ate a mortar while working ops three or four days after you left."

Tears didn't come then, but it didn't matter. They couldn't have soothed the blistering, burning hole those penetrating words had made. Patting his hand on my shoulder, Pops then quietly left me alone; never did I ever feel more painfully alone.

~

Over the prior year, even before our arrival to Phu Bai, contractors had several barracks under construction to replace the trashy trailers. With phase down underway, the Goddamn barracks were ready—five in all, with three sitting empty, never used—a future gift to some unknown entity after our eminent departure. The highly anticipated move to our new barracks was supposed to be a happy time. Robert said he would arrange that we stayed roomies, personally moving my gear from the trailer. Stunned and lost, how could I pick up the pieces? Were there any pieces left worth picking up? I did find my footlocker sitting on a bunk in an empty corridor. I blamed both God and Robert. "This isn't justice—this is not what we talked about. Goddamn this war, and damn you Robert; you promised you'd be okay! You said,

'Scout's Honor.'" How can I work without my partner? *"You ass hole,"* I shouted at the wall.

Top Kern could sense my coming unglued when I reported back for duty.

"Pirelli, aren't you due for an R&R? I guess we should have left your ass in Udorn. Better find your steel pot, might need it in the trench tonight. But tomorrow, I want your butt on the first flight out of here. I'll have your orders ready at 0600 hours. Where do you want to go, Bangkok or Sydney?"

"I want to go back to Thailand, Top."

"Done deal, now go play Army—you do remember how to do that, right?"

"Yes Top, I can play *mother-fucking Army!*"

"At ease soldier; I'm trying to help you out here. I'm not the enemy, son!"

"Yes, First Sergeant, I know. I'm sorry Top. And thank you; I truly thank you."

Awarded a week of rest and recuperation, I prayed for a miracle—to recover.

Trying not to dwell on my final few weeks in Nam, I admit to pledging with my life that Robert shall not have died in vain. Though my love could never compare to that of one who gives his life for another, I knew then I had to love enough to live a life worthy of my friend. Robert, after almost forty years, I still have your cap. I still cry on it at times. I loved you buddy. I miss you. You gave me a gift no other could, that constant bittersweet hole in my heart, always needing to be filled. You have been my drive and inspiration for a lifetime. It has been said that "soldiers never die; they just fade away." Not you, my partner. Robert, you are my angel; you remain alive and grow stronger each day—*in me*. You are indeed my brother. Thank God for brothers—in arms.

ASA Theme Song
(Music & Lyrics: 1971)

V.1   A-S-A forever
Second to none
We work with all endeavors
To see our job get done
We train to be proficient
We aim to be the best
We'll gladly go where we are sent
To support the rest

V.2   A-S-A move onward
Your duties never end
Your mind, the blazing battle sword
Your pride, the cause to defend
With loyalty and honor
Salute Old Glory high
Help Stars and Stripes forevermore
Freely fly

V.3   A-S-A the mighty
Most vigilant of all
Don't take our motto lightly
For it will never fall
We're right on top, and there we'll stay
Let lightning strike this day, Hey! Hey!
We're proud today and everyday
We're the A-S-A

Power of Love
(Melody & Lyrics: 1968)

V.1   The old have gone; the new are here
As each day scars another year
The young will burn with increasing pace
To take their place
The rapid change of our nation's hands
Invites new strength with more demands
The only hope is to realize
Some young are wise

Chorus 1   Hear them crying, "This nation's dying"
No one seems to hear the voice of youth
Speaking truth by choice
Oh, how defying, but no-one's buying
Words of peace, our hell to cease
Through the power of love

V.2   The withered plea to end this war
Before each battle spreads to more
Young minds are dying from despair
God knows they care
All routine lives and patterned minds
Will self-destruct when truth unwinds
They give no mercy, only lies
Open your eyes

Chorus 2   See them crying; this nation's dying
(Continue with Chorus 1, Line 2)

Follow with Chorus 1

Little One

Recalling my first trip to Thailand, en route from Udorn, at the end of May, 1972, our Morse Intercept test team traveled by train to Bangkok (commonly known by soldiers as Sin City) to connect with a commercial carrier back to Tonsonuit Air Base, Vietnam. Prepaid vouchers allowed us 36 hours in Sin City to explicitly conduct ourselves in accordance with the city's given name: "Bang Cock." That's all horny troops ever talk about.

Sucumvit Road promised great entertainment with the most lavish night clubs one can imagine. Block after block, each establishment outdid the last with Arcade-style entrances, remarkable illuminations, glass-lit dance floors, robust sound systems, and fabulous dancers clad in everything from traditional Siam garb to bikinis (actually, only bikini bottoms). Bottled in liters and spiked with formaldehyde, Singhai beer danced in the hands of G.I.s everywhere, each living out his individual gust-full, lustful dreams. The faceless many blocked out personal wages of war, temporarily shelving them like the M-16 rifles they grew so accustomed to having by their sides. Hotels featured well-adorned accommodations, including tiled swimming pools, piped-in American music, tantalizing restaurants, and an array of special services. One may choose room service or go out for meals, massages or miscellaneous. We, the elite, went out specifically for the *miscellaneous*.

Granted, I'd already lost my cherry in Nam on the enemy side of the Da Nang Army Compound. We (meaning American troops) cut our own concertina wire and delicately tread through land mines to deposit twenty Piaster' (South Vietnamese currency, now called Dong under reunification) and penned up G.I. savings with some old Mama-san smack in the middle of a rice paddy. On several other occasions, Viet whores were smuggled into the compound in the backs of locked RATT Rigs (Radio Teletypewriter Vans), knowing that gate M.P.s (Military Police) had no authority to inspect classified facilities. So much for security! "No money, no honey," giggled the painted entrepreneurs, who usually delivered far more than we bargained for, such as gonorrhea or who knows what else. We never worried, because two hits of penicillin and two weeks cured almost anything, including the "what else."

Procedures in Bangkok proved different from Vietnam. Sex was not on the sly, but a legitimate business and expectation by visiting military men. With itches needing to be scratched, our four-member team sat comfortably in a small, elegantly decorated lounge of red and gold that was softly lit by candles and crystal chandeliers. We relished being served drinks by a professional staff aimed to please. The lights faded into a twilight-mirrored show room. One curtained wall opened to expose several props and more than a dozen Thai natives for our choosing.

The girls flaunted flower-pinned black hair flowing down and caressing the curves of smooth sweetness. Beautifully costumed in sarongs (colorful native dress of silk & satin prints), their seducing smiles were on sumptuous show. But what's this? Youthful bare-butted brothel boys wearing nothing except tiny thongs exercised while bending and bolstering their sleek, strong, sweat-slick bodies. My heart damn near jumped out of its encasement as my thoughts ran wild. "*Sweet Jesus,*" I proclaimed, wanting them all! I'll never again have this kind of opportunity. My God, what could I do? I was with three macho guys I had to work, sleep, and shower with. I don't think they would understand. *I know; I'll act shy, stalling around until they're gone. Yes, that's what I'll do!*

Buddy Mosley, our mission leader, wasted no time. Within seconds, his dog-like panting indicated his selected pleasure. My other buddies, though more subdued in the selection process, decided without hesitation. That left me. Cautiously plotting, I patiently waited until hosts escorted my pals out of the lounge. *Now's the time, kiddo,* I thought, *If ever there's going to be one!* Looking dead into the eyes of one of the most beautiful boys I'd ever dreamed of, I whispered #8 to my host. Finally, after an eternity of delaying, I was led to a private room to meet the person of my pleasure.

Her name was Sueme' (Sue Mae). If only I had the courage . . .

~

I remained quiet for the balance of our time in Bangkok, mostly day-dreaming, but partly from having disappointed myself from an overwhelming lack of guts. In the process of saving face to others, I lost faith in me.

After flying into Saigon, we caught a hop to Phu Bai on a chopper. It was my twenty-first birthday. The bright sunshine allowed us a spectacular view of the land below. From a distance, Vietnam appeared calm and beautiful with blocks of green, gold, and blue all woven together in what resembled a warm, inviting patchwork quilt. Ear plugs prevented talking, but we were each lost in our own thoughts. Now that the Tet Offensive was over, I wondered if we had to sleep in the trenches. Robert would be excited to see me, unless he'd been transferred out already. I daydreamed of times in Udorn, such as my accidental over-dose on Buddha-grass when Buddy forgot to mention that the marijuana was laced with opium. That affair was such a common occurrence that soldiers received overnight treatment in sickbay without ever being reported. The worst part of that incident was losing my clothes, forcing me to walk barefoot to the barracks in the hospital gown, semi-exposed in the back. (Looking back, I believe that was part of their punishment—they rob you of your clothes and dignity to teach you a lesson.) I tortured myself, daydreaming of the bypassed Bangkok boy. Before the chopper even touched down, I decided to return in June, praying I would gain the guts to engage in my guilty desires. I deserved to give myself *that* gift (if only a thought for now)—after all, it was my birthday!

After learning of Robert's death, I wanted out of Vietnam. We would be working extra-long days, picking up slack for the many troops already evacuated. I didn't have to think twice when Top asked if I wanted an immediate R&R. I returned to Bangkok to explore the many wonders of the incredible Thai culture—and boys. Again I cowered in the crowd, concluding that I needed to conceal my homosexuality forever. Passing over my passion for Siamese Studs, I ventured into tourist traps armed with my Minolta. Then it happened—a miracle.

~

They called her *Lek*, Thai for "Little One." And, oh, was she petite. All of four-foot, ten, Lek, a girl selling papaya, sat on a tarp near my hotel, struggling with her 87 pounds to fill a size three. At first glance, I felt something special about her that I couldn't quite explain. She was the most delicate, delightful, delicious girl I had ever seen, but there was more; she possessed a simple, sensual purity in her mannerisms and magnetism. I was immediately drawn to her shy smile, unbridled black waist-length hair, and the soul-searching sadness locked in large, brown, deep, and mysterious eyes. Whoever created the phrase "love at first sight" knew what I had just been introduced to while bargaining for bananas. To meet Lek was to love her, and I was certain that Little One would become my bride. Six days later, she did!

My heart floated to heaven, finding love in Lek, the little lady I longed for all my life. Sharing dreamlike romance, hand in hand we journeyed through Thai treasures, stopping to exchange animal love among the

Chimps and Monkeys at the Bangkok Zoo. While photographing the Emerald Buddha Palace, I creatively captured my soon-to-be wife and newly acquired life on camera, amidst a culture of unabashed beauty. Under a canopy of natural greenery, we whet our visual and physical appetites on the open, floating market. Lastly, from Pattaya Beach to Cloud Nine, we warmed ourselves from the wind and waves of a privately navigated launch. More than anything else, I had learned to navigate my way through life's ripples into the calm normalcy of my family's expectations.

With Lek's limited English and my *nit-noi* (tiny) command of Thai, communication struggled in the form of body language, facial expressions and touch. Tearing down centuries of dogmatic and cultural barriers, two young hearts were in love, two kids from opposite ends of the world rescuing each other. I needed to deliver Lek from a forced life of pestilence and want; she saved me from wanton perversion, family disgrace, and military dishonor. It was love. It *had* to be love! With only a few weeks of Vietnam duty left, dreaming of Lek diverted my attention to life over death. Unable to call home, I pieced together a singing cassette tape to inform my parents of their newest daughter. Rightfully proud, I'd finally achieved a status even greater than heroism, because in Dad's mind, I would be returning home as a man!

~

"What do you mean, I'm arrested? And when did it become illegal to get married?" My questions had to be answered. Panicked, but even more outraged, I couldn't believe what I was hearing. Unaware that my Special Intelligence Access waived personal rights to have any affiliation with foreign nationals, marrying one without official permission breached security and violated military law. "This cannot be real." The M.P. locked me into a sweltering eight by ten room of the make-shift Phu Bai confinement center, converted from one of those old trailers. "This has got to be a joke." Joking ended two hours later when the Captain read me rights and formal charges.

"What do you mean a *courts-martial* offense? Unreal!"

I could see it all unfolding in my mind: Ten years of hard labor, bread and water, weekly strip searches, lashings, chains, beatings, and a final blow of dishonorable discharge—all because I fell in love. Worse yet, nobody would ever know or read about this massive injustice. In an effort to save face, I ruined my life, causing Dad endless disgrace. Day had given way to darkness both in time and my spirit. Debriefings were followed by lengthy interrogations as some lieutenant, claiming to be my attorney, drilled me even further. I entertained two visitors: Top (referring to First Sergeant Kern) assured me he would do all possible to mend the situation. Then our base chaplain offered everything except Last Rites. I really screwed up this time. When finally alone, I prayed like I had never prayed before. "Oh God, I need your help today!"

It was 0200 hours; though I was exhausted from heat and stress, I couldn't sleep. The buzz from a single overhead fluorescent light bore through my head as the hue scorched my eyes. Stealing my attention from the tick of an old wall clock, I heard the jingle of keys. Time had come for me to be transferred to a regular jail somewhere in country. How was I going to handle being handcuffed? I couldn't put a finger on why, but, almost like an episode of the past, I trembled in terror of being tied. Overwhelmed by the fight-or-flight response, I backed against the paneling and prepared to plead, push, pound or plow my way out of pitiful restraints. Catching my breath, I was greeted instead by the equally tired, unshaved face of my father figure. Top tossed a stack of papers on the already unkempt gray desk saying, "Well, specialist, it seems you have friends in high places."

As a team, Top, the chaplain, and my attorney had joined in going to bat for me, pleading my case to our new battalion commander, none other than Colonel John J. McPherson, former commandant of our Army Security Agency Training Center and School in Ft. Devens, Massachusetts. I was to be orally admonished, but Top could hardly conceal the personal thrill of having won the biggest battle of his career.

"Soldier, your action, regardless of reason, did not abide by Military Regulations. However, in reviewing your personnel file with the colonel, he was impressed with your unblemished record, rapid promotions, and the captain's recommendation for Soldier of the Month. More importantly, he spoke of a stract (perfectly in line) PFC, standing at parade rest in front of his desk in Ft. Devens. You're hot shit, aren't you troop? J.J. said 'We cannot arrest a Hall-of-Famer who gave us a song and piece of the Lion's Share, let alone a soldier who voluntarily came to Vietnam after being excused.' So, specialist, we have some papers for you to sign."

In specific military order of business, I signed a release from custody (which relieved them of any wrong-doing and relieved me of unwarranted tension) and a back-dated request for approval to marry; once I signed those, I was presented with a host of military orders. The colonel granted the approval to marry. Other military orders included a temporary suspension of top secret clearance (pending background investigation of my spouse); rotation orders from Vietnam; relocation orders to Ft. Bliss, Texas; assignment to a new MOS (military occupational specialty) of Radio Teletype Operator (pending training); thirty-days military leave; and travel orders escorting me back across the big drink to freedom. But wait, there's more. Now, with a grin on his face, Top read several letters of appreciation, awarding me the Vietnam Service Medal, an Army Commendation Medal, Notice of Induction of the "ASA Theme Song" into the ASA Hall of Fame and, finally, the Colonel's recommendation for promotion to sergeant. Then Top returned my passport, amended with another visa to Thailand, accompanied by a Pan Am civilian airline voucher from Saigon to Bangkok. Shaking my hand, I was heartily congratulated on my marriage and all that had transpired, but Top sternly warned, "If I were you soldier, I'd do some serious ass kissin' until you DEROS (date expecting rotation of service). You'll work for me until then, and I'm gonna bust yer balls. Now, take a shower, get some sleep, get some eggs at the mess hall, and report yer stract ass to me at 0800 hours. Got me?" (Right, like I was going to sleep after all that! No, I needed to spend that time giving thanks for answered prayers.)

"Yes First Sergeant, 0800 First Sergeant. Thank you First Sergeant."

Even though my final days there blurred from time, I vividly recall Top not having exaggerated. Sweating my ass sand-bagging the trenches was a small price to pay for the favors I had been given. It also made saying good-bye quite easy! There's not much about Vietnam to romanticize about, but I could never forget Top Kern, Peace puppy, sand bags from Hell, and Robert, my Morse-code, "Ditty Bopper" hero.

~

My week of Army leave in Bangkok vanished; parting from the Little One a second time proved heartbreaking. Married less than two months, our souls were inseparable. Upon Indiana arrival, I intended to withdraw the money I sent to Mom all year for my savings. Not yet promoted to E-5, though recommended, it was my responsibility to purchase Lek's passport and airfare to the United States. Red tape would cause a ten-week delay in starting our lives together, but at least I knew what to expect.

On the other hand, I didn't know what to expect when returning home. I imagined parades, demonstrations or riots; none of those occurred. Instead, I heard Mom, Dad, and my sisters shouting as I walked down the Pan Am ramp at 0'Hare International; that was enough. I wondered if they noticed the change in me. Two years had transformed a scrawny, screwed-up, scared kid spreading cheeks at the Gary and Chicago Recruitment & Testing Centers into a solid soldier and married man, confident and conditioned to command respect from Dad.

"Where is it?" I asked in disbelief when I found that there was zero savings upon arriving home. Trying not to spoil the moment or day, I calmly explained to Mom how I counted on my savings to transport Lek from Thailand. I had agreed by mail to loan my parents some money for stocking supplies in their new Bingo business when I was back in Vietnam, but I hadn't considered a silent partnership based on an assumed, silent approval. Dad remarked that he was building a future for me, but what about the future I wanted? Or had they expected me to die in Vietnam? My head swirled. My heart guttered. It was *my* money! Why was I being forced into becoming the bad guy?

Mom was physically shaken from guilt and the perplexity of how to bail out of this big blunder. Needing to send Lek some money expeditiously, they promised to repay $125 within twenty-four hours. *BINGO!* For the first time, I didn't care how they felt. Nor did I care how they managed to replace the funds—only that they did, and as quickly as possible, thank you!

My stay in Indiana that summer dragged on. Hampered by lack of transportation and money, I felt my independence being smothered and my future life with Lek jeopardized. All of Mom's home cooking and Dad's kind gestures didn't ease my discomfort. I couldn't get to Ft. Bliss soon enough.

~

El Paso generates many fond memories for me: the 11th Air Defense Artillery Group accepted me into their Headquarters Communication Shop headed by Master Sergeant Rawlings. He and Staff Sergeant William Phelps took a genuine liking to me, making damn sure I received the finest personalized individual development any troop could hope for. Frequently the butt of their jokes and schemes (which I always fell for), I retained a continuous daily excitement with work for month after joyous month. In addition to twelve weeks of basic teletype schooling in Ft. Gordon, Georgia, I excelled in a basic leadership course and went on to achieve top-ten distinction in the Non-Commissioned Officer Academy at Ft. Hood. All the while my leaders took me under their wings, showing me everything from archery to X-rated magazines. Receiving devout guidance, I developed into the most knowledgeable Radio Teletype Operator on base, exceeding even Bill Phelps's expertise. With the backing of these formative father figures, promotion to Sergeant E-5 proved eminent. Their lessons of life, sex, compassion, and humor, as well as their examples of stellar professionalism still stick with me today. Having missed out on a bachelor party, my comrades took me for one last fling to Juarez, Mexico just prior to Lek's arrival in the United States. The Army was my family.

~

Ten weeks had stretched to eleven long months of scrimping, saving, and believing that my dream wife and life would soon be a reality. Keeping her promise, Mom sent monthly installments on her business loan, but repayment of $100 per month didn't impact the immediate cost of air travel and setting up a household. So, following the guidance and wisdom of my leaders, I reenlisted for an additional four years to capture a variable bonus, paving the way for the Little One's landing. SSG Phelps helped me locate a pleasant apartment, secure Lek's tickets, and shop for my first new automobile, a white Datsun 1200 Hatchback. It was now nearing our first wedding anniversary. The 11th ADA welcoming committee organized a shop party, complete with practical starting gifts that included non-reported time off work to become reacquainted with my wife.

Obviously more frightened than myself, I understood the lost stare on the face of the most beautiful girl I'd ever seen as she disembarked from the Northwestern Gate of EI Paso's tiny airport. Her eyes spoke volumes of wonder and uncertainty, of sadness and hope. How do I begin expressing my love and gratitude to one who is sacrificing home, family and country to fulfill *my* dream and *my* life? I wonder what Lek saw when meeting me again for the first time.

Ours was a quiet, rather than grand, reunion. Impressed with Lek's improved ability to speak English, I simultaneously felt guilty that I had shortchanged her by not learning the equivalent ability to speak the Thai language. Getting reacquainted emotionally and physically is how we spent our first night back together as husband and wife. Shyly preparing for bed, we took turns hiding in the bathroom. When it was my turn, I asked Lek to turn off the lights while I washed up. Ten minutes later, I found Lek still fumbling around the house looking for this thing called *lights*. I chuckled; I didn't intend to, but I insulted her. I knew *then* how much hard work we had in store for us. Holding and caressing the Little One, I promised my wife nothing short of a good life.

~

Less than twelve hours after Lek's arrival we received Lek's first welcoming call, my parents.

"You're where?" I panicked. "Oh my God, Lek, my mom and dad are in El Paso!"

"Thanks for the warning," I shouted, half out of anger for invading my space and half out of shock that they had driven 1,500 miles, as if they were somehow responsible for bringing Lek to me. After giving brief directions by phone, my honey and I scrambled to be dressed in time to greet the relatives. Tension mounted as the doorbell rang. My anger gave way to pride, knowing the folks would instinctively see why I fell in love.

As if it happened yesterday, my slow-motion-video brain vividly replays, like bad news, the episode of Mom and Dad viewing Lek for the first time. Shaking and almost in tears, Mom started, "I don't know what to do. Should I kiss her?" Dad appeared equally flustered. Setting down both suitcases, he simply commented, "She's *darker* than I thought!"

I fail to understand how anyone could be so cruel, so heartless. I flashed back to a family camping trip when, for no apparent reason, Dad spat the most ugly, vile words to my twin in front of family and friends: "Of all my kids, I hate you the most!" This was on the same level of inhumanity. Dad hadn't changed. His vocal assaults always hurt more than his physical bashing. It was "Sissy" who changed. I had learned to cry inside, no longer allowing Dad to dent my self-esteem with his blows. This time, in one fell swoop, Dad managed to insult my wife, attack my pride, crumble my dream, dump on my special day, and destroy all hope of a father-son relationship. For the first time, I realized nothing was ever good enough for Dad—even my being straight.

BINGO! The old man was on *my* turf now. My actions spoke louder than Dad's hateful words. No doubt, he sensed the sudden absence of a "Welcome" mat at our door. Yes, I had changed. I was determined to evolve 180 degrees from everything the bastard represented to me: brutality, bigotry, and brandishing ways of dealing with the world.

Call on Me
(Melody & Lyrics: 1972)

(Note: To be sung, very slow and bluesy)

Chorus	I will always be around
	Yes I will always be around
	I will always be around girl
	When you need me
	When you need me girl
	Call on me
V.1	When there's sadness all around
	When your feet don't quite touch the ground
	When you know not where you're bound
	Call on me girl, call on me

Repeat Chorus

V.2	When this earth seems filled with woe
	When troubled winds begin to blow
	When you know not where to go
	Call on me girl, call on me
V.3	When your heart is touched with pain
	When all life becomes a strain
	When there's nothing left to gain
	Call on me girl, call on me

Repeat Chorus

Repeat	When you need me girl
Whisper	Call on me

Focus on the Living

Our first separation after Lek's arrival to the United States came only two weeks into our reunion when I received a mandatory month-long assignment to Ft. Hood. My friends agreed to look after Lek during the absence, but for me it was four weeks of hellacious worry. Upon returning, I heard it was Lek, not me, who went through hell. I can laugh about it now, but my heart plunged when I learned of Lek's many dilemmas. Terrorized by the murder of a single girl immediately adjacent to our Roberts Drive apartment, Lek hadn't slept nights for three weeks. She never shared that news when I called.

When I opened our new, well-stocked freezer to see no food had been consumed, I panicked. Mouthing both concern and anger, I blew my cool.

"Why in hell didn't you eat? Isn't American food good enough for you?"

Speaking in broken English, "I think that was your food and I afraid to eat it."

Not believing what I heard, I nastily questioned, "*what?*"

Now with tears, "*I sorry*; I think that was *your* food, and I so afraid to eat it."

Making me the fool, but only slightly relieved, Lek explained how she hiked daily (over a mile each way) to the nearest grocery store to purchase fruits, vegetables, and meats she knew how to cook with rice. With limited cash available, I hoped she had spent it all. She did—almost! Not knowing how to use American coin, she fetched for me a dessert bowl of mixed change, full to the rim. I hugged her with tears, pledging never to leave her stranded or hungry again.

~

What do you know? I'm going to be a Daddy—a *Double Daddy*! Call it inaugural impregnation, but not with twins. I knew Lek had cared for a small boy in Thailand, but only after we broke the language barrier did I realize it was *her* son. Lek had been married once before through the ritual of an arranged tribal marriage according to Thai custom. The family-selected husband was thirty years her senior and he lasted only until Lek's father passed, freeing her. Tradition and a tyrannical marriage died with him! I was starting to understand the Little One's hardships prior to meeting me, as well as why she left the village of Ayutthaya for Bangkok. Fearful of what might transpire in this imaginary land called America, Lek's eldest sister promised to raise the boy until Lek was better equipped to regain motherhood.

For me, it felt natural that my love should willingly and immediately extend to and embrace my new son. Look-Bon (pronounced Luke-bon) is his name, meaning "ball boy." God help us if his baseball skills would depend on me! Unable to land an assignment in Lek's homeland due to unsettled security clearance issues, I sought the support of military and civilian dignitaries to help solve our crisis. Pulling all sorts of strings, I maneuvered my way into a special congressional assignment to the Republic of China. There, at least, we could better negotiate the release of my newest family member. Without delay, the U.S. Embassy worked with the Embassies of Taiwan and Thailand to coordinate Lek's return trip to summon our son.

Complicating our mission and cause was the birth of our daughter, Melody, only seven weeks after arriving in Taiwan. Never a burden, this miracle of life did prove to be a handful for a dumb dad. In a medical emergency, my biggest Little One almost died of hemorrhaging before I could carry her back to the naval hospital. Only the responsibility of our two-day-old daughter kept this man from plummeting off the deep end of "sanity," horrified by the realism that little Lek might not live. "Oh God, save my wife," I prayed nightly, placing baby Melody on my belly in blessed bonding to comfort us both to sleep.

After several weeks of recovery, Lek regained enough pep to travel and bring our son home from Thailand. "Here we go again," I thought, remembering the many intricacies of Lek's induction into her new world. But hers was a willful change. To the contrary, Look-Bon was yanked without option from the familiar into a role of total dependency. How do I explain with love that, "It's okay to have an apple, but there's no way in *hell* I'm letting you chop it with an *eighteen-inch butcher knife*," or, "I understand your rebellion, but you *can't* pee in the bedroom corner anymore"? What was happening to my dream? I didn't know being a dad meant not only treating a malnourished kid with bloated belly, but also sifting through the toilet, making sure *all* the worms were gone!

I loved Look-Bon with all my heart. The first time he came running to hug my thigh, tugging on my pant leg when Lek announced, "Daddy's home," I realized blood could never alter the fact that Look-Bon was *my* boy.

Granted, I hadn't the vaguest notion of how to be a good dad, but that desire, no matter how wistful, never waned. Inseparable for a long while, Look-Bon and Daddy were two peas in a pod.

One day, while grappling around on the garden-fenced marble patio of our Chinese mansion, which I was able to afford on a sergeant's pay, I stopped cold when I heard Look-Bon call me "pig." Something evil snapped in my head (some of my own dad in me), causing an immediate reaction of smacking his butt. Though startled by my sudden mood change, he regurgitated "pig" when I demanded to know what he called me. There was no way my son was going to call me *pig*! Removing my belt, I wanted to teach the boy some respect early on. He was crying as we alternated my smart lashings with his stinging echoes of, "Pig! Daddy, Pig!" Then, hitting me harder than the combined strokes of my belt on Look-Bon's behind, I sensed, "Oh God, no! He's begging me PLEASE! "

It was my turn to cry—my turn to beg, but it was too late. Look-Bon didn't understand "sorry" any more than the dehumanizing terror this maniac accosted him with. I dropped to my knees in prayer, "Dear God, help me! I'm just like my dad. Oh, God, don't let me be like my dad!"

Confessing my guilt and shame to Lek, she eased my error by explaining to Look-Bon, in his native Thai, what had happened, stressing this man's vow to never again lose control. It was our tearful arm and head lock, my son's hug and kiss of forgiveness, which pulled the dagger from this heart. Thank God for lessons retained after all these years—a reminder to always temper my temper. I owed Look-Bon big time, hence years of guilty spoiling to follow.

~

The abundant riches of Taipei fall glut upon a few capitalistic elite of what I believed to be an economic caste system. Playing the hierarchy game was essential for acceptance in this unique community of less than 500 blended American forces and their dependents. Excluded? Not me! Rubbing elbows with ambassadors, formal dinners, cocktail parties, and lush night life were all part of the military way. To keep pace, Lek and I followed suit by indulging in the rewards of an undisciplined, yet conventional black market. Known as *chopping*, we finagled high-demand hard goods and appliances from the PX (Post Exchange) through legal loop holes to influential Chinese consumers. Less conspicuously, an enormous underground market yielded top U.S. dollar for perishables and expendables like cigarettes, whiskey, diapers, and dozens of other American products. Even modest involvement produced a life of elegance for everyone we knew. Beyond necessities of life, we enjoyed the spoils of a nanny, housekeeper, gardener, and errand boy, who kept my jump boots spit-shined.

I legally chopped my new metallic sea-green Datsun 510 Sport Coupe (with mag wheels, dual carburetor exhausts with cherry bombs, and white leather interior, except for sea-green velvet-lined doors and dashboard), totally pimped out, but mine to use until DEROS. The buyer also paid my errand boy to keep the car spit-shined and in like-new condition. Having reaped a thousand dollars more than I paid for the car in Texas, with half the cash up front, it may have been the sweetest deal I negotiated in all my years. It was a King's ransom, extra cash for shopping sprees to purchase a houseful of hand-crafted furniture befitting my royal lady and our heirs, Prince Look-Bon and Princess Melody.

~

Filling my life with frivolous niceties was effortless compared to futile attempts of cementing that damnable hole in this man's soul. An insatiable incompleteness wallowed within, regardless of my now over-occupied schedule. A non-typical 9 to 5 work day provided space for Look-Bon's homework, family outings, and night college courses at University of Maryland Far East Division. Needing yet more, I sought a charter to organize the first Sino-American Explorer Scout Troop, No. 197, for young men ages fourteen to nineteen. Leading the group while learning as we developed, this team of scatter-brained, pimply faced, un-coordinated, lanky teens achieved phenomenal results in converting the MARS Station (Military Affiliate Radio System, also my work place) into a functional command post for what would become a viable and critical communication link.

Built intentionally to offer our servicemen and women affordable communications, the MARS Station operated ham radio and Morse code. HF (high-frequency) radio normally has distance limitations due to the Earth's curvature. Through the use of *ring-down circuits* (meaning when one receiver is lifted, the other would automatically ring until both are open for communication), folks called us with a message read telegraphic style. We would teletype it by landline phone to a MARS Station in the continental United States. From there, the message was relayed by phone to the service member's family. Four ring-down circuits were installed: two at Combined Forces headquarters (one actually in the commandant's office), one in the U.S. Embassy lobby, and a public location at the PX (shopping center). *The latter was my brilliant idea*, I say, hot-rubbing knuckles on my chest. Prior to that, the public could only drop written messages into a MARS mailbox for daily pick-up by the USACC (US Army Communications Command) courier. At the MARS end, we had one receiver with an old-fashioned cable switchboard to connect to any one, or a combination of, ring-down circuit(s). Though antiquated, it was all *too cool* at the time!

Also stemming from my idea and crude design, Chinese nationals, under the guidance of The Army Corps of Engineers, constructed a roof-top, collapsible tower that hoisted the scouts' hand-crafted, highly technical cubical quad antenna. This room-sized configuration, built from 12-gauge wire and bamboo, permitted the first-ever full-hemispheric two-way-radio transmission from ROC (Republic of China) to the United States. Communicating from the crest of Grass Mountain, we established and maintained daily contact with a San Antonio ham radio operator. With mathematical precision, these scouts, my heroes, dangled like monkeys from the tower for hours, tuning and trimming the tail-like ground wire. In the end, the Explorers proved, beyond any shadow of a doubt, that high-frequency radio waves will, in fact, reflect from the Ionosphere, bounce off the earth's surface and skip and hop half the globe to a directed destination *without* the benefit of satellite technology. Because of the fragile nature of the actual antenna, my concept of a collapsible tower remedied foreseen problems with typhoons and natural mountain windstorms. It was a perfect recipe, allowing us to have our MARS cake and eat it, too!

Soon after its inception, the antenna earned critical acclaim during a fluke, near-shore incident. A large fishing vessel breached the beach, thereby severing the under-sea landline communication cable that linked Taiwan with the rest of the developed world. That very same day, Vice President Rockefeller arrived on island to attend the funeral of President Chiang Kai-shek. Our cubical quad antenna made emergency communications possible. (Satellite technology, even in the military, didn't become widely used until after 1980, with Reagan's satellite-dependent Star Wars program. Fiber-optic cables bloomed into full use nearly a decade later.) With our system up and running, the vice president placed a call from the commandant's office using our ring-down circuit and cubical quad to talk with his wife. Though not very secure, the V.P. could have conversed equally as well with the president or any member of his cabinet. That brought special recognition to MARS, The Corps of Engineers and, of course, Explorer Scout Troop No. 197. We were dumbfounded when the Chinese Republic later invited our troop to operate a ham radio (previously banned) during the Sino-American Scouting Jamboree. Letters of appreciation from the ambassador and commandant smiled in this soldier's personnel file.

Further honored, I was selected to be the Army's representative for the Combined Forces Color Guard on Memorial Day, perhaps one of my proudest moments. As accolades continued, my Explorers were invited to a four-day camp with a sister troop from Republic of China. We stayed in cottages camouflaged by rain forest; taught ham radio (and the renowned cubical quad antenna, in concept only, of course) to our sister troop; frolicked on the ocean-side beach, just a jog from the thick jungle-like greenery; and were guests at an all-village luncheon held on the beach. The participants in this unique annual ritual feasted at one stretch-table, about a half-kilometer long. Among other delicacies, we sampled eel for the first time. It wasn't good, though certainly memorable.

~

"FLASH—FLASH: Saigon over-run by NVA!" Declaring victory and reunification, North Vietnam took control of this southern capitol, renaming it Ho Chi Minh City. This was the *For Eyes Only* (meaning only for those with clearance and need to know) message received at Combined Forces headquarters in Taipei. Granted, most of our American troops had already withdrawn from Vietnam by 1975, but U.S. dignitaries and their families were stranded. Telephone communications had been cut off and microwave transmissions were being effectively jammed by the North Vietnamese Army. Military leaders throughout the region were summoned to expedite evacuation of our citizens and South Vietnamese political refugees.

Off shore were naval craft prepared to handle evacuees, but how could we make contact and communicate with the now-battered rescue operations on the bloody beaches and tattered Tonsonuit Air Strip? Major Branham's request came through, "Sergeant, they would never expect high frequency from this distance. Can your cubical quad zero in on Saigon? You run the radio. We'll patch you through to Headquarters, already in radio contact with the naval carrier."

Nearly two days and nights had come and gone since first alert. No time for sleep, except that in black-liquid form. Pressure mounted with each pending rendezvous with refugees, their destiny in our control. Baby Hueys, Chinooks, and C-130s all dodged strike attempts rescuing folks from the air strip, while shore patrol raced the waters, saving a number of people from several over-filled fishing junks that capsized.

"Focus on the living, not the losses," echoed Branham's voice in my ear each time a negative report was patched through. Like a roller coaster, emotions climbed and fell with each successive report. Over and over, "Focus on the living", "focus on the saved", "*Focus! Focus! Focus!*" Those words would stay with me a lifetime.

~

Leaving Taiwan wasn't easy. My life had changed dramatically in less than two years. For sure, we carried with us plenty of souvenirs—everything from teakwood-veneered furniture to wine from Matsu, the Republic's littlest island, nearest the shore of mainland China. Proudly, I carried with me Major Branham's recommendation for promotion to Staff Sergeant, E- 6. No treasures were greater to me than the small Chinese oil painting in red and gold of a beached fishing junk gifted to me by the Explorer Scouts or the Vietnamese doll presented to me by Mr. & Mrs. Sing. Mr. Sing was a journalist from Vietnam living in Taipei; Mrs. Sing was an American Liaison to the over-run embassy in South Vietnam, one of many saved by my heroes' cubical quad. Of course, we also carried home our future legacies, Look-Bon and Melody, both gifts of priceless wonder.

While the movers painstakingly crated a growing household, I thought of Robert in Vietnam and his gift of time. I dug out his cap, clenching it with all my might, while thinking to myself, "Focus on the living! Focus. Focus. Focus. Damn it, I will. I swear to God, Robert, I always will!" Theologian Meister Eckhart (from the thirteenth century) once said so profoundly, "If the only prayer you ever say in your whole life is 'thank you,' that would suffice." I believe that with all my heart. Dear Lord, thank you.

Gift of Time
(Melody & Lyrics: 2010)

V.1   I think of you each time I see the morning sun
I think of you each time I feel the rain
I cannot change your choice, what's done is done
So, for the gift of time
I will live to live; you've not died in vain

V.2   I think of you each time someone needs a hand
I think of you each time I witness love
I cannot change your choice, but I understand
I feel the gift of time
I feel your living hand, inside my empty glove

V.3   I think of you each time I hold a little child
I think of you each time I see a smile
I cannot change your choice, but God has reconciled
My guilt, the gift of time
And this life I live, proven so worthwhile

V.4   I thank you by living now as you would live
I thank you by saying things you'd say
I cannot change your choice, but thankfully I can give
My time, the gift of time
To a worthy cause, or someone else today

Ending   I thank you for the gift of time
From you through me to someone else today

Hundred Dollar Understanding

Going home is never easy, though always expected. What were we to do? Moving during Christmas holidays mandates a place for Santa to visit, and Grandpa's is better than a motel. I wasn't required to report to Ft. Benning, Georgia until January. So, Grandpa's place it was! At least Dad knew in advance that Bon would be darker than he approved of; he hadn't changed much. When I heard him ask "How can you not love this boy," my sarcastic heart believed that if anybody could find a way, he would.

Mom, on the other hand, changed dramatically. Her (our) Bingo business boomed beyond normal growth expectations. What happened to my mild-mannered mother? She leaped into the role of the *look-at-me*, liberated lady. Carrying conspicuous consumption to extremes, she beamed while boasting of her new home, luxury Continental Mark IV limousine, and extensive travels. I was deeply proud of Mom's ability to capitalize on scales of economy, to elevate her on life's scale of economic success. However, with a glance, one could see Mom had replaced matriarchal love for that of materialism. On a scale of one to ten in my appreciation, I give that zero, unlike the eleven I'd give to Aunt Ruthe.

Since early childhood, I connected well with Aunt Ruthe, one of Mom's older sisters. Second only to my sister Sandi, I was her favorite. Aunt Ruthe was the mother who almost was, never able to be blessed with giving birth to her own children. In the absence of a sense of belonging from my parents, Aunt Ruthe physically and emotionally embraced my growing family right from the get-go. Though Dad had warned her of Lek's dark complexion, Aunt Ruthe instinctively hugged Lek on their first meeting, commenting how beautiful and precious she was. It was Aunt Ruthe, not my mom, who kept in touch with us during our tour in the Republic of China, just as she did with me during Vietnam. How natural it was to look for love from my second mom, knowing for sure it would be found and abound.

Over the years, Aunt Ruthe and I shared countless laughs, letters and life's little struggles. Perhaps more than a coincidence, we also shared a hundred-dollar bill, ping-ponging it back and forth by mail just in the nick of time to solve the next crisis of "too much month at the end of the money." Aunt Ruthe shared something else with me that Christmas of 1975—the news that she had developed severe blockage of the arteries. Too extensive for bypass surgery and a decade prior to medical breakthrough announcements of angioplasty, her struggles and hope for survival rested solely on God's will, her own will to keep going and, of course, nitroglycerine to push the pulse. Aunt Ruthe always smiled, even though tears left trace-marks down her new trifocals, which were already too weak. Yet she remained happy and hopeful as she half-heartedly (sad pun intended) planned to visit us at Ft. Benning during Thanksgiving.

~

Overall, 1976 proved to be a maturing and most happy year for Lek and me. With the patience of a Siamese on catnip, I dared to teach the Little One how to drive.

"Lek, STOP…What do you mean *big deal*? Of course it's a big deal, even if it was a little intersection! Please stop crying. I didn't mean to yell, but I can't take it! I'm sorry, big time. Can your girlfriends teach you how to drive, please?" Fortunately for me, they did!

Then, in my new position as Team Leader, Staff Sergeant Vinny Pirelli knew how to strut his stuff. Honestly, nobody likes being hated, but I wasn't out to win a popularity contest. I didn't bend my strict-stract expectations, either. Simpson, one smart-ass private, always came bee-bopping to formation wearing sunglasses. They weren't even *cool* like flight glasses, but some gaudy pimp-like green glasses with glitter. If they were non-prescription and non-issue, they were non-uniform, and not welcomed in The Viper's formation! Twice, prior, I had taken them off the soldier and slipped them into his breast pocket, making sure after the second incident to lightly punch the pocket afterward, saying, "Better put these away, we wouldn't want any accidents." The last time I had to remove them, I stared the little shit dead in the eyes while dropping the glasses and shattering a glass with an unfortunate step, saying, "Oops, third time's an accident." I had an image to protect; Sergeant P's troops were going to shine, just like their boots, with or without the crap being kicked out of them—though hopefully without! Oh, I had so much to learn. In the process; I was also learning to teach. It's a good thing my guys were scared shitless; otherwise, I might not be writing this book!

Meanwhile, Melody, approaching the terrible twos, tattled on Mommy every day when I got home from work. "What this time? Oh, I see!" Lek resorted to tying the refrigerator door to the pantry door, preventing our Princess from playfully preparing pizza with pickles and powdered laundry detergent. "Aw, that's too bad kiddo; *shame on Mommy!*"

Melody chatted up a storm. She learned to say "Jimmy Carter, Jimmy Carter" more clearly than anything else. My kids were huge supporters of the Georgia Carter Camp and sweet talked me (or was it the other way around?) into driving to The Little White House to watch the Main Man announce his presidential candidacy. Okay, so *"Dumb Daddy"* got a little lost! Okay, so I got lost big time! After dragging the family out at 0400 and driving in the dark for hours, we arrived just in time to watch Jimmy Carter wave from the window of his white sedan as he was whisked away to begin winning his way to Washington. Wow, we saw his waving hand!

Look-Bon adapted well to his new world. Every night he teamed up with me to bounce balls, babysit or burn barbecue, but he never left my side. It was due time that my boy become *my* boy, legally. I remember the judge saying "This is the most rewarding part of my job. Be good to each other. Be a family. And be happy, more than anything else!" We were, but I was never happier than when I watched Look-Bon on his first bicycle, a red two-wheeler with training wheels. I wonder if he appreciated the handle-grip streamers or the spoke clicker I made from one of Lek's clothes pins. There was one thing he liked for sure. "Daddy, look at my bell," *ring, ring, ring, ring!* For a precious, gifted moment, through Look-Bon, I was six again and on a bike. I was "Mr. Hell on Wheels" and happy! "Go boy, go!" That same evening, we saw a TV interview with the leaders of a large group of cyclists doing a cross-country tour in honor of our nation's 200th Birthday. I dragged Look-Bon to see the dozens of bikers with streamers and a flag waving to the street audience in whatever city it was. "Wow, did you hear that son? Bike-centennial! Folks are biking across America. Let's do that someday." I winked, knowing it was pure fantasy.

Sparklers and mosquitoes go hand in hand on the Fourth of July, but seldom do we see the kind of spectacular scenes our nation viewed on its Bicentennial. New satellite technology, being introduced, although still sparingly used, made it possible to witness wonders from the steps of the Lincoln Memorial, the Golden Gate Bridge in San Francisco, the Chicago shores of Lake Michigan and Lady Liberty, all fully illuminated. As a teen I had seen the St. Louis Arch during visits (from ground-breaking to tour), but I sat in awe as a piper cub dared to fly under the arch without state approval. That took guts! I've heard so much about the Seven Wonders of the World, but there is no doubt in my military mind that this arch (designed by a soldier like me, first conceived in sketches and drawn from the trenches during WWII) stands alone in the wonder department. Built separately, the two sides of the isosceles triangle (of sorts) had to, with mathematical precision, meet within 1/64th of an inch in order to be welded. It exists as our nation's tribute to the pioneers, but to me it represents strength and beauty, promise and creativity, hope and strife—the one piece of rainbow creation God chose to add later. I recognized, even during construction, that it would be a symbol of greatness. I believed that arch would someday bridge all I dreamed of with all I believed in.

~

This would later become my "Philosophy of Archism" (pronounced with a "k") and my personal insignia. This concept was slowly developed as I continued my own education. I compared supports of an arch to the ever-important two legs of successful business, each with ten components. Less than coincidentally, the first letters of those modules form two (forced-fit) acrostics of management and leadership, one being the tangible scientific nuts and bolts, while the other represents the intangible visionary necessities of imagination and integrity. It compared and contrasted a host of factors, (something we did a lot of in the 1980s): masculine vs. feminine attributes, left– vs. right-brain activity, nature vs. nurture, and will vs. action, among others. Each quality of good management was deliberately matched with one trait of good leadership to form an arch. Like all great arches (and I would cleverly insert overhead pictures of arched doorways, bridges, and a wishbone), strength comes from two perfectly balanced sides, a potent force proven to be much greater than the sum of its parts. If that is true, it would not suffice to be a good manager or a good leader; why was there no college course combining the two?

My response was to create a philosophy on how to become an *Archist* (noun, an entity, be it a person or a company), applying both direction and discipline, which could be taught as a college course. An Archist appreciates the difference between inspiration and perspiration and has internalized the requisite of a stated goal and formed a plan of action. In lay terms, the value of a steam engine lies not solely in the intricate mechanics of a locomotive, but also in putting that steel miracle on tracks leading to a deliberate destination, hauling something for a purpose; therefore an Archist conceived, built and implemented a complete rail transit system. (I would end this presentation with a photo of the St. Louis Arch that fades into a magnificent rainbow to visually dramatize man emulating God.)

~

Oh, what a firecracker of a year. Like a cherry on hot fudge, it could only be topped by Aunt Ruthe's visit on Thanksgiving.

"Your doctor said you could travel? Great…What's that, money is tight? No problem! It just so happens that my promotion gave me an extra hundred dollars this month…Forget it; it's in the mail already, really…Honestly, I sent you an invitation hoping you would come…You didn't get it yet? You will by Monday…He said to take it slow? You can't be here till late Thursday? No problem! I have Friday off; we'll celebrate then, *big time*…Okay, drive safe. Give my love to Uncle Bob…We'll see you then!"

Nothing was too good for Aunt Ruthe, in my opinion. Meticulous to the finest detail, I prepared the dining room while Lek followed Aunt Ruthe's passed-on recipes in the kitchen. There comes a time in every amateur photographer's collection when they capture a picture of the perfect table setting. This was no exception. Truly fit for a queen, the international setting simply shamed the modest surroundings of our two-story military townhouse. Spread atop the hand-crafted table of teak from Taipei was fine English linen of white to enhance the glitter of Japan's famous Sango China. Our Aristocrat pattern featured royal blue designs trimmed in 18-karat gold. Bronze flatware, accented with carved wooden handles from Thailand, closely matched the freshly shined brass wine goblets from Hong Kong, and America's representation of brass and silver candleholders. Cut lead crystal from Germany completed this magnificent display. The only sparkle of greater brilliance was that of Aunt Ruthe's eyes as she lightly traced each piece of her place setting with fingertips of angelic softness. Repeatedly, she touched it and sighed, "I've never seen anything more beautiful in all my life. I'm almost afraid to touch it." Warming my heart from a distance, I watched as Aunt Ruthe gently replayed the moment over and over again. I didn't care if we lost it all tomorrow. Today, it was priceless. Today, it belonged to an angel. I thanked God for Aunt Ruthe.

It was a quiet weekend overall. Uncle Bob catered to every wish of his life's love as if each would be her last. The Georgia trip is all she talked about for months; going against his better judgment, Uncle Bob couldn't deprive her of this dream. By Sunday Aunt Ruthe's breathing seemed abnormally labored and she complained for the first time that her bodily functions were stopping. After refusing our offers for medical attention, Uncle Bob insisted they head home early on Monday.

Due to my pending orders for Germany in January, we discussed housing Lek and the kids with Aunt Ruthe while I was gone. My short assignment didn't permit family travel. I felt comforted knowing that our adopted mom would give Lek a sense of family and purpose during my absence, making this planned separation a little easier.

On Monday, as I escorted Aunt Ruthe to the front door, I couldn't help notice how she kept touching the walls. I assumed she felt weak and feared falling. She also struggled to bend low to kiss the children. Then, in a remarkable burst of energy, Aunt Ruthe reached down and swept up Melody, saying in a bold, tearful smile, "I just have to hold her one time!" How could this be? This woman, deprived of necessary breath to walk unattended, somehow managed to hoist a thirty-pound toddler to her breast. When Uncle Bob started driving away, Aunt Ruthe and the kids exchanged waves and blew kisses. Through her opened window, Aunt Ruth voiced, "See you later, alligator!"

Look-Bon replied, "After a while crocodile," and chuckled.

Melody followed suit, "See later, See later. *Jimmy Carter.*"

~

For whatever reason, I fell out of character and helped Lek clean up the guest room that afternoon. "Unreal! Lek, Aunt Ruthe left a thank-you note under her pillow...Lek, there's a hundred-dollar bill wrapped inside. Hey, I thought they were broke. That's why I sent travel money. I don't get it!" Still curious about the money, I fell asleep self-assured that I could always send it back when needed. Odder still, and also out of character, I fell asleep holding the Little One.

Both awakened and startled by a banging sound, I glanced at the clock to see the time. Exactly 0100 hours, Tuesday. It wasn't time for the alarm yet.

"Who in the hell could be banging so loud on the door at this hour?"

Both confused and worried, I grabbed a robe, heading for the staircase.

"Vinny, don't go down. Open the window to see who is knocking."

From the crank window of our bedroom, I had a direct view of the front porch. I half expected to see Uncle Bob standing there. He wasn't; nor was anyone else, for that matter.

"Some fucking punk is playing games, Lek!"

"What? Is nobody there Vin?"

I turned, looking at Lek, imprinting the once-in-a-lifetime expression from her face to my brain. It was a look of dreaded fear, as if she knew something I didn't.

She said again, "Don't open the door Vinny. There's no one out there."

I yelled, "*I can see that, Lek*. He probably ran to the carport."

"No, Vin, Thai people believe when someone dies, they don't want to be alone. Dead people knock on the door to take somebody they love with them."

"You're fucking nuts, you know that?"

"Please Vinny, don't open the door," Lek begged in a near-tearful panic.

Running down the stairs, I snapped on the porch light and peeked out the front, back, and side windows. However, after Lek ignited an unreasonable, but very real, fear in me, I didn't open the doors. I waited and watched without further disturbance. It must have been a prank. I nervously fell asleep on the sofa. In time, I heard Lek fumbling around in the kitchen, making coffee. The alarm must have gone off; there was morning light. Look-Bon dashed down the stairs with only his briefs on—backward. Starting the day out with laughter, life was back to normal. "Come here boy; the fly always goes to the front. *Fix your fly!*"

Tuesday's work proved mundanely normal. Though nobody I knew had died, I shouldn't have been harsh on Lek. "Why do I snap like that?" I silently questioned myself in disgust. It was an inherent trait I loathed. Asking our neighbor Rhonda to watch the kids for a couple of hours that evening, I offered a peace treaty by taking Lek out for dinner. I know when I screw up, and I screwed up big time! Rhonda & Bill didn't hear the knocking, but that didn't mean anything. After dinner, we took a ride around town; I finally convinced Lek that we would have gotten a call if there was a problem back home. At almost 2000 hours we returned, greeted by Rhonda.

"Lek, some lady called, asking you to call her back."

"You go ahead Lek. I'll lock up Look-Bon's bike."

Lek left her car window ajar; I headed back to roll it up when I heard her screaming, "Vinny, oh Vinny, Aunt Ruthe is dead already!"

~

Leaving the children with Rhonda, Lek and I grew ever-so-close on our long haul to Indiana. We had never talked so lovingly, intimately, and openly. Ours was a loss other relatives could never understand, those who were already blaming us for forcing Aunt Ruthe on a trip she wasn't medically up for. She died going home, but only after finding Uncle Bob did we learn the details: By the time their return trip reached Mississippi on Monday afternoon, Aunt Ruthe needed to lie down. Uncle Bob stopped at a motel just beyond the state line. Then, while Aunt Ruthe rested, Uncle Bob went out for supper, bringing back a hamburger. He found Aunt Ruthe crying, an unusual occurrence for this lady of strength. She couldn't see anymore; she told him she had lost her vision before leaving Georgia. She didn't want us to know. Comforting her, Uncle Bob sat by her bed for hours just holding the hand of a woman who had brought so much life and joy to him. Before midnight, Aunt Ruthe requested help to the bathroom. A few minutes later she started coughing, then choking, then vomiting, finally gasping for breath while falling to the floor. Uncle Bob began administering desperate CPR measures, stopping only to dial 911. Working tirelessly, he ceased his efforts only after the ambulance arrived. Aunt Ruthe was pronounced dead at the stroke of midnight. She was going to be 54 years old.

"Midnight?" I questioned in a high pitch. "Oh my God, Lek, there was a time change crossing the Tennessee border. It had to be 0100 hours our time, right?"

~

Aunt Ruthe had sufficient insurance to cover basic funeral home expenses, but not enough for her burial plot. Having been a close friend to her, the caretaker offered a wonderful location in the Hebron Cemetery for an unbelievable two-hundred dollars, half of which was donated by the American Legion Lady's Auxiliary.

"Lek, Uncle Bob said he has no money."

"Vinny, you got a hundred dollars. Give it to him to bury Aunt Ruthe."

~

Shortly after the funeral, Lek and I went, as requested, to their retirement cottage in Lower Michigan to help Uncle Bob begin organizing his affairs. In addition to a ruby ring he gave Lek, he handed me the book Aunt Ruthe spoke of the night before her departure from Georgia. I didn't want to listen at the time, but she insisted I knew which book was to be given to me someday. It contained her favorite poem; I would know which one it was. I wasn't ready to hear that gloomy crap then. The century-old book of poetry by Whittier had been gifted to my great grandmother for Confirmation by her Sunday school teacher, who passed it on to my grandmother, who willed it forward to Aunt Ruthe, who now gave it to me, Vincent Pirelli. But what was this poem I had to read?

I took a stroll to the bitter, frozen river Aunt Ruthe loved so much in summer. I bawled, thinking aloud, "I don't want your stinking book! Damn it Aunt Ruthe, why did you have to die? Don't you know we need you? You promised to always love us!" It wasn't much condolence to hear Uncle Bob's assurances that their Georgia trip hadn't killed Aunt Ruthe at all. Instead, it gave her the will to live several weeks beyond even the best medical expectations. I just wanted Aunt Ruthe Back. I found myself asking, "Who's going to repay my hundred dollars," then praying, "Oh God, why do I have to hurt so badly?"

Later that evening I sat down in Aunt Ruthe's favorite recliner, picking up my little green book. With so many poems, how was I to know which one was her favorite? Wait a minute. She's got it marked. *I'll be damned!* Oh, Aunt Ruthe, of course: "A Memorial." Only you could have been so clever in selecting the perfect book mark, too. I should have guessed as much, *you stinker*. Bet you're smiling at me! There it was—a crisp, brand-spanking-new one-hundred dollar bill. It was no coincidence; I understood!

Yesterday's Smile
(Melody & Lyrics: 1977)

V.1   Yesterday's smile
                Must it fade away?
                Why can't it last a while?
                Oh, how I need it today
                Yesterday's smile

V.2   Yesterday's dreams
                Cease to carry on
                How my life is empty it seems
                Now that my dreams have gone
                With yesterday's smile

Refrain   Yesterday's smile
                Never a trace of a tear
                The smile that gave me a dream
                Is no longer here
                It's yesterday's smile
                Yesterday's smile

V.3   Yesterday's love
                Not a love today
                Once a love, now a vanishing dream
                And a smile that will stay
                Yesterday's smile

Repeat Refrain and Last Verse

Bobby Sox

Aunt Ruthe's death changed me in a sobering way. It was one thing to offer care and love to those who counted on me, but who could I count on? Though stronger from the experience, I felt abandoned.

With too much time remaining on this hitch to reenlist, I was being shipped out on a short tour to Germany. Short tours prevented families from traveling at the government's expense. Forced to leave my family again, they would move Lek and the kids to any stateside location of choice. With Portage, Indiana being as close to a home town as we knew, packers once again upset Christmas to complete the relocation prior to my disembarkation. Mom made the effort to fill holes left by Aunt Ruthe, but her attempts were more about fulfilling Mom's need to be center of attention. Deliberately avoiding them throughout the holidays, I cherished the days I had left with my own little family.

One incident shook my confidence that all would be okay in my absence. We enrolled Look-Bon in the district elementary school, then, after dropping him off on his first day, I took Lek out for a morning of coffee and conversation. So that Lek & I could have a full day together, Mom agreed to pick Look-Bon up from school. Although within walking distance, he didn't know his way around our new neighborhood. Without advance notice, school was released early due to urgent snowstorm warnings. (Portage frequently gets hit by pockets of moist air forced in from Lake Michigan called lake squalls; they are sudden and ravenous.) Since Look-Bon was listed as a "walker," nobody at school thought to make sure he knew his way home. It took us two hours to fight through snowy streets from the out-of-town coffee shop to Look-Bon's school, only to find that he wasn't there. Noting that cell phones didn't exist, we drove to grandma's house, assuming she realized an early pick-up was necessary. Mom was counting Bingo inventory, never once giving our son a thought. After driving the neighborhood, we stopped by the rented house to call

83

the police. There he was, on the front porch without hat and gloves, crying because nobody was home. That left me with a cold feeling, to say nothing of how Look-Bon felt. Fortunately, he suffered no physical damage. Relieved at the astuteness of my son, slip-sliding through snow in a strange land to find his own way home, I was majorly pissed at my mother. I had to let it go; I was scheduled to depart for Germany the next day. Worry to the degree of paranoia prevented rest. I prayed for the safety of my little family and their protection from my birth family.

It was a fierce snow, making for treacherous travel from Portage to Chicago's O'Hare International. Trying to remain emotionally stable, Lek and I shared that January morning with a pot of java in front of the TV watching Jimmy Carter's inauguration. Good-byes are not my thing; they hurt too much. I could count on the Little One to be a giant of strength—if not for her, for the children and me!

~

Exploring new lands excites me. West Germany offered a fresh image to this man, who had long since joined the jet set. Starting with Vietnam, I spent six years in moderate to tropic climates, each hosting its unique brand of tillage and civilization. Germany felt different beyond the climatic and cultural changes. Not knowing what to expect, part of me visualized being greeted at the Ansbach train station by a group of SS Nazis waiting to escort my ass to one of Hitler's infamous detention centers. I chuckle now at the stereotyped conceptions my generation grew up with. Yet, fresh were the scars of both true and horrific episodes on a society still recovering from the grip of war-sick maniacs. In time, I would come to appreciate the rich, robust heritage of the German people, one of strength and pride, humbled, but not crumbled by a dark villain looming somewhere in the shadows. To me, the invigorating freshness of weekly Volksmarches and gala October Fest celebrations were forms of survival, not of life itself, but of history.

~

Assigned to the 141st Signal Battalion, my role would become as complex and ambiguous as the life which led me there. The last thing I expected to hear was that I wasn't needed in the capacity of Radio Teletype Team Chief. "You're sticking me where?" After all my training and experience, I was to be relegated to some hole-in-the-ground facility, pushing papers. I couldn't help but think, "For this, Uncle Sam uprooted my life? I'd rather burn shit in Vietnam, thank you," though saying this was never an option. What was all this *play Army* crap with formations for mandatory physical training at 0600 hours? I thought the Green Machine gave that up with the draft and the war for this all new VOLAR (Volunteer Army)! At the moment, VOLAR sucked a green weenie.

I've heard it said that, "the first day at anything is always the worst day." Wrong! After a week in the bowels of this pit called CMDSA (COMSEC [Communications Security] Material Distribution Systems Agency [how's that for an acronym within an acronym—go Army]), my hell had only begun. Cheryl Quinn, a twitty Specialist 4 with a bitchy attitude, frantically smothered me with an impossible sequence of files, only one of which I sufficiently understood enough to find pertinent during week one. It was called file-13, the trash! There were reams of regulations, acres of acronyms and mounds of meaningless materials labeled COMSEC that I'd been slapped with. How was I ever to jam 8 GB of information into this 4 GB brain of mine? (In the late 1970s we likely used KB for kilobytes, expanding it to MB for megabytes by 1990s. Today, we think of memory in GB for gigabytes, but that may likely expand by the time this gets published.) I didn't then accuse God of being uncompassionate, but why *me*?

At least as a Staff Sergeant I earned the privilege of a small, but private room in the barracks. Friday night finally rolled around; I looked forward to a secluded reprieve. The dayroom, complete with a Ping-Pong table, billiards, color TV, vending machines, and vinyl upholstered chairs, was a far cry from the comforts of my living room. I missed Lek and the kids. I missed that big bowl of popcorn. I missed having wheels and places to go. I longed for Lek's home cooking and laughter, the little stories of her day and her sweet, tender body to snuggle with before making love. Oh, did I ever miss sex! It had been ten days, but the tension factor approached ten years. I was a nervous wreck, not just from being in military surroundings again, but more from fear of reluctantly reverting back to old reliable. How was I going to handle the situation?

Turning down the radio blaring Electric Light Orchestra, I switched off the overhead lights to call it a night. Unfortunately, I couldn't turn off my damned electro-charged state of arousal. Sliding under the sheets of my bunk, my shaky hands slowly slipped my briefs downward. I trembled, hands and heart, almost to the point of a full-blown anxiety attack. What was I so afraid of? Surely every solitary soldier in this stinking shack sometimes surrendered to self-seduction and satisfaction! I don't know if that thought was mere justification or, scarier still, the basis of my erotic state.

Perfectly timed, there came the rap on my door followed by my "Fuck!"

"Hey Sarge, are you in there?"

It was almost a familiar voice. In a panic, I quickly pulled my shorts up while fumbling to the door. Opening it just a little, the dim hallway lighting still blasted my eyes as three half-dressed troops sheepishly awaited my response, "Yeah, what?"

"Hey Sarge, we're the welcoming committee! We want to buy you a beer."

I recognized the faces from work. Kirstoff, a giant of a man, was the appointed spokesman. All three had glassy eyes from liquid party. The others were Hefner, a roly-poly, jolly lad and Bobby Sox, a little dude with a big mouth.

"Caught ya," Sox said, referring to the bulge in my briefs.

"Just have to go real bad," I replied trying to save face, and disguising that I was pissed big time!

"Sure Sarge," Sox debated. "I know beating off when I see it."

"Ya ought to. I heard you going at it in the stall this morning," I tossed back.

"That wasn't me. It was Hefner."

By this time, everyone roared with laughter. Hefner's face glowed red and the Viper had three new friends.

All three were slightly left of center; all were humorous, even corny. They liked drinking their beer, talking crude, and jamming to the newest rock group, Boston. All of them were part of the Secure Equipment Repair team. Though Kirstoff and Hefner were older and more experienced, it was nineteen-year-old Bobby Sox who aligned himself closest with me. At work I referred to him by his real last name, Soloux (French or Native American, I'm not sure), but outside the work shop it was Bobby Sox, or just Sox (named for being no bigger than a pair of boot sox, as much as being an abbreviated last name that seemed difficult to pronounce).

Like a puppy, Bobby Sox gravitated to my side at every opportunity, be it at work, in the barracks, at the gym or in the mess hall, now called the dining facility, thanks to VOLAR. Trust me; it was the same shit with a different name. I constantly teased Sox about being my torturer, never letting me have a moment's peace. In truth, I enjoyed his company. He helped ward off loneliness and depression with his never-ending antics, sarcasm, and disrespectful mouth. My God, he had a mouth on him for such a slight fellow. How he managed to keep those pearly whites intact was beyond me. Still, I burst into life when he was around.

~

It wasn't long before my interest in communication security took hold. My work, though a technical and complex challenge, never duplicated itself, making the workday seem short and fun as time passed. Each day presented new twists with ongoing regulatory violations (uncovered and solved) and at least one minor security crises. Each evening concluded with a five-minute team meeting to discuss specific achievements and goals. By week three our facility head, Warrant Officer Bill Fleck, announced to the group that his confidence in my ability to learn while I lead was behind his decision to appoint me to NCOIC. Yes! Even though we had one repair man who out-ranked me by grade, I was now Mr. Fleck's right hand man, his non-com-missioned officer in charge.

Along with that privilege and title comes a list of responsibilities from platoon sergeant at HHC (Headquarters and Headquarters Company) to being second in charge of 1st Armored Division, Nuclear Material Control Systems. Increasingly aware of my need for broader knowledge in order to be an effective leader and teacher, I devoted evenings and Saturday mornings to a variety of military correspondence courses, coupled with continued enrollment in college. I always had the goal of becoming the first person in my family to achieve an advanced education; the European Division of University of Maryland offered that real possibility. Though I lost endless cred-its in the transfer process from Mount Wachusett Community College, Troy State, and University of Texas El Paso, I gained credit from several formal military courses and retained credit for my classes at University of Maryland Far Eastern Division.

Always firm, but friendly with my troops, I rarely allowed for close per-sonal friendships. On one hand I related mostly with officers, having com-mon experiences and aspirations. On the other, I was bound by the subordination rule, intended to prevent conflicts of interest between Enlisted Grades (E-1 to 4), NCOs (E-5 to 9), and officers on any level. If we socialized, it had to be in an official capacity only. Always, I adhered to this unwritten non-fraternization law—always, with the exception of Bobby Sox. We continued growing our friendship. Being seven years his senior, it was more like having a younger brother. Like fools, after PT we continued devel-oping our bodies daily at the gymnasium by lifting weights and playing vol-ley ball, though never coordinated enough for basketball. After work, we raced off to jog the forest trail and obstacle course. Without exception, we ended each workout by hitting the showers and each other in playful ges-tures.

On good weather weekends, we borrowed or rented bicycles to tour the greater Ansbach area, a region of southern Bavaria with some of the most picturesque views of rolling hills of fields and forests that are intertwined with hamlets, usually ending with a berg or burg. (Berg is a mountain, while burg is an ancient castled fortress; both are quaint and gorgeous.) Some of the houses were more than 500 years old and still serving families well, each adorned with flowers in boxes or on pedestals. Many original cobblestone streets remained intact; not an iota of trash or scrap would be found any-where on a public street or sidewalk. Even the back alleyways were clean and safe. I have to admit, its one hell of a heritage. Bobby Sox whined like a lit-tle brat every time he got hot, thirsty, and hungry, tired, or needed a smoke. But after our outings I'd always treat him to Cordon Bleu, Weiner schnitzel or Goulash soup (made with beef, vegetables, and paprika) washed down with local ale. Nothing could be finer, except perhaps to be able to share this with my family, too.

~

Before the summer of 1977, Lek and I realized we needed each other too badly to stay separated if we had other choices. Personnel agreed to pay my family's way to Germany if I would extend my ETS date (Expiration of Term of Service) a total of three more years. However, they were not inclined to ship household goods again. In agreement, Lek held a "Moving Sale," auc-tioning off almost everything of value to her with a plan of sending me cash to purchase an automobile. I cannot imagine the pain she endured in the process, keeping strong and devoted as each appliance and piece of custom-made furniture from Taipei went to the highest bidder. If she cried, nobody witnessed it, but I would know for a lifetime the willing sacrifice of a woman in love. Her gift to me cannot be understated!

Prior to Lek's arrival, Bobby Sox talked me into a Nürnberg (Nuremburg) trip to visit the infamous Wall. If per chance it holds some war-time signifi-cance, I'm unaware. We only knew it as an avenue of legalized prostitution.

"What the hell, Lek will never know," was the appeal from Sox. With spring fever long upon us, I didn't need a sell job to avoid another hand job. I was ready!

The train dumped us off near the Wall, but we prepped our experience by first bar-hopping the district. Not to my surprise, the Wall differed both from the swamps outside Saigon and Thai Massage Parlors. Here was a long street of bustling businesses with copious window displays one might expect to find downtown in any major city. Artistry was not in costumed mannequins, but real, live girls—many beautiful girls! That endless row of picture-perfect com-petition faced two-kinds of walls: a mammoth wall of stone and a wall of men from every land and culture—all sporting stone of their own.

While I patiently paced and smoked up a storm, Sox boy went first, tak-ing forever. Suddenly, out pops his torso from a second floor window with a head yelling, "Viper, I'm up here! I didn't get off yet! I need ten bucks more." Then, as I recall, with the squeal of a kid in his first candy store, Bobby Sox blurted out to me and all the balls of Wall World, "She's giving me a blow job!"

There was no distinguishing the shit-eating grin from that little boy as he stumbled out. I roared with laughter, hiding my even more roaring lust.

"My turn," I commanded, leaving the pup still wagging his tail from excitement. What was I going to do? I guess it *had* to be my turn.

Having missed the last train to Ansbach, we searched for a guest house to crash in. Making a deal with all but our ticket money, the frauline led us to a third-floor room. Unlocking the door, she pointed to a toilet down the hallway, speaking in broken English. *"Tis water closet 'dere', und nein noise!"* The typical guest room was equipped with two singles and a sink. Speaking and pointing again, our less than hospitable hostess pointed to the beds and spit out, *"You dere, und you dere. No smoke. No spit. No fool around!"*

"No kidding, bitch," we reverberated upon her exit. Like kids, we started giggling and mimicking *"Yes sir, Miss Hitler,"* making sure we added one-finger salutes.

In the muted light, I watched Bobby Sox undress. He sure had a cute smile. I liked the way his nose twitched on his freckled face, like my rabbits did when we talked. My baby brother tried to be so macho; even though he hardened his body with good muscular form, a certain hairless softness tamed his masculine appearance. I stole a second glance at his bubble-butt, pretending not to notice that he was going to sleep in the nude. Did he notice that I noticed? We continued talking with the lights out.

"Hey Viper, you know what?"

"What, Bobby Sox?"

"I didn't get off tonight."

"Then, what was all that shit about you getting a blow job?"

"I needed more money, because I couldn't get off."

"Probably drank too much."

"Yeah, I guess. What about you Viper? You didn't take too long."

"No, I couldn't even get it up. I kept thinking about Lek or something. But I wasn't fool like to toss good money after bad!"

We laughed. Then Bobby Sox started joking, "Better not roll over. I'm so horny; I might think you're a woman."

Tossing my pillow at him, I jostled, *"You fucking faggot.* Get near me, and I'll have you for breakfast."

"Bet you would, you queer." Then he started singing like a third-grader, *"Sergeant Pirelli is a queer."*

"Oh shut up and beat off."

"I already am, man."

"So am I."

The room fell quiet. My head whirled. It was bad enough that I noticed him, but I truly liked what I saw. "Oh my God," I prayed silently with mist in my eyes, "I'm in love with Bobby Sox. That can't be. I love Lek. I love my kids. I love my sisters. I even love my parents, who don't deserve it. I loved Aunt Ruth so much it hurt, even though she deserved more. I even love my job…Who would have guessed that? But this can't be; oh God, help me. Bobby Sox can never know. No one can ever know. I love him big time; no, I love him *more*!"

We never spoke of that night again, but our friendship flourished long after Lek and the children joined me.

~

Totally intended, therefore not surprising, Lek became pregnant on her arrival night. Mr. Fleck teased, "Everyone leaves Germany with a cuckoo-clock, baby, or both." The Little One was a big hit with my boss and subordinates alike, except for Bobby Sox. However, they got along for my sake, as well as out of necessity, because once our family settled in at Katterbach Military Projects, Sox became a permanent fixture on weekends. It was non-negotiable!

Miranda Marci, our Valentine sweetheart, made her formal, but premature debut just after midnight on the 15th of February, barely missing Valentine's Day, but winning everyone's heart regardless. With glistening eyes and bursting chest, I assisted in the delivery and witnessed the miracle of birth. Raptured by every second, I clumsily followed a list to clean up the baby by the numbers and checking for missing parts: eyes, ears, nose, fingers, and toes; counting them, there were ten little piggies. "Yep, she's all here—*and beautiful*, like her mom." I could tell she was cocky & smart like her pop. Dads somehow know these things.

Look-Bon and Melody celebrated the addition without jealousy. We had just gotten home from the hospital less than an hour before. Like always, the biggest Little One and I shared coffee and conversation in the kitchen for a bit, when suddenly Lek shrieked. In came Melody, our three-and-a-half-year-old bucket of love, dangling her real live dolly by one arm. Momentarily traumatized, we quickly recovered once we ascertained no physical damage had occurred. A quick lesson of care was in order for Melody, but scolding was not. Her actions were an expression of love. It wasn't long before we taught Look-Bon to change diapers and permitted Melody to hold the baby bottle. Our thoughts on babies were no different than televisions or stereos: If you don't want the kids breaking them when you're not looking, teach them early how to handle them correctly and with respect, then trust!

(It would be tempting to sensationalize the recollections of this man who loves his children so dearly, but I don't need to. Distinctively recalling all their growing pains of bumps and grinds during adolescent years, I swear that as children go, they were remarkable. For years, their giving, loving, sharing, playful, and respectful attitudes toward one another were noticed by friends and relatives to the point of unsolicited comments to their credit. To this day, that bond prevails; though normal in most regards, these children would prove to be the true strength of our family. Each so distinctive, yet so well blended, they form a magnificent arch—the Pirelli Rainbow.)

~

Ah, those were happy years. I chose to savor the moment, knowing I had it all—all except my dad's respect. Lord knows I tried, but I just hadn't achieved his narrow definition of success. Certainly, if I were an officer, he would approve. Since I was a better fit with the elitist crowd, I submitted an extensive application for Officer Candidate School, believing I met all the requirements. "What do you mean there's an age cut-off? I'm only twenty-seven, big deal! What's a year anyway?"

Disheartened by that rejection, I played sour grapes to save face with my troops at CMDSA; they had all rooted for me. Then, following Mr. Fleck's recommendation, I requested a direct commission to warrant officer. Warrant in the officer ranks equates to Specialist for the enlisted. Pay grades for warrants are delineated by technical skill level rather than realm of authority. Once again, I prepared extensively for applications, testing, and standing before a Board of Approving Officers, similar to a Senate confirmation hearing. I received the *highest* recommendation of the Board, a key word Mr. Fleck said was necessary for acceptance...

"What? How could I be denied? I have what it takes, Mr. Fleck!"

"All except educational requirements, I'm sorry. Brand new regulations elevated standards of applicants to having achieved a minimum of three years' college equivalency."

"But, I have three years; I'm sure of it." Fighting tears, I kicked file-13 all the way into the next digit.

Grasping my shoulder, Mr. Fleck firmly said, "Look at me...apparently not at the time of your application. We can appeal this decision if you want, but for now it stands! And you, Sergeant, will stand as well. There isn't a solitary soldier on the base who doesn't respect you for who you are—and that's the finest Goddamned Sergeant we ever knew. And don't you forget it! Do you hear me?"

My silence must have spoken volumes, because Mr. Fleck sharply questioned, "Comprende' Sergeant?"

My eyes swelled, but I wasn't about to cry. I was more angry than hurt.

"Yes Sir," is all I could say in a cocky way.

"I didn't hear you." He needed to counter my attitude.

"YES SIR!"

"Okay. Now go home, get some supper—and a little nookie."

We both smiled. I couldn't help but giggle as I said, "Yes Sir!"

"Oh, by the way, Sergeant, you should know we've already recommended you for promotion to Sergeant First Class E-7."

"You're kidding!"

"No Sergeant. You have more than enough promotion points, but you don't have enough time in grade yet. That can be waived if you re-enlist at the end of your tour. You may end up one of the youngest E-7s in this man's Army. Hell, at this rate, I could be looking at the future Army Command Sergeant Major!"

"I doubt that, but thank you, Sir."

"Now get the hell out of here before I put you back to work."

There was no doubt Mr. Fleck knew exactly what he was doing, a talent I absorbed for later years. He managed to do more for my ailing esteem through that rejection than any recognition I had longed for from Dad all my life. Guess Dad was wrong after all; success cannot be rated solely in financial terms or placement on Dad's fictitious totem pole of hierarchy. Mr. Fleck said I had *respect*, so there! God, what a feeling I had driving home. I could hardly wait to tell Lek. She would be happy for me—she was *always* happy for me. Gee, this was even better than Warrant Officer...NOT!

~

Near inseparable, Bobby Sox and I shared our mornings and weekends. It was never easy walking that fine line of dividing friendship and necessary superior/subordinate roles at work; on the job I'd take no flak from the twerp, often expecting more from Specialist Soloux than the others. Off duty we were pals, like playful pups; Viper was a dog who wanted to play with Sox. Though I kept my feelings in check, subdued like the OD (olive drab) uniform, I tingled inside whenever Bobby Sox was around. Having become part of our family unit, he tagged along everywhere: Volksmarching, touring castles, outdoor concerts, and on vacation. Ours was a connection like none I had ever experienced. It was love, for sure—as pure, innocent, deep, and enduring as love can be. It was inspiration and imagination all rolled into one, but very carefully managed. I was living proof of Archism. Bobby Sox completed the circuitry necessary for my brain to convert AC to DC, if you know what I mean; my emotional batteries were ever charged. Though I had never once touched him inappropriately, he caused me to accept with comfort what I wanted from life. With Lek, the children, and Bobby Sox, I felt whole and happy at home and at work. I gave and felt love. I was completely and utterly in love!

Love for My Friend
(1979)

Love
For my friend
Oh, where does love begin, and friendship end?

Heart
All confused
Should I give my heart, or just get used?

Feel
Never touch
Is it okay to feel, just not so much?

Soul
Let it bleed
Hiding what I know, or what I need?

Need
Deep inside
Will my cries be heard; why must I hide?

Love
For my friend

Going Home

(A
t this juncture, I will depart from the original story to talk
about the process of writing it. So far, I've shared with you my
recollection of events that both shaped my life and were my life from age six
(1957) through age twenty-eight (1979). If you haven't yet put this book in
file-13, you might be interested in knowing that virtually everything you
have previously read was written in 1996. Before I can possibly go forward
with the story of "Going Home," I must go back to 1996 to explain why I
stopped writing. I simply didn't have the heart to begin telling about the end
of my military career. I didn't want to let go of the happiest years of my life.
The time I spent in Ansbach, Germany with HHC, 141st Signal Battalion
and 1st Armored Division CMDSA, with all the family, friends and work I
lived for and-loved, were beyond special, even sensational. They were
sacred. Permanency is not the military way, but somehow writing about
some changes made them seem all too permanent. I didn't know how to say
good-bye.)

~

Once again, controversy has been ignited around the issue of DADT
(don't ask, don't tell), with President Obama pushing (or not) the Joint
Chiefs of Staff commander, Admiral Mullen, to publicly support ending this
insane course of action. Now that the act has been repealed by congress, gay
Americans may serve openly and honestly in the armed forces. My readers
might quickly surmise, "Ah ha, some insidious incident was cause to end an
otherwise extraordinary military career." Not so! In fact, when I cashed in
army fatigues for civilian fatigue in 1980, we were still a dozen years away
from implementation of President Clinton's creative DADT policy, intended
to appease both the conservative armed forces and progressive Democrats,
especially those Democrats in the gay community.

During my term of service, the Green Machine openly asked; I more-than-willingly lied. I wasn't ready to give up a career and family for a man I loved—the timing for me to come out was not right. Even though I graduated high school in 1969, a historically rebellious and liberating year, I still came from an ultra-conservative state in the Bible Belt. For me, venturing into the mysterious state of New York that summer was all about Woodstock Festival, not the Stonewall Rebellion. My rainbow colors had everything to do with tie-dyes and nothing to do with Dorothy's rainbow at the end of her yellow brick road. Besides, I wouldn't have traded a military moment. While escaping a seriously dysfunctional family, this scrawny 130-pound weakling with an impoverished and sickly history found freedom, purpose, and manhood in what we called "This Man's Army." I feared my yet-unfulfilled secret side, choosing silence as a means of sustaining what society called a "respectable self." Like my Dress Greens (formal wear), my colors were protected in the closet. I was proud of, but seldom donned, that classy uniform, knowing someday I would also wear my rainbow pride.

Although it may have been true only in my eyes, I had seen more in my twenty-eight years than some dudes had in a lifetime. There is a saying, "The world is a wondrous place; it's the people that suck!" Though it's true that there are assholes about everywhere you go, I have always found more good folk than not in all the places I had been. This great Earth is a marvel to behold for anyone choosing to explore it. The Army offered me a way to afford exploration and experience. I was richly blessed with an incredibly unique Army career and life.

Growing up, I appreciated the great city of Gary, Indiana as being a place we loved visiting at Christmastime. I memorized my last drive down those same avenues, which you cannot call a ghost town; a ghost would be too fearful to bunker there. Hidden among the boarded-up buildings are drugged-up gangs, ready to gun you down if you dare stop at an intersection. Gary is only fifteen miles, yet a world away, from Leroy, where I was lucky enough to get an early childhood education that seriously mattered in a three-classroom, red-brick schoolhouse built by French settlers in 1882.

My most recent plane trip seemed problematic with endless searches and scans, thanks to the "no-longer" Osama bin Laden, but I flew on a jet before even five percent of the U.S. population had done so. I witnessed firsthand the earliest transistor radios and color televisions, experienced the very first intercom systems. Today I'm operating an antiquated Gateway 350S (though upgraded, and perfectly reliable and sufficient) to connect myself to the world with an out-of-date, all-in-one scanner/printer/fax, and I suffer with less than 100GB hard drive memory. Adding insult to injury, I watched the Super Bowl recently in HD (high definition) with commercials for some device that gives one a G4 phone, answering system, camera, video recorder, streaming TV, radio, MP3 player, portable e-book, Internet access, email, and links to things called apps (for Applications) I'd never heard of. You can access them from just about any spot in the universe one might try to hide in, but you can't use it on a plane for safety and security reasons! In this Information Age, that G4 will likely be obsolete by the time this book could possibly make it to e-formats. That's a lot to witness.

By 1979, I'd been blessed to view a floral spring in New England, eat clam chowder on the Cape, climb the Leaning Tower of Pisa, fuck in the rice paddies of Vietnam, dodge mortar fire from the trenches, see the snow-like glistening of a few acres of White Sands in New Mexico (which never, ever mix with the brown sand surrounding it), and taste the waters of Hot Springs, Arkansas. I was able to see Bob Hope in a USO Show, Red Foxx on stage in Italy, and Bob Dylan, Santana, and Chicago in concerts in Nürnberg, Germany. I even laughed with Johnny Carson in a live show before his retirement. Who would give that up?

I ate, drank, and smoked who knows what at Woodstock (although I cannot say for certain I saw the entertainment there), then did it all over again a few years later with buddies in Udorn, Thailand, where I saw stuff that wasn't real, like lamp posts following me to the dispensary. During travel I couldn't afford dinner for my family at a restaurant in Tokyo, but fit a mansion easily into my budget in Taipei later that same month. I hold fond thoughts of my first car, a baby blue, 1963 Chrysler Imperial with push-button transmission, and my first brand new car that I paid for with cash, a 1972 white Datsun 1200 Hatch-back with 4-on-the-floor and a heater. It carried me through the Smoky Mountains, Arizona deserts, Montana wheat fields, and every place between. What smart person would give that up?

I had been a respected worker since age fourteen, impressing my friends with jobs and promotions normally outside my age and education level, like going from cook to manager at Burger Boss at age sixteen, stock boy to marketing manager at age eighteen, high-speed Morse Interceptor and Army Security Agency "Hall of Famer" at age twenty-one, Radio Teletype Team Chief at age twenty-six, and Communication Security Nuclear Control Chief at age twenty-eight. I had run down the snowless Giant Slalom in Innsbruck, Austria; hiked the Black Forest and toured Ludwig's Castles in Garmish, southern Bavaria; played on bumper cars at Riverview Park in Saint Louis; went camping in the Ozark Mountains; dined with the ambassador to the Republic of China; ate shit in mess halls; burned shit in Vietnam; and personally shit in all but a few states, in everything from marble bowls to nothing but holes!

I sipped Heineken on tap before most people knew what it was and sucked on suds of all brands in many lands, including warm brew at a genuine October Fest. I was the Army's representative for an all-branch honor guard (Memorial Day, 1975), waved to Bobby Kennedy down Portage Avenue (summer, 1968), ran from tear gas during rioted demonstrations outside the Democratic National Convention in Chicago that same year, and lived through some things so horrific I couldn't even think about them until many, many years hence, even though they might make a good book. I married one of the most beautiful girls I'd ever seen; adopted my son from Thailand; witnessed the births of my two daughters, one in Taiwan, one in Germany; and was head-over-heels in love with Bobby Sox. I'd rather eat shit and die before I'd give any of that up!

Now I had a dad that proved his love by making a trip to Germany, to the place he served during WWII, to take his son on vacation—just the two of us. We slid down the slide of the salt mines in Saltsburg, Austria; ate authentic pizza on the beaches of Largo de Garda, Italy; played chess at the base of the Leaning Tower (my second visit there); and talked about life, both his and mine. We spent more quality time together in two weeks than we had in the composite of my lifetime. After all the years of fearing his fury and feeling that to him I was a failure, this man, my dad, came all the way to another continent to ask me to bring the family home. Did I hear him right? My dad said, "Come home son, where you belong. We're proud of you. Your mom and I want to retire. It's time to turn the family business over to you—we owe you that much."

Was it an epiphany? Was he dying? Was he really talking to me, "Sissy"? Yeah, he was talking to "Butch," his junior. Oh, I loved my job and my life, but I needed to hear this, big time, from my (wanna-be) hero. I prayed before sleeping, "Thank you God, thank you world, thank you Army; Dad wants me, Vinny Junior, his son, to come home!" That was in September, 1979, and it was all I needed to hear, all my life. On my very first day back from leave, I submitted my notice to ETS (End Time in Service).

~

Lek and the kids were excited about the prospect of settling down in Portage, Indiana. Perhaps they could finally have a normal life; I know Lek tried very hard to be family to Mom and Dad since our marriage. It was all going to be good. It wouldn't be easy, starting over with virtually nothing of our own except a well-used Plymouth Volare. Lek had sold everything of value we owned to bring the family to Germany and to buy that Volare. We were resourceful; we would generate a nice income with the Bingo business booming. After all, I was a business man long before I was a soldier.

Bobby Sox didn't react to the news as well, but he was expected to rotate to his next assignment in December, anyway. Wouldn't you expect he'd want to spend every possible minute with his best bud? There was pretty much nothing we didn't share, except a bed, and even that was borderline questionable. Countless weekends, when Sox crashed at our pad, we invariably babysat and played with the kids on Friday night while the wife went out with the girls. We baked pizza or would make my own creation from Rice-a-Roni, peas & carrots, hamburger, and mushrooms (a dish we called Rice-a-Ritzy). We drank Miller or Bud and jammed to our favorite rock groups on vinyl LPs. By the time Lek returned, the youngsters were off to bed; I'd retire to the bedroom for my weekly duty as husband. It was a routine.

Equally as regular, I would come back out to the living room to hang out longer and get "stupid" with Bobby Sox. Lek followed with two pillows and a blanket, kissing me good night, knowing we planned to zonk out on the sofa. She willingly retreated back to our bedroom for the night, never acting selfish about my time with Bobby. Before the night was over, Bobby Sox and I would share the sofa and blanket with our heads on pillows, opposite one another. We would surrender the turntable to Armed Forces FM Radio, turn down the lights, get down to our skivvies, and snuggle in with our legs in somewhat of a criss-cross position. Like school boys on an outing, we'd talk trash with foul language and explicit sexual scenes, and never, ever admit to one another, to my wife (who must have known), or to any other living creature (until now) that we both sported boners by night and stained briefs by morning.

Knowing this, why did Bobby Sox start making excuses about having other things he needed to do on the weekend? He *never* had anything to do! Why, too, did he ignore me at work? Worse still, why did he openly disrespect me with his big mouth, in no fun way? Profusely irritated, it wasn't long before I no longer invited him over, causing several less-than-civil arguments at work, one of which led to some pushing and shoving. Two weeks before Christmas, Bobby Sox didn't bother to show up at the CMDSA Christmas party, which was also a farewell to him. He headed to Frankfurt the next morning for rotation across the big drink, back to the USA. I didn't get to say goodbye to that asshole. You know, big boys never cry. I'm sure that cocky twerp didn't; neither did I. Goodbye Bobby Sox...or was it good riddance? Did it really matter which it was? I'd never see Bobby Sox again. That was that. Like Robert in Vietnam, he was dead to me. Focus on the living, Viper. There *will* be life after Bobby Sox.

But life *wasn't* the same for me after that. Instead of dwelling, I concentrated on going home, as well. There was so much good to look forward to, but the Army, church, Bobby Sox, bicycling, my guitar, and music (all big parts of my life) would no longer be part of the mix. Mr. Fleck, too, had long been transferred out; a new warrant officer, named Sally Lockwood, was now in charge. Mrs. Lockwood became my first female supervisor since Gracie at Short Stop (convenience) Store. There were some adjustments, especially since she was four years younger than me, but I transitioned well; before long, Mrs. L and I were trusted team mates.

We handled nuclear codes so sensitive that they required two-man control to prevent them from being compromised. We laughed because military regulations made no provisions in the manuals for other than "two-man" control, yet it was Mrs. L and Viper (secretly, Sally and Sissy). When a mission required us to transfer said material to Stuttgart (which is a full-day's drive), we were in a highly precarious situation, entailing ingenuity in maintaining two-person control. That necessitated leaving our metal briefcase with double combo locks on the floor under the bathroom stall door, each of us keeping eyes on it while the other stood or sat on the opposite side while trying to avoid excessive toilet noise or smells. Naturally, more embarrassing was that Mrs. L had to use the men's room, or Sergeant P the ladies room; even more embarrassing was the necessity of posting an armed guard outside the latrine to stop others from entering and a second guard inside as double-security to ensure we were not ambushed unawares by the SMLM (Soviet Military Liaison Mission).

We took it all in stride, protective, but not overly absorbed by regulations requiring us to travel with front– and rear-armed vehicles, loaded to the hilt with M-60 sub-machine guns to guarantee the safe arrival of our material *with or without* us. Was there any wonder, then, that our facility was underground, or that I went through three bank-style safe-combination doors to get to my desk in the morning and had to unbar steel file cabinets before going to work? Sally Lockwood had yet another safe door beyond to her office, which held a double-combination safe for our two-man control. There is also no wonder why that bitch (SP4, now Sergeant Quinn) who patiently taught me the basic administrative control system ended up being one of the most trusted and respected soldiers I ever had the privilege of working with.

~

Now, who in their right mind would give all of that up? I would, because I was going home. In April of 1980, that's exactly what Lek, the kids, and I did, carrying both a baby and cuckoo clock. Just before departing Frankfurt Airport, Warrant Officer Sally Lockwood pinned a WO1 Warrant Officer bar on my collar, handing me her official recommendation that I be awarded the Meritorious Service Medal (MSM) for unparalleled service during my entire tour in Germany. Generally reserved for high-ranking officers, we speculated it would get downgraded to Army Commendation, which was still quite an honor, but that never happened—the down grade, that is. In June, after I was a settled civilian, I was summoned to an Army Reserve post near Green Bay, Wisconsin, where the MSM was smartly pinned on my suit-jacket lapel. Can't say that kind of thing happens very often; it came as a really needed boost to morale.

We had taken a short vacation after arriving stateside, first to visit my wife's sister, who was married to an Air Force Sergeant working on Air Force One in Virginia, then to see my Grand Mom in Trenton, New Jersey to deliver a Catholic Rosary that was blessed by none other than Pope John Paul I. (It was his first Sunday public audience at the Vatican. We happened to be in Rome on vacation at the time, me, Lek, and Bobby Sox.) He was the Pope of Change that mysteriously died a month later, if you recall. If it's true that the good die young, dare I ever talk about surviving? By the time we drove to Indiana, it was May and my birthday. The folks had one hell of a birthday present for me—not exactly the business they promised, but something almost as good.

We were given the news that Mom already retired and bought a house in Tennessee (where Dad would join her a few months later when he retired), but that they got a good price for the business (already sold) in order to put a nice down payment on the Tennessee home (which they could hardly wait for me to see). To reward me for helping with start-up costs with the business (yeah, like a year of my income stolen, which caused an unnecessary year separation from my wife...duh), they wanted Lek and I to have a new washing machine and dryer to help us get started. Not just any set; it had to be the latest Whirlpool extra-large capacity with double rinse. I'm *so* overwhelmingly blessed.

Yes, a Goddamned, mother-humping washing machine...what a second-place prize I won for giving up my ten-year Army career and a chance to become one of the youngest Sergeant First Class E-7s in what was now "that man's Army" to me—all on a promise made by my "hero," my dad.

When I got called away from bussing tables (a job I took in order to initially feed my family while searching for a real career) to receive a Meritorious Service Medal, I went, holding my head high, *big time*. I did not cry! There was no time for such nonsense. I was needed to scrape dirty plates, empty trash, and scrub toilets later that evening. I had one more feather to put in my hat. I went from two-man nuclear systems control chief to *busboy*, all by age twenty-nine. Happy Birthday! This is the kind of stuff that will make you a man—the kind of stuff one simply cannot make up. Welcome home, Vinny Pirelli, to the *real* world! Welcome home!

Marks of Honor
(1980)

I wanted to win the soapbox race
Building a car from junk in the yard
But boards and buggy wheels couldn't keep pace
My prize, a bloody knee, scarred

I wanted to star on my baseball team
Batting a homerun for all to see
But balls bounced off me, afraid it would seem
The only thing battered was me

I wanted to be liked in my teenage years
The smart one they all could praise
But in one stupid move, I ended in tears
Torn and left in a daze

I wanted to be a successful man
Recognized for all I had done
But a good faith trust was not a good plan
Callused hands scrubbing toilets; no fun

I wanted to win the love of my dad
An Atta-boy is all it would take
Not hearing it, I slunk, intensely sad
An injury one cannot fake

Goodbye to sadness and much that I love
Remember the past, but move on
Focus on life and things you dream of
Your scars become skills, a new dawn

Starting over, I want to just be me
Keeping time to my own song
That boyish stupidity has now set me free
Marks of honor, proving me strong

Pardon My French

O ne of the most difficult jobs in my role as platoon sergeant was to motivate my troops, many of whom had more education than me, to do all of their tasks with the same kind of attention to detail as they would give a complex COMSEC transceiving (both transmitting & receiving) device. A soldier's job goes way beyond the actual work station. Platoon sergeants were responsible for troops and their quarters, including maintenance of barracks and sleeping areas, personal fitness and dress standards; all troops below the rank of sergeant had to take turns policing the compound (picking up trash); KP; cleaning company, battalion and division offices and, the most difficult of all, cleaning the dreaded latrines (bathrooms).

Frequently, I'd tell stories of how I won notice and earned special privileges, even being recommended for Soldier of the Month on a few occasions, when my superiors witnessed that all my tasks were done with excellence. I especially liked to tell of the time when a colonel at Ft. Bliss, Texas went to use his latrine: he made a point to acknowledge me (still polishing away). He said, "Soldier, the only thing in this latrine that shines more than the chrome on this urinal is your pride; thank you." I always pointed out that it didn't hurt me a one iota when that same colonel sat as head of the E-5 promotion board. If none of that worked to raise work standards, I would joke, "Well, I'd do it myself, but I've already cleaned more urinals than you will ever use." If they still weren't completely convinced yet to do a good job, I might resort to, "Well, how about if I kick your pansy ass, then?" They'd laugh, half believing I was joking, but they usually ended up doing a job that made us all look good.

Why, then, was all of that no comfort to me at Yorkshire Steak House, where, in addition to bussing tables, I was responsible for cleaning the men's room? What do you think, Dad? Could it have something to do with not expecting to go from platoon sergeant to crapper cleaner? "Swallow your pride, Viper," I would tell myself, knowing that I could someday say, "Do as I say, because I did it that way—all over and over again."

My extra effort got noticed quickly by Jim Black, our area supervisor. After briefly talking with me one day, he realized I had more to offer than a clean men's room. I mentioned that I could use a good word to our general manager, Mr. Reynolds, to get some needed time off for a trip to Green Bay Army Reserve Post to be awarded a post-service Meritorious Service Medal for my leadership in military intelligence. That's pretty much all it took to clench an interview; the interview was all it took to cinch a better job. Well, what do you know, Dad, as manager-in-training, I get to learn how to clean bathrooms the Yorkshire way! Granted, I had to qualify in each job position both by performance and with a written exam, but at least I had hope for my family.

Starting over, even with a glorified busboy job and a new home laundry system, was a struggle for a family of five. My salary was $225 per week, slightly more than I was making eleven years earlier as a marketing manager for Pratt Drugs at the ripe old age of eighteen. As good a wife and mother Lek was, I believed she had no marketable skills of her own to seek ordinary work outside the home. (No doubt I was undermining her abilities, or at least overlooking them, I wanted her at home.) Besides, our baby wasn't even school age yet. Therefore, in hopes of feeding our family, we approached our landlord (Mr. Patch) for permission to use a small section of the backyard for a garden. There wasn't much grass for the kids to play on, anyway. When he said, "I don't care if you till the entire lot, including the attached apartment, if you pay rent on time," well, I was in my glory.

Wesley, my brother-in-law (Sharon's third husband), owned a rotary tiller, so he volunteered to help me work the soil on my one day off. It was a late start for gardening, but by nightfall we had planted a variety of vegetables, also planting hope with each and every seed. I gathered much of what Mom had taught me from back at the Merrillville farm, passing on what I knew to the Little One. Lek learned well; she worked hard by day to keep it fertilized, weeded, and watered, as if she had nothing else to do. Same for me—after work (though usually dark by then), I often went to the garden with a flashlight to help pick weeds; they were easier to pull with moistened soil. As I plucked, I prayed big time, "God, please bless our garden and give us a good harvest. And God, help my kids to learn the value and pride of using their hands. Amen." Looking back, God must have answered those nightly prayers, because our "Patch Garden" kept our family full during some very lean times that year.

Meanwhile, I asked University of Maryland College Park to complete a transcript evaluation of what I needed to finish my Bachelor's Degree in

Business Management, as well as if they would accept transfer credit from Indiana University Northwest. I lacked only about twenty credits, which was too much for one semester, but could be done if I applied myself in night courses for a year. Without delay, I enrolled at IUN by late August, 1980. As if my fifty-five-plus hours at work were not enough, I added four night courses; I whittled time for homework right after pulling weeds. Sometime between 0200 and 0530 I squeezed in shut-eye, but I had to be ready for and on the job by 0700 sharp. Accomplishing the near impossible, I pulled off that schedule for about five months before I ran into a tiny snag.

While teaching a broiler chef class, I asked the guys if we could hold our training in the dining room, saying in the third person, "Mr. Pirelli had a hard day and needs to sit down." I wasn't feeling normal—strangely weak, I would say. After work I went home, instead of school. Being the great wife she was, Lek suggested that I take a nice, warm bath to relax myself. Little did either of us know that's *not* the best remedy for one in the middle of a HEART ATTACK!

I could barely breathe and had chest constrictions and pains. The Little One had to drive me fifteen miles to the hospital, getting me there amazingly quick. (Which of her friends taught her how to drive, anyway? Thank you!) Lek damn-near carried me into the emergency room, where they quickly ascertained that her husband, not yet thirty years old, was in the middle of a heart attack, presumably brought on by over-exhaustion and abnormal stress. Ten days later, I was back on schedule with a bottle of nitroglycerin in my pocket, but I dropped two of my night courses in order to get more, if not proper, sleep. I gladly followed the Doc's orders to combat stress with a favorite physical activity. He suggested hiking, but I knew it had to be biking. There's nothing better to help unwind a stressed-out, muscle-constricted heart and over-extended mind than to breeze down the road on a bicycle, letting the wind massage body and brain—my next best alternative to sleep.

~

By the end of 1982, I had been promoted from manager to senior manager, then to general manager in charge of the Yorkshire Steak House at Southlake Mall in Merrillville. Mr. Reynolds was a casualty of my success. That's the way the ball bounces, the cookie crumbles, or the steak flips! I took over in December, 1982, knowing that our restaurant had lost about $1,200 for the year. Not a truly stellar performance, but I knew the place had potential—what it needed was good management and great leadership; it needed an Archist. I intended to put an "army" of lessons to work for me.

One of the justifications I was cited for in the Meritorious Service Medal was my creation of ". . . a highly acclaimed systems management program" that caught the professional eye of the National Security Agency on one of their inspections. I'm not referring to computer systems here, but the physical in-out flow of equipment repair and COMSEC material distribution. I determined that if identifiable flow could help with accountability of equipment and security, people and product flow charts for a high-traffic cafeteria-style steak house with virtually all home-made products might help productivity, food safety, and employee accountability as well.

The trick, in part, is to know your business. That meant getting to know your resources: employees; customers; responsibilities; overall potential, including limitations and all direct or indirect competition. I knew the best approach for each and every position within the restaurant because I had been in every position; I knew the placement of tables and each storage spot for every item or product used within the four-thousand-square-foot dinosaur of a facility. Not only was there a specific place and utility for everyone and everything, but employees memorized exactly where all was supposed to be. I learned to maximize employee effectiveness and customer perception, if not satisfaction. Not until years later did I need to learn more about the Ray Crock's (McDonald's) rule for success—*location, location, location*. One thing I imparted that could be taught and contagiously caught was RESPECT for the customer, fellow employees, oneself, and the business that kept us all receiving paychecks. Respect begs the difference between having a job and working, giving lip service or helping, being in the game or on top of your game. There is no substitute for respect. When I counted rewards, I thought in terms of devoted coworkers on all levels, teaching them: "Earn a dollar, and you have a dollar to spend; earn respect, and you have something of value no person can ever take away—except you." I am blessed that my teachings were well respected.

Ours was a unique, high-end cafeteria-style steak house, which was similar to others of that era, but unique in that it was "perfected," I was taught. We located Yorkshire Steak Houses in high-traffic malls, guaranteeing that we had a hungry, money-spending population waiting to eat out of our hands in our French-speaking American restaurant with an English motif. We were international in that our president, Bernie Gresham, was from Germany; he toured the world to share the finest recipes for everything from delectable honey-glazed roast chicken to our renowned chocolate whoopee cake and coconut-crème pie.

The show our employees put on for the customers was not to be matched by any competitor in any style of restaurant. Our line service workers communicated with our broiler chefs in French, and not only for show.

Language distinguished workers from customers in that incredibly fast-paced environment. A flurry of *pomme de terre por la poulet, pomme frites* or *excusez-moi, ferma la bouche, s'il vous plait*, and *merci beacoup* filled the air because timing was critical—not unlike military communications. We had limited opportunities to maximize our customer flow when hungry folks wanted to eat.

That entailed streamlining and refining departmental floor operations in order to serve more than 300 customers per hour, which, by the end of my first year as general manager, we did routinely on weekends; this carried on throughout the next December holiday season. If you don't think that's a trick, try doing that in a dining room with a maximum seating capacity of 240, plus highchairs (designed to be bulky, I'm sure, to block walking paths). Bussing tables became less of a job and more of an art form of mass turnover. Our dining room servers often doubled as line pullers (literally meaning they pulled the trays down the cafeteria line for the customer to keep the flow going). It became regular procedure to ask names on the way to the tables so that, when necessary (usually on weekends), servers could approach a table with a smile and say, "Excuse me, this is Jerry and Kathy, who graciously ask to dine with you today."

Our customers loved the game we played, though there were rare but funny accidents we sometimes caused. The time I dropped a tray full of food onto a customer in line comes to mind. He was not just any guest, but a suited gentleman in a wheelchair. The situation was hilariously funny, but, too horrified to laugh, all I could say was, "Forgive me, sir," as I reached to pick up the T-bone from his lap, knowing I had absolutely no intention of retrieving the mushrooms down his crotch. "And sir, I will of course replace your dinner at our expense. And please allow me to pick up the tab for your entire party to repay you for what will certainly be a dry-cleaning bill. I'm very, very sorry. Now, was that medium rare?" Our corporate policy was, "The customer is never wrong." Our unwritten local policy was, "The customer is never wrong, no matter how fricking wrong they often are." Viper's military policy was, "Pardon my French, but don't say fuck it, just fix it, but do it very, very quickly *s'il vous plait*."

~

Every workplace has its stories and secrets; ours was no exception. I recall one customer having met the grim reaper in the dining room early on a Saturday afternoon. Having heard his head smack the floor, I knew he literally bit the dust (not that our carpets were dusty). He appeared to be in his late 50s, partly bald, and seemed to have a neck so stout that it left no definition between his bulging cheeks and fat-layered shoulders. He was one of those guys that were so heavy (easily 400 pounds) that he snorted more than talked. He probably choked to death while chugging steak, but was too large to consider the Heimlich maneuver—who could get their arms around him, let alone pick him up? The EMS team was unable to revive the jumbo man, saying he presumably had a heart attack. The man had to lie in the dining room with a tunic draped over his head for what seemed an eternity because the ambulance crew did not have the strength to carry him out until a second team arrived. The customer (who brought a new definition to *dead weight*) wasn't with others; therefore, he was either a bachelor or he had eaten his family. I hate to lose customers that way.

A crowd gathered outside the restaurant, straining to look through stained-glass windows over dining guests to see the action. I thought for sure the man's untimely demise would kill business that afternoon, as well. The fickle American public never fails to amaze me. Droves of families with young kids scrambled to eat at Yorkshire that day. I even heard one freckly faced boy, about age ten, shout, "I've got dibs on the dead man's chair," as he pushed his younger brother away. It was quite an eventful, yet profitable, afternoon, even if we did lose one potential repeat guest.

As general manager, I spent quality time in the dining room getting acquainted with my customers and, in essence, building my own client base. I had dozens of couples and families that hallowed in their own VIP complex (a higher self-image resulting from a demonstrative display of knowing others they perceived were in a superior status). I was certain those customers became regular patrons in order to say they personally knew the boss. Although I tolerated a lot of consumer arrogance, I played the game well because they were important to our success. They were the most likely folks to spread the good word of Yorkshire Steak House—they were indeed Very Important People. In truth, our food and service was exceptional for a cafeteria; once past the cash register, all guests were made to feel valued, because they all were.

When I heard that a major competitor, Ruff's Buffet (a free-standing, rotunda-style mega-restaurant), was being built adjacent to the mall, I knew my own future business rested on consistent quality, superior service, and a preemptive marketing strategy. For months, I went from table to table greeting guests and thwarting future competition by telling them what I knew about Ruff's.

As the story goes (which I believed and sold as fact, whether or not it was), old man James Ruff was a native Hoosier like me; he, too, grew up on a farm. His family had a pig farm that he hated. Later, after college, J.R. (who inherited the farm and the initials people loved to hate from a popular TV show at the time called *Dallas*) sold the farm to chase his dream of becoming a restaurateur. He was a pioneer in the big buffet business, but instead of having employees out front to service food bars, he developed his buffet with two colossal rotating tables, one for cold food and one for hot. These gyrating tables protruding through the kitchen wall could be serviced from the back. A restaurant journal touted that his concept goal was to save footsteps, and man hours, of buffet service workers. The customer only saw the rotating buffet from the dining-room side. It really was quite appealing, a marvel to behold, which I made sure to point out to my own customers as I guaranteed their desire to taste-evaluate with my blessing. "You'll come back to where you are appreciated," I would say.

Being a fierce competitor myself, I chose a less subtle, proactive approach to undermine my competition by highlighting a few lesser-known facts to my faithful customers and captive audience, such as, "For starters, Ruff fashioned his buffet after the infamous revolving pig's trough that worked very well on the farm—so gorging hogs could only get so much!" Then, with no hesitation, I contrasted how Ruff's *hid* their workers, while Yorkshire proudly professed professionalism by placing our employees on show for our guests, asking with a wink, "Who really knows what goes on behind the wall?" Off course I mentioned how we prided ourselves by adhering to our slogan: "Our hot food is hot, cold food served cold; all food is fresh, none of it old!" Then I'd compare by suggesting, "On the other hand, Ruff's had the perception of fresh, because it always appeared to be coming straight from the kitchen, right?" Tossing in my limited knowledge of heating and refrigeration, "Is there really viable technology to keep heating elements and cold compressors working strong while spinning like a top?" If I hadn't flung quite enough competitive dirt, I'd ice the cake with, "Unfortunately, food-borne bacteria that make people violently ill are seldom thought of a day and a half later; please consider that when you choose to dine at J.R.'s, okay?" Whispering further, "that's a bit of inside info from a Board of Health-certified food inspector—*me*—you knew that, right?" By responding to my questions, they bought into my story.

Ruff's Buffet, the biggest of its kind, opened for business in December, 1983. I often peered across the mall parking lot to count a handful of cars in their mammoth parking lot. Ruff's Buffet, the biggest of its kind, closed its doors in February, 1984. "It's a marvel," I would say, adding while shaking my head, "what a shame!"

Though I genuinely loved our business and our regular guests, there is always that one or two that pissed and moaned about everything. One wrinkly, cantankerous old biddy always came in on Sunday night right before closing. Always, she asked for her steaks "very well done." Always, she would send her steak back because she could see red in the middle—*always*, except one time.

We simply had one of the finest broiler chef crews in any restaurant, anywhere. Although our system of operation allowed for quality steaks without waiting, we sometimes had a short delay near closing time, especially on Sundays when we closed early with the mall. During those slow periods, I'd give one of our closing chefs a break, taking over his spot behind the broiler. That Sunday as I took over, I saw one very old, dried-up T-bone still sitting on the broiler. Nolan didn't want to toss it into the destroy bucket—it was a T-bone, and we did add up destroys by the shift. Flinging the leather into the bucket, I declared, "this is your destroy, boy!" Just then, I heard the old gal at the order station already bitching about her steak never being done enough. When the order taker called over, "T-bone, extra-well, with fries," Nolan and I just looked at each other as I reached with my tongs into the destroy bucket to guarantee the old gal a perfect steak.

"Perhaps it was your 'destroy', but this is my save...*Biftek d'aloyau*, extra-well, *de pommes frites passez*," I announced as I spun the plate across the serving table with heat lamps in the Frisbee fashion that became part of our Southlake Yorkshire Steak House show.

"No, Mr. P, I can't look!"

As he turned to leave quickly, I added, "And you hear no evil—and Goddamn better speak no evil, you hear me Nolan?" We were both laughing our asses off, knowing it would be our secret. That was the only time the lady's steak never came back, even though that memorable and loyal customer regularly did.

Speaking of T-bones, there was one Fourth of July during an episode of our own *As the Steak Turns* when we maintained a minimal crew for what was historically a very slow day. That holiday it happened to rain wickedly, preventing most picnic plans. To make up for loss of celebration, droves of diners come to Yorkshire for steak. They did not want budget steak; the vast majority ordered T-bones. There is a normal three-day slow-thawing procedure in our walk-in coolers which allows for steaks to properly age and marinate to perfection. My counterpart that day was Barbara Handell, who had infinitely more restaurant experience than me, having spent much of her life in greasy-spoon operations. Barb had an answer for almost any critical situation.

"What the fuck are we gonna do, Barb? We can't cook frozen T-bones, unless we want to compete with Firestone."

"Don't you have any creativity," she snapped as she ran to the kitchen. I followed her to see what this wondrous woman wielded up her sleeve.

"No, Barb, you can't do that!"

"Why not? They're sealed in plastic."

Then Barbara loaded one sleeve after another of frozen T-bones onto dish racks, running them through our humongous Hobart Dish Sanitizer. I clearly recall what she said in the process: "Twice through, and they're ready to chew!"

I shook my head in disbelief; they were, I'm certain, less than ideal steaks, but, beyond a doubt, wonder woman saved the day.

That was also one of the exceptionally rare occasions when we were short-handed to the point of customer self-service. Seeing how overextended we were, one of my regular guests yelled from the dining room, "Vinny, you go on with what you're doing; the wife and I will serve coffee—you can repay us next time." If I hadn't been stretched to the fricking limits already, I might have responded with something other than, "God bless you Chuck—big time." Eva and Charles were seen talking with guests, making coffee and bussing tables *all* afternoon. I promise that they were amply rewarded over their next few visits.

~

I believed my restaurant was blessed with a motivated, dedicated crew. Jim Black (our area supervisor) and Bill Wolf (our regional director) credited *me* with creating an incredible crew. Either way, it was remarkable to watch the show. How busy is busy? Only when a workplace is refined to a point of maximum efficiency and effectiveness will one witness extraordinary results. Cliché as it may be, our restaurant ticked like a finely tuned clock, each stroke of effort happening exactly as it was intended.

I loved and lived for Friday nights at Yorkshire Steak House. I had a hard-working team of hourly employees that permitted me to be fair with my managers. I arranged schedules so that each of my three supports would get two consecutive days off every week, but I wanted a half-day off on Friday for myself. I expected all of my mangers to work that day to set us up for a solid weekend. I demanded flawless food figures, superb scheduling, and maximum motivation for what would always prove to be a wickedly wild and wonderful weekend.

I wouldn't show up on Fish-Friday until after the dinner rush stampede began. I grew into a star of the show, even though I have to admit the addition of Bernie's Baked Fish Almandine was the main attraction. One by one, starting with our broiler chefs Nolan, Robbie, and Carlson, everyone would yell, "good evening, sir," or, "good evening, Mr. P," as they would turn to salute me. Though a show, it was no joke; they were courtesies and convictions so stupid, but sincere, that they stuck. It caught on; down the line, the order takers, dessert gals, line stockers, steak servers, and cashiers all took their turn. I'd walk into the kitchen, only to be greeted by the dish washers in similar suit. Even in the dining room, the busboys, headed by Jim Genofrey, a mentally challenged lad who proved to be the fastest busser this side of Texas, greeters, seaters, and servers all stole a moment to salute and be recognized. Barry Boesky and Steve Sullivan (two subordinate managers) also joined in on the party. Only Barbara Handell would give me a hassle (and nose flip), but I loved Barb for being the tyrannical bitch-of-a-butch boss I needed when nobody else wanted to be. Every now and then I'd bring my own family in to dine, because Friday nights put Yorkshire on parade, with victorious Vinny as grand marshal. All I had to do was walk around, thank our guests, give thumbs up to every single right thing I saw, and be visible to my customers and crew. Every once in a while, one of our fans (usually an older retired military man or young wanna-be soldier) would play our game by jumping out of their seat to salute the boss—always by name, of course.

If I were lucky enough, I would come in to find Mr. Black or Mr. Wolf already visiting us (mostly because they liked having a great place to say was theirs, too). They would tease me about the ridiculous ranting and silly salutes, but, deep down, I knew they were envious, never having witnessed that anywhere else, even in their own restaurants some years back. I wonder if they knew I bribed some employees to salute them as well. After all, they were still my superiors. I wanted them in good spirits.

Whenever there was a special event, which was my forte, Bill Wolf would fly in from St. Louis and Jim Black would drive in from Illinois to participate in our day. Managers dressed in tuxedos on Valentine's Day while we served Cherries Flambé in the dining room. On Halloween, we persuaded most of our employees to volunteer time to convert our restaurant into an alternative event to trick-or-treating: a haunted house with games galore and fun food for all. We sold tickets at a handsome price, which covered our costs and permitted us to contribute a notable check to a popular local child rehabilitation center operated by Easter Seals. That only brought us more free advertisement and good will in the community. For the holiday season, my sweet spouse hand-crafted intricate pompom-style décor that we draped along wall sconces throughout the dining room as well as around our "Christmas Tree of Hope."

I had this bizarre idea to decorate our tree with "hope". Having hundreds of business cards printed in red and green with the Yorkshire logo on one side, we offered our guests a chance to write their wish, dream or hope for the world on the back side of the card, which had a few lines and place to sign. Everyone I worked with told me this was the most ridiculous idea they ever heard. There was no gimmick, no coupon, nothing whatsoever given to the customer except opportunity to participate with our pledge of hanging their "hope" on our tree. Within a week, I saw new customers returning to read the "hopes" of others, to bring friends or family in to write more or just to see if what I had done was something inane.

My idea, soon labeled *brilliant*, was more of a success prediction than a hunch. I sensed a shift of genuine good will in our country when an anthem known as "We Are the World" stormed the radio waves and everyone rushed to buy a copy to support efforts in ravaged Biafra. Timing is nearly as important as location, you know! Our Tree of Hope was up by mid-November. We were closed on Thanksgiving, but by Black Friday we were again running lines out the door, down the corridor, around the corner, and past several other businesses in the mall. We continued pumping people through our cafeteria line like a finely tuned conveyor, resulting in customer counts in excess of three hundred for several hours back to back. We made it impossible for other Yorkshires to claim our figures were fictitious. Our Tree of Hope had so many tags that it took on a life of its own. Customers marveled at the wonder of it all. Unlike any marketing device ever conceived, it preceded the copycat gimmicks some places use in the name of charity today.

Remarkably, even though I had high expectations for our Tree of Hope, I solemnly swear that profit was not my motivator. I wanted Yorkshire to be a genuine part of the "we" in "We Are the World". Not that I didn't appreciate those profits that were making me rich! I received a whopping $8,000 bonus that quarter, an amount equivalent to a half-year of my former military pay. As a recorded fact, our restaurant, which lost money before my tenure, managed to generate a twenty-six percent margin in 1984, which made us at the time the most profitable Yorkshire Steak House of one hundred fifty-seven nationwide. We, by financial analysis, determined that we achieved a distinction of having more customers that year than any other restaurant reporting to the National Restaurant Association, of any type, anywhere in the country, including the busiest of McDonald's.

~

I decided to throw an awards ceremony for my employees to give something back in gratitude. We had long established an "Employee of the Month" program that included gifts or dinner with the managers (the most sought-after reward). Everyone fancied my idea of, "Can you get caught doing something right," in which I would take time to write a public note of appreciation to an employee I saw doing something stellar while not knowing that they were being watched, to which I would attach a Polaroid picture. I believed they all earned a reward—an evening to celebrate the lives and work of every employee on our team. The managers created one-of-a-kind awards (serious and silly) for each and every employee. They were treated to live music and good food served in style by none other than us managers. It was a night to behold for sure—one I hope a few might remember fondly after all these years. They were a team to be reckoned with.

After we got credit for closing Ruff's, with statistics to show we were beating our own figures month after month from the previous year, I was summoned in July of 1985 to meet Bill Wolf and Jim Black at Chicago's O'Hare International in one of the First Class lounges. There, it was announced that Bill had been promoted to vice president; Jim was promoted to regional director (replacing Bill); I was promoted straightaway to area supervisor (replacing Jim Black).

Pardon my French, but, "Fuck you, Dad." Who needs the bingo business?

I Choose Love
(Melody & Lyrics: 2004)

V.1	I learned that joy would come from giving
	Then you took it all away
	I learned that life is unforgiving
	I need to work, no time for play
	I learned that names would never kill me
	Only make me hide in shame
	I learned that if I cry it will be
	Because I am to blame
Chorus	But I choose hope; I choose happiness
	Goals and dreams and worthiness
	I choose living with a purpose
	And I will pave my own success
	I choose bigger, more and better
	Don't let little setbacks matter
	I choose always to believe
	And I choose love
V.2	I learned that love is something fleeting
	And trust is an empty word
	I learned that *progress* implies "you're cheating"
	And *white* means "you are preferred"
	I learned that faith is for weak of mind
	Hope is for weak of heart
	That speaking *truth* suggests we "be unkind"
	We live with pain from a slapping start

Repeat Chorus

V.3	I learned that boys must behave as boys
	Got to kick them while they're down
	Boxing gloves are proper toys
	Jump, then swim, or you will drown
	If you get smacked, don't turn your cheek
	Real men will settle a score
	Survival of the fit, not weak
	Strong and mean to the core

Repeat Chorus

Ending	And more than anything else, I choose love

Location, Location, Location

Being the general manager of Southlake Yorkshire provided my family with the means necessary to finally purchase our own home, with a mortgage, of course. We found an affordable place between Portage and Valparaiso in a moderately priced subdivision called South Haven. It was a working class area with families—a solid, friendly place to rear children. To be perfectly honest, however, I spent very little time in South Haven for a few reasons beyond taking plenty of time to bicycle, dream, pray, and stay healthy.

First and foremost, I worked endlessly to earn big bonuses to give my family many of the nicer things in life my friends all seemed to have. I was caught up in "keeping up with the Joneses," even if my keeping up was out of love more than greed. Another factor was that I loved my work, or, at least, I loved having a life so full that I didn't have to think much about what my life might have been had I the courage to look for Bobby Sox. Part of that full life, of course, was wrapping up a degree. Messy as it now seems, I did manage to complete a Bachelor of Applied Science in Business Management through the University of Maryland.

Then there were our "Mr. Macho" neighbors, who were forever playing football, basketball or baseball with their sons, working on automobiles or remodeling their homes. I was out of place. My own son needed to be with them to learn "boy" stuff, unless he wanted to play army; he had long lost interest in bicycles. When attempting to remodel our bathroom myself, I knocked out two walls before realizing I lacked the skills to rebuild. Luckily, we had money-hungry neighbors available for hire to complete the job. It was a great bathroom that our neighbor Danny built for us. All I needed to do was paint, but I slipped off the ladder, landed my foot into the enamel paint bucket, and sprained an ankle, to boot. Danny salvaged most everything, but the new floor had to be replaced. Hiring others was a better plan for the future.

~

With a promotion to area supervisor, I was in new territory, both literally and figuratively. It's one thing to climb from busboy to general manager in one facility where everyone you worked with knew your trials and triumphs, which produced an element of respect that is earned rather than assigned. It's something completely different walking into another's restaurant and introducing yourself as their new supervisor. The label *enemy* was thrust upon me, and rightfully so; how could I expect anything more than defiance at first? Worse was the fact that they all loved Jim Black. I can understand that; I loved him, too! He was a genuinely all-round fun and congenial good guy to work for. He had to be good; he hired me, right?

Troubles abounded elsewhere in the area. His restaurant, in what they call The Brickyard, Chicago, was clearly an inner-city operation, not unlike inner-city housing—kind of substandard. It was moderately clean until one examined the coolers, under the booths or in the storage room. The office, too, was a mess. The management looked sloppy, so why should the employees appear better? There was a standard belief, still true today in a different context, that our work performance often matches our personal appearance. If we care about one, we generally care about the other. Today, looking good might incorporate earrings, designer jeans, and sneakers, but the concept still applies. If one likes how they look, they do better, a psychological fact borne out by business statistics and performance appraisals.

I picture the face of the young general manager (let's call him Jock), a playboy sort who was highly athletic and buddy, buddy with his employees who was more likely than not doing their jobs while they were fucking off. I'm certain he was doing a little fucking of his own with some cute girls he hired, but my focus had to be teaching him the difference between "setting a work example" and "being an employee crutch." Jock was single and fresh from college; he was as green as some mold I found in the salad prep area. Why wasn't it conveyed to me in advance that this Yorkshire was losing green? Not a lot, but it was in the red for the year, kind of like my own restaurant before I took over. Oh yeah, that's the similarity; it was the same sloppy operation I walked into as a new manager-in-training back at Southlake.

Onward to Fox Valley, where I found an almost-new Yorkshire Steak House that had been in operation for less than a year. It was like a pair of shoes still on the rack, not yet to be tried on. I knew beforehand that it was a money sucker, but it had a good, solid management team that cared and sincerely tried to nudge their way into the market. They were on the tail end of the up-scale Fox Valley Mall, a hidden business at the end of a lonely, eerily quiet corridor. Only destination diners, intent on eating at Yorkshire, could be enticed down "Quiet-Ville," but that meant lugging

116

all of their purchases back through the mall to find an exit following dinner. Being less than a comely scenario, it shot holes in the theory of putting our restaurants exclusively into malls to capture foot traffic. Location within the mall proved equally critical to survival. We were the best kept secret in Fox Valley, a delightful, but dying dinosaur.

Also in charge of my old restaurant, I was advised to pay only infrequent visits there to give the newly implanted general manager (from St. Louis, I think) an opportunity to take over unimpeded by my history with the employees. What about promoting my own managers? Surely, Barbara Handell had the qualifications. Oh, I get it; general manager was not a woman's job, right? Warrant Officer Sally Lockwood of CMDSA might disagree. Was this new era of equal opportunity restricted to the military? As directed, I drove by Southlake nightly going home, rarely stopping in to hear the old gang tattle on the new guy. I almost felt sorry for the sucker...not! He inherited a rocking business and bonus.

My furthest restaurant in was in Racine, Wisconsin. It was possessed by a team squandering profits without regard for the future, theirs or mine. They had a moderate customer base that lacked motivation to come to Yorkshire. They also had unmotivated employees, which says a hell of a lot about the management. It was so bad that on my second visit I fired one of the managers for showing up several hours late without a good excuse and without calling in advance. I surmised that type of flagrant, irresponsible practice was a common occurrence. It wouldn't be long before I found a replacement for the general manager, as well.

What does that say about Jim Black? He was promoted to Bill Wolf's job as regional director. Things were always great for me at Southlake; we were setting records for the company. I had no idea until assuming Jim's prior territory that none of his other restaurants earned a buck. I understand he gets credit for putting me in the right position, but how can he account for his other clutters? I was facing a living example of a theory I read about in college, The Peter Principle. Lawrence Peter theorized that institutions generally promote people to their level of incompetence. That described my boss to a T-bone. I give credit to my employees for helping me get repeatedly promoted, but I was certain now that *my* performance earned Jim Black his new title. I inherited more than his title; I acquired his fermenting cesspool.

I wanted to prove myself. My work was certainly cut out for me; I had to install proper management, young believers willing to follow my lead. It required a deluge of dirty details, a torrent of retraining, a monsoon of military methods, plenty of patience, and a ton of travel, but by the end of 1985, both Racine and Brickyard carved their first profits, along with another nice revenue from Southlake, although marginally less, for which the new G.M.

got full and proper credit. In December, I had the unpleasant responsibility of bolting the doors on Fox Valley. We would waste less by paying minimum rent than rent plus an impossibly high operating overhead. To be honest, there were days they didn't have enough sales to cover the cost of electricity, let alone all other expenses. The management and employees received severance packages. I now had only profitable restaurants.

Two weeks after closing Fox Valley, Jim Black busied himself with converting that beautiful Yorkshire into a facility for making commercials. Located in a Chicago suburb not far from O'Hare International, it was ironic that a market that could least afford TV commercials now had an ideal place to shoot them. I was invited to help monitor the quality of the food featured in the new advertising campaign. The main star (other than my chocolate cream pie and perfectly grilled steaks) was a very familiar face on television, a family guy who previously made commercials for A-1 Steak sauce. It was a good commercial and a great concept connection. We exhibited A-1 bottles on the tables, wrangling in promotional cash, but I cannot imagine the A-1 people being pleased to be devoid of their "exclusive-actor" contract clause. That scored Yorkshire Steak House a fricking A-plus!

Usually, I would plan my trips to Brickyard, leave in the afternoon, head to Racine, work through closing, stay over at the Holiday Inn, and return in the morning to oversee early operations. I was driving a fleet car and the company covered all my travel expenses. My only difficulty was being home even less. I carried my trusty Apple IIc in an attempted modernization of what had yet to be a computerized restaurant chain. As a company, we were still using outmoded, manual inventory, sales, and operating cost systems. I mimicked our formats to create Apple Basic programs (thanks to classes at IUN) in order to get better control on inventory and expenses. My general managers each purchased their own Apple IIc computers, with a little supervisory arm twisting, to put my programs to use, thereby saving management hours and maximizing efficiency and accuracy. We were far and away more advanced than other restaurant areas in the Yorkshire chain, leading to receiving my first Supervisor of the Year award. A nice bonus package of cash and General Mills stock accompanied that distinction. Until now, I hadn't mentioned that Yorkshire Steak House, Inc. was a wholly owned subsidiary of General Mills—you know the Betty Crocker people! (A host of other retail establishments that were born to Betty in the late 1970s through early 1980s included Red Lobster, Eddie Bauer, and Talbot's, but I'll let others tell those stories.)

~

Regardless of how much success I enjoyed, I accepted not being able to reclaim my days with Bobby Sox. During my nights away from home, I often wondered where Bobby was now, who he was hanging with, working out with or sharing a beer or a couch with until I drifted off to sleep. I missed him so much, pondering what my life would be like living openly gay in the safe haven of San Francisco. That was a distant, different world to me (living queer *and* being Californian). Recognizing that being gay was never a choice, my only option was to live a lie—or not. South Haven was my safe place of choice; until I left Southlake Yorkshire, venturing into new territory, I hadn't considered other options. I wallowed in emptiness, torn between a safe existence and living. Fearful of the queer stigma, nobody ever saw me eyeballing the cute guys coming down the cafeteria line while my male counterparts' eyes were less inconspicuously targeted on tits.

It was during those travels to Racine that I first saw (and later frequented) an adult shop alongside the I-90 when entering Wisconsin from Illinois. Terrified that someone might copy my license plate and report me, I made sure to park in the rear, backing in for quick escape and not exposing the license plate (Indiana is a one-plate state). I avoided gazing at anyone square in the eyes, and I sidestepped entirely the 10% corner...you know, the 100% queer stuff. Now I laugh at the prospect of actual moral police, although history is full of self-appointed moral dictators. Admitting that I ever went to those places is laughable, yet I was fearful, no, terrified then that someone might know the real me: this guy who liked guys. So I carefully selected magazines that were primarily straight, with perchance a kinky trio, hiding even from the cashier my intent to drool over the male models. To not belabor the point, that kind of guilty cover up went on for a few more years. There was some gay cancer thing in the news that I wanted no part of, as well. As long as I worked hard, nobody would suspect the secret side of Vinny Pirelli.

~

By 1986, I was branded "trouble-shooter" throughout the Yorkshire Chain; the company started adopting many of my ideas. I taught my teams to focus on energy efficiency more than a decade before energy conservation was a subject companies entertained seriously. Advertising scarfed up my notions for affordable local marketing promos, while Personnel lapped up my employee appreciation programs, each unveiling them as some grand corporate advancement under the Yorkshire label. None of that mattered, because Yorkshire restaurants were starting to struggle everywhere. There was indeed an explanation for this—location, location, location.

How could that be, when Yorkshire had such a captive customer source inside mega-malls? Two things were at play. First was a national decline of mall traffic in the late 1980s in lieu of a newer trend to shop in what we call strip malls (a chain-link building complex designed to give each business an independent feel and road frontage). That caused mall operators, who had mass contracts for a small base rent or percentage of sales, whichever was greater, to begin floundering. To reverse that drift, malls introduced fast-food operators into the mix, triggering instant success and making way for entire wings or corridors to be dedicated to what we now identify as "food courts." It was a mall phenomenon within about two years. Yorkshire could combat a regression in mall traffic, as I did in Southlake by actually having more than half of my customers as destination shoppers, meaning they came to the mall to eat at Yorkshire Steak House; shopping was secondary to them. But as each new Burger King, Dairy Queen, Pizza Prince or Chinese Dynasty picked a percent off the top; we began straining to have much, if anything left on the bottom line.

General Mills suffered from their deteriorating mall-based retail outlets of all types and commenced dabbling in free-standing operations in an attempt to recoil. My creativity won me a unique opportunity to join a team in developing and opening the prototype of Italian Fiesta, another General Mills first concept which was located on International Drive in Orlando, Florida, right down the street from our Restaurant Group headquarters. Experimenting, I did some constructive learning and training before declining a job as manager. Though they offered to roll over my area supervisor salary and add a few perks and the whatnot, why would I swap a proven supervisory position for what I was certain would be a major cluster-fuck? And my bosses would be those dumb-fucks in marketing? Thanks, but no thanks! Secretly, I knew all those bastards would be looking for work within a year. Let history prove me—oh shit, do I even need to go there?

So the Viper was called to the Yorkshire's rescue, headed first to Indianapolis. This entailed relocating my family, which was not an option on my part. Having purchased our South Haven home in the early 80s when finance rates exceeded eleven percent routinely, there was no hope in a five-percent market of making a dime. We would have lost our asses had it not been for General Mills buying us out to make the relocation rapid. While having a new home built in an upper-middle-class suburb, I began working in our restaurants in Greenwood, Lafayette Square, Bloomington, and Lexington, Kentucky, of all places. For three months I was on the road, living in hotels such as the then-new Super-8 chain. Even after the home was finished and family relocated, I remained on the road, spending time in Lexington, a restaurant situation silhouetting the once-troubled Racine. I saw fit to replace a couple of managers to give my teams a wakeup call. Then I broke our glass ceiling to promote the first woman, Ms. Melanie Toler, to general manager of our Greenwood restaurant. By that time Yorkshire was experimenting with a new concept called York-shire's Choice, a "less meat, more vegetable"-oriented cuisine for the uppity (and healthier) crowd in high-fashion malls. I applaud that woman. She was damned near infallible. She became my right hand man—can I say that? Kind of reminds me of two-man control.

I couldn't salvage them all; Lafayette Square, the only Yorkshire inside Indianapolis city limits, became the first casualty. A few months later, it would be Bloomington's turn to go bust. That was the corporate plan before I arrived in town; I just wasn't clued into it at the time. I played along (as if I had a choice), to my benefit. Yorkshire was again reorganizing by the end of 1986; I was elevated to a new position of regional manager (a median replacement for regional director and area supervisor positions). It involved a welcomed stock package for me in lieu of salary increase and about twice the work load—whoopee! I did get a new car, having driven the other one into the ground, and an opportunity to remain employed. Regional manager was a step up from area supervisor for me, while some poor bastards were either demoted from regional director or terminated outright. My new region included Lexington, Kentucky; Greenwood, South Bend, and Marion, Indiana, and Benton Harbor and Kalamazoo, Michigan. I seldom saw my wife and kids since I was always on the road. I managed to rescue all of those operations.

Marion, in particular, was a thrill. It was a retirement community; the chief employer there was (at the time) the VA hospital. We capitalized on our customer base by dedicating one of our side rooms to "Local Heroes". We also invited our guests to post memorabilia of servicemen or –women who honorably served in any of the Armed Forces, including those currently serving as well as those who have passed. It was a double-draw for us, and mammoth success. But I had a doughboy (meaning flaky) general manager. I needed someone who could kick shit and take charge. Since I couldn't find Sergeant Quinn, I had to rely on Barbara "Butch" Handell. Reluctant to relocate at first, Barb did, in fact, give it her all; she developed into a first-rate general manager who built yet another team I respected so much.

~

Life was re-emerging in the stock market. I seemed to be advancing nicely on modest investments and General Mills Stock. By 1987, "Big G" was reconsidering the retail market altogether; one-by-one, they sold out or spun off their non-restaurant subsidiaries. General Mills stock soared with each sale, while I profited from windfalls. I never imagined that they just as handily could unload restaurants. (A fireman dousing flames doesn't consider future property value during rescue; I might have served myself well by also being an actuary—or a mental telepathist.)

By 1987, only a year after completion of our home, I was tasked (a nice way of saying forcefully asked) with going to resuscitate the Boston market. I had to supervise six of the most gruesomely operated food establishments to ever call themselves restaurants. I packed my bags again after negotiating a much better salary package. Thank God I did, because I was about to learn that the cost of living was skyrocketing in New England. In fact, housing was so expensive in Boston proper that year that I had to locate my family thirty miles west to a town appropriately known as Westboro. For the modest sum of $1,250, I could afford to rent a three-bedroom apartment. Ouch! (Comparatively, in 2011, nearly a quarter-century later, I am paying $1,130 for a place even nicer in Rochester, New York...but I digress.) General Mills' pockets were only so deep. I couldn't finagle another buy out, so, unable to get a fair market price for a brand-new home with little equity, I decided instead to rent our home in Indianapolis. Once we repositioned, Lek had no choice but to find employment to help make ends meet. Our lifestyle had already afforded her a new car each year. Now, she needed transportation to go to work to pay for her car!

My restaurants included Danvers, Revere, Burlington, Medford, Natick, and Foxboro. They were all different, but equally dreadful, sparing Foxboro, perhaps. Some turned a profit, some did not, but all had trouble keeping employees. It was an employee market, in that there were more jobs at the time than people to fill them. We maximized high-school student employees, but they, too, knew they could get a job anywhere. Because of this, most of the time they didn't work at all, with Foxboro, again, as the only exception. (Some communities have strong work ethics; Foxboro is an example.)

I witnessed an employee in Revere slapping a customer and walking out. There was one instance when half of the Burlington employees called in sick on a Monday football night. Wouldn't you expect that from Foxboro, home of the Patriots? Natick had its cooks go on strike... we didn't even have unions. Medford was known for table sharing with cockroaches. Once, while in Danvers, I saw a man jump hysterically from his booth, stomping around and screaming, "A mouse ran up my pant leg." He all but undressed right in the dining room. What did the employees do? Did they run to his aid, to ask if he needed assistance or if they could do anything whatsoever to help? No, of course not! Instead, they gathered by a bus station and, as a group, started stomping around, mimicking the poor old soul with the mouse up his house. I simply could not terminate them all, no matter how inclined I was to do as much, but I, Vinny Pirelli, someone who thought he had seen it all, was shocked! This was not the dreamlike Massachusetts from my Fort Devens days. Where had they gone?

Yorkshire had a grand notion that they could revive the company in the Northeast by remodeling and adding buffets to all restaurants in New England; we required more drastic measures. First, I needed a mass of dedicated employees, because what I had just didn't work, in every conceivable expression of the term. What could I do? Pay more, that's what! In the spring of 1988 I raised Yorkshire's entire Boston market minimum wage to $7.00 per hour, a move so courageous that it made news, *big time*! We, who could barely afford TV commercials during dinner news hour, were now literally the dinner news story. Nobody else in the faster-food segment dared match my move. It was like playing chess, and I won! We depleted our stock of applications in less than a week, and were able to be more selective than anyone dreamed. We knew we damned well better get the guests in the door to pay the price, which included a reasonable product price hike to offset my gamble. It became a matter of, "do it well for us at seven dollars an hour, or do it anyway you want somewhere else for four something an hour." Within a month, our restaurants rocked. I had a few hurdles to overcome, such as a few cooks who already earned that much and needed yet another bump in pay and a corporate office that was ready to chop me into firewood if my plan went awry. Instead, it was awesome, back when *awesome* was still reserved for remarkable events. Yorkshire had good cause to reinvest in these restaurants.

~

Ernie Gresham, my regional vice president (the nephew of our nepotistic president, Bernie Gresham, who had undergone forced retirement), was ousted as well right after the presidential shake up. Before departing, Ernie told me about General Mills' plans to sell off all Yorkshire's Steak Houses and Choice Restaurants, which rationalized the new face lifts. I wasn't expected to be privy to this, but I latched onto that arm-twisting lever to squeeze my choice, for a change. I could alarm my market by sharing the news that all of our restaurants would soon be sold or closed or Yorkshire could make a deal to evacuate my family back to Indiana where I belonged. I hated my assignment in Boston. What they offered me was an opportunity to enter Italian Fiesta management in Indianapolis, a city which then operated three of those chain restaurants I had no faith in. I negotiated to keep my salary, but gave up the fleet car and current bonus package. It was déjà vu, starting all over again, learning each department, each job, each nuance of a restaurant concept I once helped originate. At least I could, indeed, go home. There was only one snag: the folks I rented my home in Indianapolis to caused considerable damage, enough that I had to delay moving my family back. Italian Fiesta granted me paid time leave to go to Indiana ahead of my family to re-service my own home. I did the best I could with my limited refurbishing skills while I camped on an air mattress for a month.

~

Meanwhile, I craved entertainment beyond patching and painting walls and unclogging toilets and drains. I resorted to visiting an adult book store. It was there that I met a man in his late twenties, who followed me to some sleazy motel. He stopped to pick up a six-pack. We spent the next hour getting to know each other a little. He was married and a brand-new father. He worked as a bartender for a sister company, Red Lobster, and never before had a man-to-man experience. He said his name was John, that I would be his first. I was thirty-eight; John would unquestionably be my first. There seemed something innocent and honest about him, but I guess that defies logic in that we were about to cheat on our wives—a first for both of us!

There has to be a first time for everything. John and I held each other in exquisite bliss; neither of us expected how splendid it would be. I had read stories of how gay men often found their first same-sex experiences totally unfulfilling, even wretched. We didn't. There is no fair way of describing our inexperienced experience—an all-night, breathtaking moment to keep close to heart. Nothing can compare to the first time I was freely able to intimately touch and be touched by another man. The sensation was more than explosive; it was magical. It seemed to me both natural and pre-ordained to happen. Both of us shed tears as we simultaneously unloaded our pent-up inhibitions, our mutual lifetimes of disguises, emptiness, and lonely feelings of being incomplete or outright inferior. We were made whole again, the total male package God intended us to be. I prayed with joy and gratitude, "Thank you, God, for leading me to this moment. Amen." Neither of us wanted to let go, but we each knew we had to, at least for now.

I never saw John again after that night, but I thought about him nearly as often as Bobby Sox for a long while. I had with John the one thing Bobby Sox couldn't give me—fulfillment of being the gay man I was meant to be. I never wanted to, or thought about, hurting Lek; it was only about giving something to me for once in my life; it was the one thing I had been longing for…the freedom to be me. (It's similar to the freedom I feel when I'm on a bicycle, exploring new trails of bountiful beauty like those I found throughout Cape Cod and Provincetown. I, of course, had to return for a farewell visit to reclaim my family and bike the trails one last time before retreating to Indiana. I had seen two worlds in Massachusetts, one of glory and gorgeousness, the other despicable and dreadfully loathsome. The two co-exist naturally. Life is like that it seems…my life in particular.) I knew from that day forward that I would someday be in another place entirely; I just did not know where or when. After all, it was about location, location, location and, for me this time, an opportunity of relocation within my heart of hearts. At age thirty-eight, I, Vincent Pirelli, knew there was no turning back; I was now on a true journey home.

How Can I Say Goodbye?
(Melody & Lyrics: 1972, Rewritten: 1990)

V.1   How can I say goodbye
How can I tell her not to cry?
How can I desert her?
When I don't want to hurt her
I find it hard in giving
The reason why I'm leaving

V.2   How can I say fare-thee-well?
Maybe time will only tell
It isn't easy, knowing
One void is gone, another growing
Though my heart is truly aching
It will be her heart that's breaking

V.3   Lord, help her see through my eyes
I love her still, but won't live more lies
Then maybe I'll not be so sad
And maybe she'll not hurt so bad
When we say final goodbyes

Repeat Verse 3 (Speaking first 2 lines; sing the last 3)

Enterprising Entity
(Melody & Lyrics: 2010)

V.1
While some accumulate money and toys
Amassing wealth, without restraint
Trading freedom and people's trust
Nothing left of integrity
While earnest news gets drowned by noise
Each hero proves to be no Saint
Stepping over humble folks they bust
An enterprising entity
An enterprising entity

V.2
While some are driven to politics
Gambling lives to wage a war
Trade jobs for under-table cash
Nothing left of integrity
While breaking spirits to get some kicks
Leverage all you have and more
Then pulling out before the crash
An enterprising entity
An enterprising entity

V.3
While some are living beyond their means
The mass succumb to bitter ends
Trade their dreams for broken backs
Nothing left of integrity
While skimming life without routines
Enslave them all, make no amends
Then sneak away, but leave no tracks
An enterprising entity
An enterprising entity

V.4
Until one day, the banks are gone
Your toys are all in disrepair
No office left worth running for
A breath of fresh integrity
Nobody left to tread upon
Barren land, polluted air
Your assets gone, you can't restore
An enterprising entity
An enterprising entity

All Things Impossible

P hil Nelson (the former marketing executive who directed Orlando's Italian Fiesta groundbreaker), now vice president of Operations, assured me I would love what had become of the concept since its inception. Phil was right. Italian Fiesta was a national sensation in a few short years that featured virtually all homemade appetizers, sauces, pastas, and sides. It offered a full-service dining experience, including imported wines and specialty drinks, and an intimate, separate waiting lounge with a bar. It featured their signature all-you-can-eat dinner salad with homemade Italian dressing and breadsticks warm from the oven. Every single table was accented with a fresh carnation. Complete with table covers, cloth napkins, Italian décor of rich greens and reds, and some then $15,000-worth of exotic indoor plants, it offered an upscale experience at a midscale price point. It was indeed everything Phil said it would be, but it wasn't for me!

Don't get me wrong; I thoroughly enjoy the unique Italian Fiesta experience, even though much about that chain has been modified significantly. Uncooked eggs were dropped from the salad dressing due to salmonella problems; pasta-making machines were abandoned entirely with similar issues. Gone, too, are fresh carnations and some homemade sauces, I've been told, but Italian Fiesta is still a nice place to eat for the slightly-upper-middle class crowd, since the working-class affordable dinner menu is also gone. America has a vibrant middle class (although it is dwindling) that is living on credit, which manages to keep a waiting line at every Italian Fiesta almost guaranteed. It is a genuine success story. I, on the other hand, was not—at least at Italian Fiesta.

I would equate my fit to someone shopping for a new pair of shoes. Once in a while, you fall in love with a pair that would look terrific on you, but when you try them on, they seem awkward to the point of hurting your feet. You try larger sizes, smaller sizes, and wider sizes, all to no avail. To your downright chagrin, you leave those shoes behind, though still liking them, because there is no advantage in making a force fit. There is no need to cause suffering, but it's a damn shame; they were magnificent shoes.

Thus it was with me and Italian Fiesta. Serving alcohol is one clear example, because managers were required to hold bartending licenses. I really enjoy an espresso with brandy, but if I aspired to be a bartender, I'd open my own tavern. I totally had fun with the employees, but often clashed when I exerted authority. These were not high school kids, eager to learn what I could teach. These were independent-thinking college students of legal-drinking age; others were young family bread winners. They boasted of more full-service experience than me and were keen on showing me up. I was okay with that, but the management seemed to dump all the difficult chores on this newcomer. It was their goal to break me. I'm sure they were doing as instructed by the area supervisor (let's call him Mr. Slimes). He was, of course, aware of my supervisory background, pay level, and inside connection with Phil. Perhaps I was a perceived threat. In many ways, he was much like me, except that I never isolated one individual to be rude, inconsiderate or arrogant with, unless that person had truly deserved it.

Life at home wasn't much better. Without a company car, I stretched the budget to allow a second auto for myself. It was important to me not to let my family suffer a setback. Whatever they wanted, they got, especially the Little One, who had long developed a big appetite for name-brands and new cars, like her (then) $30,000 all-white Grand Marquis with every option of the era available. It was categorically my fault she wrapped herself in super-ficial, expensive niceties. I wanted her to have all the trappings a good wife deserved, because deep down, I knew she could no longer have me. Most nights, I slept on the made-to-order sofa with our dog Cupid wrapped in my arms. I made excuses like having to work late, which was often the truth, but I would go from work to an adult book store in hopes of meeting someone like John or Bobby Sox. Physically exhausted and emotionally unfulfilled, I indeed traipsed home very late. Guilt, more than anything else, drove me from the bedroom. Sure, I could *do* it again, but I couldn't *feel* it again. I earnestly loved and appreciated Lek for the great wife she was, but she could never be the man-lover I needed her to be. Providing the Little One with her own unlimited ATM card would hopefully keep her preoccupied, therefore unsuspecting that I was living a double life. That was my plan; it worked well for an extended period.

Slimes had the upper hand, but I played his game of "follow-the-leader" with my own cutting, overtly diplomatic and snide quips of forced respect. That infuriated him, causing his attitude toward me to worsen. After six tor-turous months, subsequent to my rapid training, I allowed that scum to get under my skin. The persistent irritation festered until it drew to a head one day when I gave that slimy bastard a piece of my mind and one-month notice. I knew policy would give that much in severance, so within minutes, we agreed it would be in our mutual interest to part ways.

~

That fiery relief lasted about as long as the last guy I picked up. Now what the fuck was I going to do? Unemployment seemed a less suitable fit than Italian Fiesta. I didn't know how to begin discovering a new career, how to handle the sudden loss of income with an upper-middle-class lifestyle to uphold. I was kicking myself emotionally. "Crap Vinny, you lost your cool just like your old man did." What a heritage I received. What kind of impossible situation did I inflict upon myself and my family, with Christmas only a month away?

Fortunately, I had "reasonable cause" to be on the job market. That's what I explained to Old Southern Buffet, an up-and-coming family-style buffet restaurant. Perhaps they were impressed by my overall positive attitude about Italian Fiesta. Maybe they liked my ability to convey a clear and concise collision course of a man with solid family-style, faster-food credentials swimming uncomfortably in unfamiliar waters. It was a true scenario they bought lock, stock and, barrel; OSB stock was a discernable feature of that agreement. Rapidly coached undercover, in that nobody was to suspect my irregular contract details, I took lead position as general manager in a newly launched Old Southern Buffet on the east side of the I-465 loop around Indianapolis.

In less than a year from my departure with Yorkshire, I maneuvered my way back to Indiana and was now in charge of one restaurant with unlimited profitability potential. Our incentive as owner-operators was to assume some risk (like an owner would have) by accepting a small salary in lieu of a significant percentage of bottom-line, pre-tax profit. It was a prime opportunity for me to break free of the traditional corporate climate while making myself paymaster, in the sense that my income rested solely on my own ability to build a business, and thereby be my own boss.

Work was fun, partly because I am well suited for the buffet-style business, partly because I was wildly successful. By July I doubled our guest counts and started reaping respectable monthly bonuses. I was blessed with incredible Hoosier help, young people and wives (even two heads of households) that responded to consistently good operations as a matter of insistently good management and leadership. I was in my glory. Fulfilling the dream of an Archist, I was making what Dad would call "a lotta mullah." I worked scores of hours, but I had a terrific time both at work and after hours, disclosing now that Lek believed I dedicated even more time than I did at the workplace. Still preserving my *other* cover, I crammed in a sensuous, but self-ishly sleazy night life…before crashing on the sofa. Never once was my deceit aimed at wounding the Little One; it was about fantasizing a fabri-cated life I couldn't possess, thereby continuing to live a lie.

If one can lie about who they are, they will falsify other matters far eas-ier. I didn't always reveal to Lek how much income I was generating. We had a long-standing arrangement that I would manage the checkbook and she could exploit the ATM card. Before I seized a career with OSB, while facing uncertain unemployment, Lek took an outside job to help make ends meet. I sensed a happier woman when she was contributing, and, in fairness, Lek did spend her own paychecks, mostly on the extras she wanted for our chil-dren. She liked unleashed independence; I liked having her attention diverted. The kids liked the new swimming pool in the backyard, two new cars in the garage, and a humping dog on the porch. It was James Truslow Adams's illusionary American Dream and family, epitomized and projected. We did have many fine moments together, but like the beautiful waves of Lake Michigan, it's the undercurrents that pose the most danger. My under-world of liking guys in and out of underwear was our undercurrent. I was taking the Little One for granted.

Endings were becoming habitual, but seldom as abrupt. My regional manager (let's call him Dudley Dudd, who may as well have been Slimy Slimes' brother) previously promised my restaurant to some giant of a man from Georgia, nicknamed "George the Giant", so the more successful I became, the less Dudley liked me. Possibly, I presented a threat to him, but Dudd was too thick-headed to let my success help pave his path—he was no Jim Black. Besides, I excelled at and loved my work and the solid, but secret, life I forged for myself. That fucking Dudd fixed my finances by bringing in George the Giant with general manager benefits on top my own. George was clueless about directing any restaurant, let alone mine, but I could find no clause in my contract to prevent Dudd from burdening me with this bum. George's salary took a giant slice from my bonus, and I simmered, big time—longer than any kitchen recipe—until my attitude was scalding.

It was October, 1989, and once again the portion of "my dad" in me spilled out when I all but told Dudd to go fuck himself; perhaps I told him that, too! I even tried the "I'll give you one-month" approach, which worked with his wanna-be slimy "brother," but Dudley Dudd had a different idea.

"If you leave now, I will give you a two-week severance; if not, I'll fire you on the spot and you'll get nothing, you son of a bitch."

"Then, *goodbye*; it's been a genuine pleasure *undoing* business with you," was my final remark as I stormed out, tossing my keys in a table slide that slammed his briefcase for effect.

Instead of going home, I went to pray in private. "Oh dear God, what did I do? What am I going to do now? Help me; this is simply impossible! Amen."

~

It was relatively easy to explain leaving the military after a decade and even General Mills Restaurants after almost another ten years, but I was employed less than a year with Old Southern Buffet. I knew it would be a formidable challenge for me, in my late thirties, to sell myself into another solid restaurant position, especially with a ten-month defect tossed into the conversation. But having had my fill of restaurants anyway, it was time to explore other income avenues. It was high time, I thought, to spend more time with my family—at least that was the plan.

My youngest daughter (Miranda) had a birthday party the prior August, so Dad got to play deejay in a highly memorable garage party. It occurred to me that, with a moderate investment, I could deejay for a living while being my own boss. OSB stock was sold to purchase more portable and durable speakers and other rugged gear, including this new technology called compact discs (CDs). I owned mostly cassettes, so an updated quality deck for that seemed reasonable. As not to let the LPs go to waste, I was easily suckered into a second professional turntable for spinning. Quality entertainment required equalizers, audio mixers, microphones, and a new thing called a *Snap, Crackle & Pop Machine* that would reduce any flick of sound brought by a fleck of dust, nick or scratch on records or tapes. What about a reverb unit for an acoustic echo and dynamic range expander to accentuate the highs and lows? When I wanted to spin mostly for show, I could have premade tapes running from a reel-to-reel camouflaged under the costly, but efficient, homemade equipment stand. I knew I could build something!

There was also the matter of lighting. Fire lights, disco balls, black lights, strobes, and floods were added. I needed manual controllers for some and hype controllers, which would ignite other lighting by the beat of a drum or squelch of treble, for fun. Lighting cannot be pitched on the floor, so elaborate light stands, which developed into a filthy-expensive priority, had to be strategically placed for effect, thereby necessitating specialized cable extensions. Then, all I needed to do was promote myself as "The Viper" through local newspapers, fliers, and business cards, and acquire seed money to get my name out to bars, schools, and clubs. It was more cash outlay than I ever dreamed it could amass, all while keeping up with the mortgage, two cars, three kids, a wife addicted to ATMs, a swimming pool with multi-level deck and new cover since winter was coming, and a humping dog on the porch. It was indeed going to be another bleak Christmas.

To bag the best, most-prominent and highest paying gigs, I needed to sport a union card, which cost all but my left nut. Before obtaining that, I faced union stipulations for a broader music inventory (which had to be all original purchases to prove royalty loyalties). All of that compelled more credit cards, because I was fresh out of cash, and remaining investments were less than liquid. I managed to contract some respectable gigs: bigger weddings, birthday bashes for brandish bitches, and high school sock hops, but my leading event was an after party for the Rolling Stones at Union Station (paid for by some marketing company), in which Mick Jagger actually appeared for at least five minutes. (Hired hands didn't get introduced.) On a couple of occasions, I inadvertently double-booked engagements, but I solved those situations by splitting equipment and music. I entertained one booking, while my daughter Melody and her boyfriend kept me from getting sued by the other.

Though playing deejay gave me immediate cash flow, it wasn't enough. On evenings when I wasn't "The Viper," I sold family photo packages for Rainbow Studios, having linked up with them through a photographer's connection made at one wedding reception. Still struggling, I ventured into yet another endeavor, a pyramid scheme I fell victim to through late-night TV. It was called NSA—in this instance, Natural Stream Association, who developed a trustworthy water filtration system for homes. It was a laudable product, but there was defective initiative. I took a bath on that water deal and needed an abusively high-interest loan to cover that cost. In truth, I ended up giving away most of those filters to friends that helped me achieve success over the years, which was not such a bad thing, except that it perpetuated a cash flow leak, like water down the drain.

Still clinging to good credit, I was bondable for work in an overnight check-sorting facility for a major bank. It proved to be one of the most physically demanding, manually mundane, most unappreciated jobs I ever held. Money weighs a lot when in the form of paper checks packed 10,000 per crate, ten crates per bin and ten bins per pallet. I couldn't count the endless bins we processed through some electronic scanning and sorting machine each and every night. Invariably, one or two checks from each batch would refuse to be scanned or a staple slammed and jammed the machine to a halt. Unless you've handled that much paper, you cannot fathom what dry hands are about; each and every finger splits and throbs. Add to that a hundred paper cuts, and you can almost feel my insanity!

Though check sorting paid pittance, it was full-time work with mandatory overtime. I labored from midnight to about 1000, slept and sold at the photo studio from 1600 to 2000 a few evenings per week (wishing sales of NSA water filters on the others) until weekends, when I had DJ Viper contracts. Knowing I was on a first-class track to a second heart attack, I soon ceased selling photos and water filters, but I tried my best to hang onto the name I was building for "The Viper." My secret social life ended after Old Southern Buffet, but the family time I planned for never came to fruition. I teetered on an impossible dead-man's cliff for what seemed an eternity. I broke down one morning after work, begging God to help me out of this impossible situation. Lek was already off to her place of employment; only Cupid cared if I cried. "God, what is it you have planned for me? Please show me. Amen."

~

In March of 1990 I received an unexpected and highly welcomed phone call from my old boss Jim Black. He and Bill Wolf jumped ship, following me during the sell-out phases of Yorkshire Steak House; they were involved in a new buffet venture called Newstyle Family Buffet, an operation fashioned uncannily similar to Old Southern. Jim quickly injected, "We are ABC, 'A Buffet Cadillac', Old Southern perfected, and we want the best people we know to run our operations—naturally we thought of you." Okay, I'm still a sucker for "I Want *You*" campaigns, but I really welcomed the thought of a bailout. (I wonder, years hence, if they knew beforehand of my financial predicament.) In reality, it was OSB in a different flavor, in that Newstyle's Operations vice president came from Old Southern, bringing all the recipes. Newstyle's director of Facilities came from OSB, bringing all the blueprints, as well. Wouldn't you guess that Newstyle would be in totally unscathed markets? How fun is that?

My location was to be Baltimore, necessitating another move, but I was more than ready. I asked for a small signing bonus and a week to settle business in Indiana. The following Friday I was packed and I proceeded to Maryland. Lek and the kids stayed in our home until school was out. (I say with tongue in cheek, since I was already two months in arrears with our mortgage, car payments, and several credit cards, unbeknown to them.)

It was a brand new day at Newstyle Family Buffet—hip, hip, hooray! At least I didn't have to agonize about a back-stabbing boss. Jim Black was loyal if nothing else. (Let's say, competent?) My presence didn't instigate a management fight. They fervently awaited their new general manager, who, with welcomed assistance, brushed up on procedure. What a firecracker crew they had already trained! It was a decent restaurant in the Essex suburbs of Baltimore; it simply lacked adequate customers to turn a profit. That's simple enough. Immediately digging out and dusting off a variety of previously proven local marketing programs found effective over the years, we captured our first black numbers within sixty days and were neck deep in having fun.

~

[Allow me this vital tangent pertaining to fun in the workplace: Over the years, I can recall only two associates that were bright and cheerful from the moment they woke until (presumably) the time they lay down to sleep. One was Sergeant Suzie Hicks, back at CMDSA in Ansbach, Germany. Though I hadn't mentioned her before, Suzie's influence was that of humor with a positive Christian spin. She taught me how to laugh at myself, especially when she convinced me that this introverted guy named Staff Sergeant Pirelli could, indeed, put on a Santa Claus suit. Though I had long been a Christian, Suzie also reminded me, through her gift of Og Mandino's *Greatest Miracle in the World*, that I was irrefutably one of God's one-of-a-kind miracles; that realization was a genuine spiritual awakening.

Suzie further apprised me, after the Christmas party that rumors previously circulated throughout the battalion that Bobby Sox and Viper were having an affair. That gossip, both inaccurate and unfair, shook my workplace, but never my confidence. It explained why Sox abhorred me. I prayed that his esteem and spirit had not been punctured. Suzie taught me that, "perception is reality when reason fails." Then, with a usual funny quip, Sergeant Hicks whispered the only vulgar word I ever heard from her Christian mouth, "Do you know what I really think? He's gone; so, does it really matter what people say? Fuck 'em, if they can't take a joke!" Then she laughed, holding a guilty hand over her mouth. Suzie was my friend, my teacher, and right on all accounts.

The other person in a humor bubble was Ms. Millie Freeman, my senior manager who was second in charge at Newstyle in Essex, my friend till the end. When I would approach near panic if more than one employee called in sick on a shift, Millie taught me to, "laugh, have fun, and make the best of all the rest." Her employee instincts were second to none, exceeding my own. Perhaps I brought business experience and practicality to our team, but Millie was the laugh-given, life-driven star of our show. She's one of the few natural comedians that could literally make you "wet your wear" with colorful, laughable wisdom. Millie, not unlike Suzie, brought fun to the workplace. Fun is an essential ingredient for a food business to prosper and profit from. Millie was also my friend, my teacher, and right on all accounts. Millie would also become the first woman at Newstyle to be general manager, but only when I was again advanced. I liked leaving a legacy of promoting promising "lioness leaders."]

~

During my first five months in Baltimore, I lodged in cut-rate motels, a portion of which was expensed; living was not cheap out East. I cashed in some "Big G" stock to help cover basics at both ends, but I still had mounting debt on credit cards with late fees from my former existence in Indiana. I also needed fresh credit to fund my current ventures and work-related family separation. Everything simply cost more: laundry, dining out, entertainment and the growing demands of three teenagers back home. To momentarily relieve myself of the stress, I started enjoying a beer or two after work. I inquired where the gay establishments boomed and discovered the more seedy part of Baltimore, where a closeted gay man could find hunky, hung, young guys to party and romp with, sometimes for cash, other times for mutual satisfaction. Yes, I found Washington Street. I became part of Washington Street. I employed Washing Street big time.

Not surprisingly, I ran across one of my own employees in one of the bars; let's call him Peter. He wasn't twenty-one, but certainly not jail bait. On the other hand, Peter was "off limits," since he was my employee. Though I wasn't aware of any written rules at Newstyle, I knew not to mix work and play. On occasion, the thrill of doing the taboo takes precedence over professionalism. I was using the proverbial wrong head; I knew it. I didn't care! I made my bed and gladly slept in it. It wasn't long before Mr. Pirelli was also providing for his boy toy, by choice, fearing only that it would end too soon. It never developed into a problem at work; because Peter left my employ of his own accord, let's say to pursue other interests or pleasures.

Let me not suggest for a military moment that the willful involvement of a married man with any employee should be justified or condoned, but it explains part of who I had become—one side of me, either the false side or true side, depending on point of view. I lived two consecutive lives for a long while.

~

By the end of August, 1990, it was time to bring the family to Baltimore. It was also time to put my financial house in order by obtaining an attorney who arranged a necessary bankruptcy in Indianapolis. We endured the shame of having Lek's brand-new Bonneville repossessed, the house recaptured by the mortgage company, and my assets frozen, liquidated, and dismantled piece by frivolous piece. We even hawked our jewelry to get money to retain the attorney. I convinced the Little One that we'd leave this impossible mess behind and start anew in Baltimore. I was lying, of course, because I knew another impossible mess of my making might soon materialize.

Home life in Baltimore doesn't ring a bell because I didn't spend much time at home. The apartment was your average three-bedroom townhouse in some middle-class west suburb of Baltimore. The wife took work at a major department store. Look-Bon already graduated from high school, but he wasn't college inclined, so he opted to stay in Indianapolis to live and work. My eldest daughter Melody took her first job in a mall food court; little Miranda concentrated on studies. By September, I was already supervising two restaurants in Baltimore and picking up two in Pennsylvania, one at York and one at Lancaster. It was also time to confront my fears and my wife about the double life I was living. This time, I had no choice. I had become a carrier of at least two venereal diseases, one which was a third-world parasite that required the state of Maryland to notify the Little One officially. I advised her first, but the damage was already done. She ultimately proved positive, and was treated successfully, for both. Peter, too, was infected; though I undoubtedly contracted my disease from him, I was to blame, being the older, more responsible partner. His treatments were willingly paid for by me, yet the unforgivable scene was enough to end a short-run relationship. Peter moved from the apartment I provided near Essex; I shuffled in. On the job, I was constantly on the move.

The Washington Street Park is a romantic place by day, but an unfit place to roam by night. It was a beautiful, but overcast, autumn afternoon on the winding walk, dusted with maple and oak leaves. The Little One and I walked hand in hand throughout the park, as I beat around the bush in owning up to more than just infidelity. We stopped to sit a spell on a park bench that was also in the autumn of its days, with crumbling cement legs and missing a wooden slat or two. Lek wept, softly, but very deep and inward—the kind of cry one hears from the survivor of a lost loved one. For all her frailty of frame, her spirit was eternally strong. She was not a girl to often cry; I only recall a few times before when she had. They all involved learning of the deaths of those she loved: her brother, who was killed in a skirmish along the Thai-Cambodian border, two sisters, Aunt Ruthe, and now our marriage. Hers was a cry that will haunt me until my very last breath.

How could I possibly explain that my love for Lek, from the beginning through that day, was honest and strong? If it had been another woman, she might have known how to react. I had to explain that the very first time I ventured outside the marriage for sex during extended travels was not with a girl, but with a boy...well, that kind of thing I hoped she would understand as nature. Didn't she see the signs all these many years? No, she didn't! I was a consummate liar, the best there was! It was so ingrained in me to lie that I knew nothing else. To lay down the truth of my lies over recent years to the only woman whom I ever found sexually charming was a wound for her beyond anything I ever sustained. She was crushed; how could I envisage understanding and sympathy?

(Looking back two decades, I now identify with the pain I caused—the selfishness of my words and actions. Pain supersedes unintended hurt. Why couldn't I see that it wasn't only our marriage under assault? I had, at least in

Lek's mind, attacked her womanhood. She blamed herself for not being woman enough for me, but the realism was quite the opposite: Lek wasn't man enough for me. No words in the world would be truer than what I said to her: "That doesn't make you less of a woman, Lek, it makes you Super Woman. You are the only girl to ever turn me, a gay man, on!" She didn't hear me. She still hasn't today. Little One, I never meant to hurt you, let alone hurt you that badly. I will always love you. I choose to overlook your own misgivings to praise the good wife you were to me and good mother you were to our children. I do miss you so.")

At the time, however, I was more self-absorbed. With or without Peter, it was time for me to divulge the real me and uncover my new life. After living alone a few short weeks, Lek begged me to come home to her and the kids. She sought a compromise to our marriage; it was her offer not to question my whereabouts on Saturday nights as long as I would come home on Sunday. The new week would be normal until I would be gone again on Saturday. Did I say normal?

There is nothing whatsoever normal about such an arrangement, but we gave it a fair try in November and December of 1990. Oh, who am I kidding? There was nothing fair about such an obscure arrangement to either of us. When I would get home Sunday morning, I realized that Lek was still awake and sitting in the same corner of the sofa as when I left. How fair was that? How cruel it must have seemed to her; how heartless and insensitive I must have seemed as well. I couldn't endure the traces of pain streaked down her cheeks. I would rather die, however, than give up my newfound freedom—an opportunity to be the man I was born to be. It was justifiably impossible to keep torturing ourselves this way.

~

In January, 1991, Newstyle offered me an opportunity to head up their largest, most prospectively hopeful, albeit not so profitable, market in Buffalo, New York. After they had just transferred my family to Baltimore, it appeared they knew about troubled waters at home, though I assumed they did not know why. It was a remarkable offer made by our human resources manager directly to my wife, not to build a bridge over troubled waters, but to burrow a gulf between her and one of Newstyle's key employees.

Following is the message, as it was relayed to me: "Mrs. Pirelli, we understand the difficulty of your marital separation; we sincerely empathize with you. However, we need to protect our business. It is not in the best interest of Newstyle Family Buffet to relocate you and your children to Buffalo along with your husband. You may, of course, go on your own accord; however, it will be without corporate assistance. We also think your presence in Baltimore could prove to be a company disturbance. Therefore, we are offering you a one-time opportunity to relocate yourself and your children at our expense to anywhere in the Continental United States that a Newstyle is not currently located, provided that you sign a written agreement to never interfere with your husband's work or workplace in any fashion whatsoever."

Lek scurried at that chance. She chose none other than my own home town. Even if my parents were no longer there, Lek knew Portage, Indiana. She felt safer there because she had my sisters nearby and some of her own friends to lean on when her world had seemingly come to a stop. She made the best of an impossible situation. I helped her secure a used car, but it had to be on her own credit; mine was in the gutter. After nearly nineteen years of marriage, we were fully and legally separated. Divorce would follow eighteen months later. Thanks to me, our lives had become an impossible mess. The only thing we had left was hope of a better tomorrow.

Kindly Understand
(Melody & Lyrics: 1974)

V.1   By the time you find this letter
Darling, I'll be gone
Understand, please understand
But a man must find his place in life
Instead of drifting on
Understand, kindly understand

V.2   And though my love for you
Will never parish
Understand, try to understand
If not, then for the memories
We still cherish
Understand, kindly understand

Refrain   Though my search in desperate sorrow
Must take me away from our home
Understand that tomorrow
A better life will come

V.3   And for all of the promises
I have broken
Understand, I beg you understand
And if all too many words
Remain unspoken
Understand, kindly understand

Repeat Refrain and Last Verse

Broken Dreams

[Please be advised, this chapter would be rated R (Restricted) using the movie rating system. It contains graphic language, adult subject matter, violence, and both sexual scenes and innuendo. Some early readers have found it disturbing; others proclaimed it objectionable; therefore, if this book is being read by persons under the age of 17, parental supervision is encouraged. That said, the content in Broken Dreams is an integral part of the story; if kept in context, it may well be used as an effective teaching tool when guiding gay youth.]

Everybody who knows anything knows the saying, "I love New York." Whether they are talking about the Big Apple (New York City), Niagara Falls or anyplace between, the saying applies. Once you're here, born into the state or transplanted, you are from here; once you are from New York, you'll always come home. I am no exception, and I am at home in New York—anywhere, New York. I love every nook and cranny. I am especially fond of Buffalo and Niagara Falls, Rochester and Syracuse, Utica, and Albany, Adirondacks and Catskills, Manhattan and Binghamton, and Finger Lakes and Cornell. Let's face it, I love New York. It is here where I spread my rainbow wings and flourished in my flings, flightiness, fantasies, fetishes and future. Here is where I flaunted my feminine side, fretted my biggest fears, fucked up, fucked off and fucked almost every available fairy in sight—even a few that weren't even queer.

I was what we would call back in the day a pig, a big time pig, to boot. One shouldn't be so proud, I guess, of being such a slut and sleazy man-whore. At the time, I liked laying the field, the whole field, and nothing but the field, so help me God. If any of this sounds cliché, borrowed or stolen, all I have to say is tough shit. It was real, expansive, expensive, and, for both better and often worse, it was part of me, the gay part I dreamed to live out. I wasn't only making up for lost time; I was making up for all time, lost or not, yours, mine, theirs, friends of theirs, and friends of their friends. Some guys, and now gals, I hear, keep black books, possibly now on an iPad. Back then I kept several books of rainbow colors. I'm fairly sure I had listed over 300 fellows I personally sacked, and I don't mean fired, although some of them needed to be in *that* book, because they sucked, and not in the good way. That was before I stopped keeping track! I was the gay epitome of pig, but I didn't discriminate. I played top, bottom, butch, prissy, passive, aggressive, lover, pimp, master, slave, boyfriend, and asshole. I played with every race, creed, color, age, and sexual variation. Have you heard the expression, "I fucked my brains out"? Well, I had become so addicted to sex that my ability to mentally function was vastly impaired, to a point of mental fucking illness. It was all-encompassing, the most glorious, most graphic, most grievous part of my life, away from work, that is, because I had long learned to compartmentalize my work and play lives, absent a home life.

~

Work was another story. I don't know if I had the Midas touch, if I was one of the lucky chosen few, or if I'm actually that damned good at running a business. Immensely successful in converting pits to profits, my opportunities in New York would be no exception. All four of my restaurants were the pits when I took them over. Only Niagara Falls made money; that was because the exchange rate fell in our favor on this side of the Canadian border. Canadians came over in droves to shop at the outlet mall and eat at Newstyle. The restaurant crew was a rough bunch to manage, but I won their confidence, and, in time, earned their respect. That only came after I taught them to win the battle of buffets, thereby winning awards and bonuses, as well. My teams, all of them, willingly became the finest restaurant teams anywhere to be found. One by one, they embraced my Philosophy of Archism and embarked on sizeable profit making.

One of my secrets of organizing in the service industry is to invest in training sessions that broadened the scope of the workplace by teaching employees some lessons on existentialism, internalizing motivation. Also, young people need to hear that their decisions and performance impact the lives of others as much as their own. It matters to fellow employees whether or not they arrive as scheduled, on time, or early and do a good job. A smile and kind word matter to the senior citizen they encounter that has possibly gone an entire week without having someone to talk with. I often spoke using theoretical "What if" scenarios, refusing to dumb-down my crews.

"What if that mom, dad, and their five snotty-nosed brats you just complained about, needing so much extra attention happened to be on a once-this-year celebration because he had been out of work since the steel mill closed? What if this is the only place in town they can still afford to go for a special family event? Wouldn't you *then* want to bend over backward to help make their day spectacular? You'll forget the dollar tip the minute it's spent; you'll never forget the feeling inside when that mom thanks you, with tears in her eyes, for helping them have such a good time. And what about the old buzzard that barks at you for no reason? What if he might not be able to verbalize the hurt of having recently lost his wife of forty years, and now *nothing* seems right without her? If you could draw a smile from him, would you not carry that in your heart all day? Everything else you encounter that day will seem easy."

I would challenge managers to "see and hear" the little achievements of their employees, and remind them of how an encouraging or uplifting word is all that is required to gain repeat excellent behavior. I would reinforce that notion by reminding the manager of the time I complimented him on his unusually crisp, white shirt, at how professional and dignified it looks, then point out that they have worn crisp, white shirts ever since. Perhaps I taught Pollyanna at times, but in my heart, there are no hypotheticals when it comes to customer service; there is no shame in serving others well, only pride. If I can cause someone to internalize that sense of accomplishment and pride, I will have given them something for a lifetime. If I can teach another to cause the next person to internalize pride, I have set Archism in motion. It is what I believe. Positivity can positively be taught. Leaving that imprint is the trademark of an Archist.

Why would my local marketing ideas be any different? We couldn't afford TV commercials, but I could afford even less to not promote our business. The ideal is to create a win-win program, meaning that both the customer and business wins, but what if we could expand that rationale to include employees and a charity of their choice? Would that be a win-win-win-win situation? That was my plan. Regionally, I had the employees select a charity by vote; there was a clear winner, a teen refuge home, called The Villa, for recovering drug– and alcohol-dependent youth. I went to The Villa to inquire what our employees might contribute, other than cash to the coffers that would make a viable difference to their clients. They suggested gymnasium equipment: boxing gloves and punching bags, dumbbells and weight belts, and basketballs and hoops. The employees could visualize what they were working for, which was always an incentive to success. The task was to sell dollar-off coupons for a dollar; one hundred percent of the proceeds went toward gymnasium equipment for The Villa. Employees were permitted to sell coupons at school, at home or in their places of worship. Each coupon could be cashed in for a dollar off the contributor's next visit to Newstyle. The customer had a vested interest in returning. What about employees? The top-selling employee of each unit won a paid trip to The Villa for the ribbon-cutting ceremony. The top selling unit won an after-hours 50s party, where managers would serve the unit cheeseburgers, fries, and milkshakes, none of which were on our buffet menus.

What the employees didn't know was that I also talked an independent, local sporting-goods dealer into a cross-promotion. If Elmwood Sports covered printing costs and sold our coupons for the charity, its name would be printed on the coupon as a contributor. If the company sold $500 in coupons during the month-long promotion, we would purchase all of the equipment at that store. Do I need to ask if we added another "win" to the mix?

The sales promotion and two-month redemption period did more for bringing new guests in our doors and building repeat-customer loyalties than any single local marketing or advertising campaign I witnessed of any type in all my retail years. We enjoyed nothing less than region-wide astonishing results. More customers meant more tips, better pay, bigger staffs, happier employees, motivated managers, cleaner restaurants, fresher foods, and a dining experience that perpetuated more customers, thereby putting a stranglehold on some competitors. I guess there were a few losers, after all. What a shame!

Within a year, my region expanded to include two restaurants in the Rochester market, one each in Syracuse and Utica. I also remotely guided a distant Newstyle in Long Island, although it was technically in another's region. In short, but in fact, I was running one-fifth of our corporation, turning in 200% of all corporate pre-tax profits. In other words, the other four regions managed to somehow lose half the profits my teams were generating. I surpassed all expectations, winning awards, recognition, special stock negotiations (for me and my managers), cash bonuses, amazing trips, and bragging rights that I will never relinquish. My work life was equally a real, progressive, and important part of my life. Let there be no mistake, though: I had long since learned to work for a living instead of living to work, like I had done for most of my working days.

~

By April of 1991, I sent a memo to my teams announcing that, "From this day forward, there will be no acceptable discrimination, in mindset or practice, within my region. All men and women of every race, creed, color, family or financial background, neighborhood affiliation, education level, age, and sexual origin will be openly and absolutely accepted and embraced as part of our valued New York Newstyle Family Buffet Team. You are hereby notified, officially, that you are working for a hardworking, qualified, fair, and impartial regional director that so happens to also be gay. This will be the end of that discussion, and will hereby immediately and permanently end any and all possibilities of leverage against me, should this knowledge have come to you by other means. I am and will remain your supervisor, unless or until you are no longer able or willing to work for me or my management staff. Also effective immediately, both men and women within my employ will have equal rights to wearing earrings, provided they do not dangle and cause food-borne hazards. Thank you and God bless us all."

You can imagine the flak from headquarters. Jim Black flew in from our offices in Tampa Bay to confront me on the issue. He was angered, not that I had made such a statement, but that I had not trusted him long before to accept me as gay *and* professional. He actually felt somewhat betrayed, having worked with me on and off for more than a decade. He left with a clear understanding that I was out and proud, not about to go back into the closet for him, Newstyle or any "he-man" that thought he was going to kick my pansy gay ass. Jim assured me the company would accept me, as well as look at corporate policy on equality, but there were to be no earrings on my male employees. He also wanted me to run future policy by him first; he was fair! Jim Black was always fair, but especially so on this Friday. That's why Jim Black is so loved.

Sure enough, the very next business week each unit and supervisor received an updated policy, by fax, on Equal Employment Opportunities, which included "sexual origin" as an added category. Also sure enough, at our very next regional director's meeting held at Virginia Beach, I was informed that men in Newstyle will not be permitted to wear earrings. Our then-president, Jack (let's call him Ass, former president of Mandy's Burgers), was emphatic, pounding his fist on the table to reinforce his loud statement of, "no Earrings!" I told him it was outright discrimination against men, but he shut me down in front of everyone. They were all quiet, except me. I appealed on the basis that New York was not like other territories, that earrings preceded me in my region and had been long accepted as part of the young culture in my adopted state. All I heard was another resounding, "NO!"

Of course, that's not the end of the earring story. Looking back, was it foolish of me to argue the point? Maybe it was overconfidence in my relevance to the company? Perhaps it was my total arrogance; I'm not sure. Whatever mindset it was that drove me to drive during lunch break to the local mall to have my left ear pierced; I'm here to tell you it all but drove Jack Ass over the cliff. He totally lost his cool, and threatened my job, verbally assaulted me by calling me every gay fornicating name in the book, and admonished me in front of all my peers. I was not fired, though, or asked to resign. Jack Ass threw up his hands, slammed them both on the table, and said, "The very first time I get a complaint of an earring in someone's soup, your ass is grass, and I'll be the mother-fucking lawn mower. You better believe that Mr. Smart-Ass Pirelli." That was the last supervisory discussion of the issue; Newstyle employees all across the country were forever permitted to wear stud-style earrings. Jack and I considered each other an ass, but to the rest of the company and corporate staff, I was a hero—the one man who dared stand up to the president and won. Or did I? Was he actually afraid that he crossed the line, risking the chance that he might be sued for discrimination based on his own, now improved, Equal Employment Opportunity Policy? I don't want to know, but we were never great friends from that point on—goodbye, stock deals! It wouldn't be long before Jack Ass was ousted by the board of directors. Rumor was that Jack's thoughtless outbursts were a detriment to the company. I was cruising in dream territory.

~

Among my testosterone triumphs, I tethered a handful of genuine boyfriends, including a couple that I truly cared about. I was addicted to play, as were they. Only a dream could be short-lived in such a lavish and lustful lifestyle. True to their policy, Newstyle embraced me fully. When I won a regional quarterly food-control contest, which involved points based on independent, unannounced food-quality evaluations coupled with some formula involving our food cost percent, I and my boyfriend of the time were given a first-class Bahamas cruise, complete with airfares, spending money, car rental voucher to tour Cape Canaveral after the boat trip, and the opportunity to swing by for a grand welcome at corporate headquarters before heading home. It was a week to die for, more than anything I had dreamed of at the time. Of course, my new vice president of operations (Jim Black) and president (Bill Wolf) were also onboard the big boat with their wives. That was in April of 1992. By July, my dreams turned into nightmares.

Beyond being Buffalo's biggest slut, I wore a professional reputation of respect that I diligently tried to preserve in western New York. My rapport with product purveyors, both dry and perishable, was (borrowing from Ronald Regan) "trust, but verify." I could negotiate regional food deals with companies like Frysco Foods and Bills Poultry; sometimes I did not sign agreements for weeks on end. One time, I even scored a thirty-grand produce contract on a handshake alone, without signing a single document. My word was good, appreciated, and honored by our suppliers. Some managers believed it was because my Italian name preceded me, in that the Mafia influence on the food industry was not too far in the distant past. They would joke, "Hell, yeah Mr. Pirelli; you can always make an offer they can't refuse," or, "I don't think they want to wake up next to their horse's head," both references to *The Godfather*.

Then, out of the blue, one of my stores was refused delivery unless they could pay in cash.

"What the hell? There has to be a mistake. What do you mean we are ninety days in arrears for my region? I'll call accounting; there has to be an error." There was no mistake. Cash flow had pretty much flown out the door; we had to stop deposits to pay in cash if we wanted to stay in business. The situation straightened itself out in a couple of weeks. Then, I heard rumors from an old rival in Old Southern Buffet. Newstyle was going to get squeezed by the stock market until we were in a leveraged sellout position. Old Southern simply wanted our markets.

Bill Wolf was replaced by some faggot hater nicknamed "Sam the Sham" for worming his way into our company without a discernable history. Sam gave me verbal instructions to call headquarters, reporting my location, every two hours. Jim Black was demoted to regional director again as Sam did away with his position entirely; we were facing new problems. Newstyle had set up its own building company (operating separately, of course), which secured leases and constructed new facilities on behalf of Newstyle throughout the Midwest and East. The right hand was paying the left hand twice or three times the going rate for planning, construction, and equipment, with private stockholders reaping countless profits while the original Newstyle was left carrying the credit bag. We owed more than double what our business was worth; now, with our cash-flow problems, our credit rating was about to get slashed to bits. Because we only recently started trading publicly, word hadn't yet gotten to shareholders. In retrospect, this was insider information. Although not understood by everyone, the term "insider trading" from the 1987 movie *Wall Street* had been tossed around.

Unable to draw concrete answers from corporate, or what was left of it, I quit and sold out my stocks as quickly as I could latch onto my broker. Immediately following cash out, I sent Sam the Sham a tele-message about being discriminated against, saying that I intended to sue if I was not given proper and immediate settlement by Newstyle. This, of course, was crazy, because I was not terminated or even threatened outright by the Sham, only harassed. It worked, however, because our human relations manager called to confirm that my severance package was shipped by FedEx and that I should turn over my keys to Betty, a general manager I promoted who had already been verbally elevated to regional director, replacing me. My fat check was contingent on not sharing any further communication with my restaurants. I signed and returned their documents without delay. This was all a bad dream that I couldn't shake. Newstyle went belly-up shortly after I was gone. Could I and my region have saved it? Not a chance! But at least my guys got sold, not closed.

~

Intertwined with all my work and play life was an ongoing divorce and custody battle. When I first received a subpoena to court in Indiana, I hired an expensive attorney that was familiar with gay rights in Buffalo. Shelly Reicher negotiated agreements with my wife's attorney, namely that she could represent me in court and that the gay issue was not to be brought up. I signed a contract to pay my attorney to pay all her expenses, which amounted to thousands, to go to court with me in Valparaiso, Indiana. Keep in mind, this was the original alimony and custody hearing in 1991, a full year before the divorce became final. We showed up in court. There we were my attorney and me on the defendant side. My wife, her attorney, my mother, sisters, former neighbors, and friends were all on the plaintiff side. I was looking for the humping dog, too! This is precisely how it went down:

Judge Waxer, pointing to my attorney, asked, "Who are you?"

"Shelly Reicher, your honor, attorney for the defendant."

"Are you licensed to practice in the state of Indiana, Miss Reicher?"

"No, your honor, but I have an agreement with the Plaintiff's—" She was cut off before she could explain our deal.

"I didn't ask you about agreements, only if you were licensed to practice in Indiana."

"No your honor, but I have Mr. Theursosis's signature—" Once again, my attorney was cut off mid-sentence.

"In that case, Miss Reicher, I want you to take your notes and your briefcase and move to the back row of the courtroom. You have no business in my court; do you understand me?"

"Your honor, please—"

"*Now*, Miss Reicher, or shall I hold you in contempt?"

Now there was only me against all of them, with no notes to draw from. It doesn't matter, because I wasn't allowed to speak, except to respond with a "yes" or "no" as directed. Mr. back-stabbing Theursosis flailed away at me with one unsubstantiated claim after another; all I could do was agree to mail the court proof otherwise. ("Gee", I wondered, "will this bastard accept a hand-delivery from my attorney after court? Not a fucking chance!") Wouldn't you guess that the first thing out of his mouth was that my wife was seeking legal separation and divorce because of my homosexual activity? There you have it, a matter of public record; I was declared guilty of homosexuality.

In 1991 (even today, for all I know), Indiana had laws on the books that made homosexual activity illegal; Judge Waxer let it be known in no uncertain terms that, "If you hope to be a free man, Mr. Pirelli, you will comply with all court orders and requirements without delay, without rebuttal. You and the likes of you disgust me!"

I was sentenced to:

> No custody
> No visitation
> No contact without court approval
> $600 per month, per child, for support, through the court
> $1,200 per month spousal living costs
> To pay all existing debt, even that incurred since physical separation
> To pay my wife's legal expenses, which no doubt doubled upon this order
> To indirectly retrieve my clothing and my dog Cupid, but nothing else

Can you believe it? I wasn't even entitled to the balance of my personal effects, like the dozens of blueprints from a high-school drafting course, personal gifts from military friends, the Chinese fishing junk or Vietnamese doll or childhood pictures and keepsakes, nothing but the humping dog that I couldn't take care of and had to leave behind. I'm really surprised I didn't end up paying support for him, too. I didn't even get critical items like my baptismal certificate, college lettered degree, sheet music, and lyrics, which were all hidden from me. (In fairness, years later my daughter Melody smuggled a handful of documents back to me, including one copyright without music and a few hand-written lyrics, but all the music, my lettered degree, and photos for the first forty years of my life were gone, even destroyed, I was told.) "All I got was the shirt on my back and the bills" was more than a joke; it was a living nightmare. To grind salt into a seeping wound, Aunt Ruthe's book of poetry by Whittier was burned. Little One really gave me the big one.

I was served up one whopping invoice from my own dear Miss Reicher. The entire deal still reeks of unethical odor if you ask me, but she claimed to file a grievance against the plaintiff's attorney to the officiating board. That and a dollar would buy me a cup of coffee at the time, if I had a fricking dollar *left*, that is. Any money I had tucked away for my own emergencies was soon history, as was my marriage the following year. Now Newstyle, for me, was history, too. What a stinking streak of nightmares.

~

By November 1st, my then-lover (Clark) and I sold out, packed our cars, and headed to Las Vegas to forge fresh lives for ourselves with new friends, opportunities, and careers. Were we nuts? I had passed through Reno on vacation with the wife many years earlier, but I'd never stepped foot in Vegas. We owned a few personal belongings, cash from selling major furnishings, our bicycles, the residual of my severance, and a dream. Setting up home and office in a raunchy, roach-infested, rat's nest of a room, we began pumping out resumes and hand-carrying them to every casino and foodservice place in town.

Las Vegas, Nevada is not just a different city in a different state. It may as well have been a different country. We were locked out of Vegas, or, as my dad would say, "Shit out of luck!" One had to be a union employee and "city certified," which meant taking special courses for Nevada residents only, whether or not we needed them, to work in the city. This involved paying exorbitant fees before most companies concerned would even accept applications. We had to prove residency before getting driver's licenses, but a hotel was not sufficient proof of residency. We couldn't open checking accounts without Nevada driver's licenses. We found every catch 22, 23, and 24 out there. We estimated a four– or five-month process of getting qualified and settled and gaining employment. The problem was we had about three months' cash on hand and no friends in this foreign land—not a pretty scenario.

We did what any two foreign gay men would do in that situation; we lived up to the slogan, "What you do in Vegas stays in Vegas." We ate in cheap buffets, drank free drinks in the casinos, laughed and cried our fool hearts out, played the slots, and played like sluts. We played together and apart, in couples, threesomes, foursomes, and moresomes. One month later, we left Vegas together, headed for Indiana with nothing but our cars, clothes, crumbled dreams, and a lot less cash—like, none. First selling our bikes, we could hustle (sell ourselves) for quick cash at truck stops along the route home to pay for gas. That was our plan, so we stuck to it—together.

~

We arrived at my sister's duplex in Portage in December, 1992. Marci was the only family member, other than my kids, still speaking with me; she invited us to live with her for a while. Marci had about as turbulent a life as my own. She, too, was on the verge of independence, surviving battles and wounds of her own; she didn't need two gay men sharing her pad. However, generous as she was, my almost-twin made room in her heart and home for us both.

Marci was working for an Indiana State Prison as a guard, and encouraged Clark and me to apply for jobs there. Clark passed the written exam, but not the psychological part; he was too much of a clown, laughing through the interview. I, on the other hand, passed both, but I stalled taking the position while hoping to learn my fate through a professional career counselor, who was paid to find upper-level jobs for persons with upper-level skills. Ha, neither of us had the balls my sis was known for.

In the nick of time, I signed an agreement with Pit Stops of America to run their Gary restaurant. I didn't know the first thing about twenty-four-hour, greasy spoon establishments, but it was ferociously busy, and looked like a place I could fit in. My only experience in truck stops was—well, you know, the trip home from Nevada. The general manager was Kurt Klemm, who was a former Baptist minister, honest to God; he had a mouth on him befitting a truck stop's darkest corners. He took a liking to me right away. I dived into the pit, ignorant as sin when it came to my responsibilities.

For running a single restaurant, I was contracted to make more hard cash than I earned in any prior supervisory position. It was going to be my dream job; who knows, I might get big tips by some big-riggers, hopefully in the rigs! Corporate training is part of any new position. They taught us their brand of systems and operations; we were to bring refreshing thought and leadership. I was actually having fun, convincing the boss to set up Pit Stop's first one-table buffet, half hot, half cold. The cooks learned quickly that I was utterly useless in the kitchen. I couldn't flip an egg for the life of me, but oh, did I ever try! It's in the *wrist*, and you've either got it, or you don't; I clearly didn't. (Maybe that's why I passed so easily as straight?) I went through the management crash-training course in Akron, Ohio, and was fully entrenched by the end of February, 1993.

Clark was not as fortunate. Unable to find concrete employment even working as a restaurant waiter, he needed to return to Buffalo, which was a necessary, but emotional split. He was a man with pride, young as he was at the time, perhaps twenty-six. Clark was not a Hoosier, and he hated being hated. Gay men in Indiana were nothing to most people, less than nothing to some. Clark couldn't take the pressure of having to play housekeeper to me and Marci while relying on us for his pocket money. With my blessings and love, Clark Whittner boomeranged home to western New York—alone.

~

My eldest daughter Melody had graduated from high school only months earlier. She was engaged to marry her best friend, Oliver West, who was about to complete Marine basic training. (We joked that Oliver North was the bad marine; Oliver West was the good guy. He is!) They planned a March wedding, in which my first born asked her "daddy" to walk her down the aisle. Little One would have nothing to do with the planning, and, taking cues from my parents, threatened to boycott if (in my dad's words, I'm sure), "the degenerate was permitted in the church." With a shoestring budget to work from, since my employment of late had been erratic, to say the least, Melody and I put our cash and heads together to shape the nicest wedding possible. Others helped, for sure: the soon-to-be in-laws, some distant aunts, and, of course, my beloved Marci, who single-handedly prepared all the food for the buffet-style dinner reception. Melody conservatively selected her gown and bridesmaid's dresses, while I inserted veto power on the latter. Cutting corners, we crafted decorations for the church hall, designed and printed invitations, and squeezed the florist to limit flowers to those with creative flair. With a little compromising on the cake, we threw one hell of a wedding for a bargain-basement price. Her mom showed up last minute, shocking us all, but we never spoke, even though we stood side by side in the reception line. Melody's grandparents (on my side) were conspicuously absent, testifying travel troubles from Tennessee. I did all I could to comfort Melody on her grandest of days, dampened by the damned heartlessness of my parents—some malice leaves an unforgettable sting. As Marci sang a wedding hymn, my beautiful baby (once comforted on my belly) strolled comfortably steadfast by my side to become a breathtaking bride. No father could be prouder.

(Not all things go as well as Melody's wedding. Not all marriages are as good as hers and Ollie's. Whatever problems they encountered over the years with family, military service, children, employment, home, and a life of their own, Melody and Ollie West, to this very day, appear to be as united as they were on Saturday, March 6, 1993. Being proud of both of them, I am grateful they have included me in their lives, as awkward as it was on many occasions.)

~

It was an early wedding and reception. Everyone was gone, and everything cleaned up by 1800. It was a gorgeous, warm, and sunny day in March, unusually so. It was still light out. Marci had already come home, changed clothes, and was gone to work at the prison in Westville. I had the remainder of the weekend off, and was at home, gratified by the day's events, but melancholy. I had no one to be with. From a distance, the Little One looked as lovely as the day we first met. I was missing Clark terribly. I needed him to make me laugh. I wanted to be loved and held; I craved sex, big time. Newer friends were not available to hang out with, so I ventured to the gay district of Halstead Avenue, Chicago's version of Castro Street in San Francisco. Living required being with someone—anyone. It was one of the loneliest times in my life.

I braved one club called the Vortex only minutes after an unannounced visit by Marky Mark. Body-to-body tight is how to best describe that scene. With barely breathing room, there was a lot of sweaty-slick bare skin pulsating in one massive motion. Seemingly not safe from pocket-pickers, I headed to the next joint for a multi-male lap dance, then another club promoting an underwear party—a gazillion gorgeous guys in the slightest of garb. After doing the strip, I reached Unicorn, one of two bath houses I knew of in Chi Town's district called Boyz Town. There are play dens, but I had never before, or since, for that matter, witnessed anything like Unicorn, which was the place for one-horned fairy stallions.

There were the typical single-bed stalls, hot tubs, steam baths, showers, TV lounge and snack shop, plus several play rooms, each more erotic and mind blowing than the last. One was nothing but padded floors and cushioned walls with cut-out and pillowed cubby holes in three walls, in rainbow colors, of course. The fourth wall had a theatre-sized screen to broadcast XXX gay porn with no sound other than the thumping beat of cyber music, low enough to hear the raw sound of the naked men in action on the floors, along the walls and in every cubby hole. The erotic groans and moans only amplified the lust of delicious duos.

One room was a peephole room called the Pig's Pen. It was built for guys with oral-visual fixations and fantasies. Comprised of a split-level balcony/basement arrangement, the balcony was a mere three steps up to a narrow L-shaped walkway with a half-wall (with pre-cut holes) and a railing facing below. It was all black and had a second stair case on the opposite end. The lower section was three steps down to a square tiled area of black and white check with more lighting, so all could view the men in the pen. One could go atop to simply watch or to make use of the wall by probing his pecker and pack through one of the peep-holes. The lower pig's pen was reserved for hungry hogs that could feed to their delight at just the right height. Suffice it to say, the design was deliberately tiled for easy hose cleaning.

Another space was for hard-core S&M (Sadomasochistic) players. It was pitch-black with black lights to find one's way to racks, slings, cages, stockades, whipping blocks and the dreaded fucking-horse (a contraption resembling a saw-horse), where a slave could be strapped down safely, exposing both ends to be used or abused by his master. Warnings visibly posted required participants to, "Play safe, sane, and consensual." Strategically located throughout the establishment were condom bins, cigarette tins, and "trash-ins" equipped with huge rolls of paper towels. It was the Sodom and Gomorrah of bath houses, the gay man's play palace—a health club that made orgies look like third-grade recess.

I waited in the long line outside, bought the one-time membership and paid a room fee (which gave the member up to twelve hours to play, rest, and shower before handing in the towel on the way out through a turnstile exit). I checked into my plywood single-bed cubical, stripped, put my clothes in the open-faced locker provided, strategically dangling my wristwatch for rapid time checks, swathed myself in a towel, locked the room, and put the key around my wrist with the plastic slinky-like key holder before touring open doors and playrooms. But that night, I was feeling vulnerable, and desired, for the first time in a very long time, to surrender to a man's man. Spotting, then signaling to my mate, Mr. Right (for a night) followed me to my cubical.

He was a burley, heavy set fellow about half my age, but not so big that I couldn't handle—or should I say, be handled by. He wanted me mission style, gay version, which is face down, propped up by only a pillow under the lower abdomen. I handed him lube and a condom. He forced one squirt of lube in me with his thumb, tore open the condom wrapper and held my head down with one hand while he rolled the condom on with the other. Then he slapped my ass, and whispered in my ear, "Are you ready for the fuck of your life?" Then he rammed me full force, one stroke, all the way in. I screamed into a second pillow, pleading in a whimper for him to take it easy, to let me adjust to his size. Instead, he began whaling at my head and shoulders with one fist while holding me down at the neck with the other. Ramming me with the might of a bumper car, he yelled profanities such as, "You know you love it, you fucking faggot whore!"

I demanded, "*Stop now!*"

"Tell me you want my big cock, you mother-fucking queer!"

I may have momentarily passed out, because I experienced flashbacks to a time when I was strewn over some makeshift table as a boy of sixteen, being brutalized in a dingy-gray basement in Gary, Indiana. I remembered it all, every dirty detail, and I shrieked while fighting my way out of the memory. I kicked my way out, again, and pushed this ravaging maniac off me. In an instant, he was gone, but oh, my God, I finally *remembered*! While wrapped into a naked ball in this cubical stall, trembling from a lost memory regained, I cried for my lost childhood; I cried for my mom—why didn't Mom love me? I cried for Aunt Ruthe—why did she abandon me? I realized something else at that moment. Burley didn't use the condom, because it was lying on the floor, open, but still rolled up—and I was bleeding profusely. I knew as sure as I'm writing this event today that I had become the newest statistic. My dream of being loved had turned into one of life's worst nightmares. I looked through tears at my watch dangling on the locker hook. It was 0323, March 7, 1993. I wonder how many people can pinpoint with accuracy when their dreams ended with certain destiny. Mine were broken—as was I.

~

How does one begin to recover from such a violent assault? Too ashamed to report the incident to either the establishment or authorities, I stumbled about my business in a fog of humiliation the remainder of the night, and for weeks to come. I hated going to work, because work meant being around and talking with people. I strived to be alone; counting cans in the stock room, cleaning refrigeration coils in the coolers—anything that kept me out of sight. The last thing I needed was for Mr. Klemm to send me to yet another corporate school, this time to learn cooking the P.S.A. way with a few of my employees. Off we headed to Louisville, Kentucky, where I was pitted against relatively uneducated, but highly skilled cooks throughout the Midwest. I never liked cooking, nor did I yearn to be there. My inattentive attitude was apparent. Therefore, when I was carted to a nearby emergency room with horrific flu-like symptoms, which were substantiated medically, it was nevertheless perceived as some ploy on my part to avoid class. It wasn't influenza season; doubting foodborne illness under the training circumstances, the doctor asked me in private if I had any history of intravenous drug use or homosexual activity. Hesitant at first, I answered openly and honestly. The physician recommended that I take an HIV (Human Immunodeficiency Virus) test. I promised to, as soon as I got home to Indiana. Keeping that promise, I underwent testing the following week at a free, anonymous clinic in Gary. My results came back two weeks later.

The nurse, after comforting me, said, "Your test results are indeterminate."

I asked, "Now what exactly does that mean?"

"It might be an early indicator of positive results, or it might be a false reading of negative. You need a second test called Western Blot to confirm results."

"Excuse me, but no thanks. How can I know it would be any more accurate? Trust me, I'm fine! I'll get rechecked some other time." I left in a breathless panic, thinking, "Put this out of your mind Vinny—go to work—forget this *indeterminate* thing."

~

Did I mention the mouth Kurt Klemm had on him? He enjoyed spitting one queer joke after another the entire time I knew him, with a rare womanizing or Jewish joke in the mix. He discriminated in his jokes, never imparting slurs on blacks, Poles or Latinos. Of course, all of those types are a big part of Pit Stops of America; therefore, the vast majority of his evil comments were homophobic. Since the Louisville Flu, it was obvious that the boss had a grievance against me, some chip on his shoulder. I asked Kurt for a meeting on my way home the evening following the blood test results, to question his "Kurt-ness." He said I disappointed him with my deliberate class cutting in Louisville, but that he'd get over it. Meanwhile, I should focus on my work. Then, out of the blue, he told another faggot joke. I didn't laugh!

"Kurt, why do you tell so many gay jokes? I never hear jokes about blacks, trailer trash or anything but slams against gays. Why always gay jokes?"

"Why do you care? We don't have any faggots working for us."

"Yes, we do, Kurt!"

"Who? Do you have queers in your restaurant? Who's in the faggot fruit basket?"

"We don't have any faggots, Kurt, but I'm gay, and I don't appreciate the constant bombardment of slanderous slams against us gays!"

He was, for once, momentarily speechless. His eyes bulged with hatred and disgust as they burned a scarlet "Q" on my brow. After the most uncomfortable thirty seconds of silence I can ever recall, Kurt rolled his chair back from the desk and stood. With one hand grasping his belt and the other pointing at me, he said softly, but with all the contempt of a war enemy, "I told you we don't have any fucking queers working at this Pit Stop, did you hear me? Now give me your keys and get the fuck out of my sight, you God-damn faggot."

"You can't do that, Kurt. You don't have just cause."

"Your contract says I can fire you for any reason or no reason within the first ninety days. I'm entitled to a replacement by the Management Procurement Center. I don't want some mother-fucking faggot working for me today, tomorrow or *ever*!" I may never forget the deranged, vile twist he put on the word *ever* before he continued, "I want your keys *now*; get your stuff from the restaurant office, and get the fuck out of my sight. Don't even bother coming back for your severance pay. I'll mail it to you. Now get out of here, you stinking piece of filth."

As I turned to head out, I heard a definite spitting sound. Turning back and tossing my keys across his desk, sliding them into home base against his groin, I forcefully chuckled and grinned, saying, "Spit Stops of America. I get it—homophobe. And I bet the Baptists dismissed *you* for being the Anti-Christ. Ha!"

I casually strolled over to the restaurant, knowing my turtle's pace would increase Kurt's blood pressure by twenty points. I kindly asked another manager to retrieve my jacket and cap from the office, and then left that facility, never to show my face there again. His Kurt-ness did mail the severance check, which arrived a few days later. I had no legal grounds, or desire, to fight that homophobic, faggot-hating ex-Baptist.

Strangely enough, I found my voice again, having once been slapped alive and now slapped down in my birth town of Gary, Indiana. I needed to stand up and be counted. By May 1st, I offered Marci what cash I could to help with current expenses, but she declined. She wished me well as I headed back home to the great state of New York, to Buffalo, my hometown of choice. I love New York!

Clark had managed to get back the same eastside apartment he occupied when I first met him. It was small, but he offered me refuge until I could get on my own. With Clark already dating someone else, the situation was anything but ideal, but at least I was home where I was wanted and belonged. For the first time in my life, I felt like the chains and shackles had been cut. I was free: from physical constraints, insults and injuries, from the nightmares which haunted and tortured me since childhood. Free to start a new life. I knew that someday I would return to the place I was born as a man people would look up to, not spit on. I wanted so desperately to make my kids proud again. At least, that was my dream. Are all dreams meant to be broken?

Nothing Man
(Melody & Lyrics: 1972)

V.1   Do you know what's pounding in my mind?
Will I lose the only life I hope to find?
Do you know what I am bound to be?
Not a success, because that simply wouldn't be me

Chorus   And I'll be happy just as I am
Doing what I'm doing just as long as I can
I've had nothing before
I see nothing ahead
And there's nothing in all the words I've said
If I can, I'll stay a nothing man

V.2   Do you fear the future that I long?
If nothing is right, whatever could go wrong?
If no lessons are learned, what can be planned?
So if it's nothing you want, honey; come take my hand

Repeat Chorus Twice (Note: Slight variation on the 2nd singing)

Chorus 2   And I'll be happy just as I am
Doing what I'm doing just as long as I can
I've had nothing before
I see nothing ahead
And there's nothing but jumble in my head
So, if I can, I'll stay a nothing man

Biking Dreams and Angels

Transient lives are lived by both ends of the social spectrum, the rich and famous and the deadbeats. Mom would call them the "wherewithal-s" and the "we're without-s." I was, for all practical purposes, without: without a job, nest egg, place to live and, for the most part, without a family. Though it seemed an inevitable fate at times, I know in my heart that I did this to myself. We are ultimately the product of our own choices; I obviously made some horrendous ones. I did not choose to give up my family and wealth in the process, but those losses were consequences of my choices. I have nobody to blame but me; however I am not someone to give up, roll over, and die. A Buffalo Bills optimist always hopes for a better tomorrow. Go Bills!

Fortunately for me, prior generosities and social connections left me with a handful of friends in Buffalo that I could lean on until a plan or strategy could be formulated. I remain grateful to Clark for initially taking me in, but it was a hurtful situation for me and his new boyfriend. I meandered from friend to friend until securing employment and my own efficiency apartment on North Street in July of 1993. As part of my employment strategy, I excluded everything that had transpired the previous year from my resume and approached new employment prospects with a highly probable story: that I remained with Newstyle Buffet until they went defunct, when I took a needed sabbatical and married off my second child, then decided on using my strengths to enter a related and more stable, albeit different, career field." I was offered a management training position in the deli department of a major grocer in western New York; let's call them "Shoppers Supermarkets."

Shoppers claims to be one of the finest employers in the country, and near best in western New York. We each did a good sell job, so with barely enough money for gas left in my pocket, I dived into deli. Even management works shifts at Shoppers, and I was to spend my training months on the early

159

shift, 0600 to mid-afternoon, in their newest venture near Galleria Mall. Although it is true that "Vinny is a morning person," I found out quickly that deli work was far more physically than mentally demanding; the days grew from tiresome to gruesome within several weeks. I started missing my alarm clock by a few minutes, starting to get "the eye" from employees and supervisors when I'd show up even two or three minutes late. Tardiness is not tolerated at Shoppers. Then I caught cold from working in and out of the walk-in coolers, accompanied by a cough and chill that I couldn't shake. By October, I lost so much weight that my size-36 slacks needed to be replaced with 32s. I was on the verge of collapse from loss of energy, so I decided a visit to the Buffalo VA hospital was prudent. My Shoppers's medical insurance had not yet kicked in, since I had less than ninety days on the job. I was hoping against hope that the Veterans Administration would honor my military service and offer me some temporary assistance with medical costs.

The emergency room determined that I had an unusually low white blood cell count. I urgently needed an injection of Neupogen (commonly called growth factor), which forces the bone marrow to produce more white blood cells. Meanwhile, Dr. Griffin admitted me for three days to recover; he personally notified Shoppers that I would be absent. I opted out of most procedures, but Dr. Griffin seemed to take a personal interest in me. Once again, I was asked about my lifestyle; once again, I chose to be honest. The Doc suggested an HIV test, and I reluctantly agreed, sharing with him those indeterminate results several months earlier in Indiana. Waiting for HIV results (not unlike cancer screenings) usually results in your imagination going wild. Two weeks passed before I got a call at work to come to the VA Emergency Room and report to Dr. Griffin. This time, I wasn't imagining the result.

"Mr. Pirelli, there is no easy way of telling you this. Your HIV results have come back positive. Although we are required by law to inform your sexual partners of their possible contact, it will be done anonymously by the New York State Division of Health and Human Services. Expect them to contact you shortly. We are required also to protect your privacy on this issue. Meanwhile, you have been approved for medical care at the VA hospital, and will be billed according to the income guidelines by the Department of Veterans Administration. You do understand this is serious, right?" After I nodded, he continued, "but it is *not* an automatic death sentence. Your CD4 cell count is less than 200, with normal being 1,200-1,500. Should you acquire an HIV-related illness, you will be certified as having AIDS (Acquired Immune Deficiency Syndrome). There are approved and experimental treatments being used, and I will introduce you to Phillip Sorenson, one of our finest physicians in Infectious Diseases. He will take over your primary care from here. Mr. Pirelli, you are not saying anything. Mr. Pirelli, are you okay? Do you understand what I am telling you?"

All I could do was nod with tears in my eyes and say, "I'm going to be sick."

The Doc responded with an upbeat, "Well, for the moment, you are healthy."

Then with a gurgle, I proclaimed, "Oh no, I'm sick!" At which point, I jumped out of the chair, aiming for the trash can to extract any life giving substance from my belly. "Oh God, I need help!"

Dr. Griffin stooped down, putting his arm around me to help prop me up as much as for comfort. I knew at that juncture that he and the VA were not your ordinary care providers. "Mr. Pirelli, we'll work with you. You served our country when we needed you. We'll not abandon you now when you need us. Let me help you up, then let's get you cleaned up. You need to get a grip, Mr. Pirelli. From this point on, your will to help yourself is paramount to any medical care we provide you." That's when I heard the rap on the privacy door.

"May I come in?"

"Hello Phil; this is Mr. Pirelli, the man we discussed. I'll let you take it from here."

"Hi, I'm Dr. Sorenson. Why don't we head to my office, and we can get acquainted there? I'll be able to answer some of your questions, and then we can discuss treatments currently being used. We have an excellent staff in ID. Come on, follow me." Dr. Sorenson addressed me with a smile on his face. Dr. Sorenson was a tall, handsome man in good shape, near my own age. His gray-blue eyes sparkled, and his smile was not unlike his department— "infectious." He had bristly, reddish hair, albeit thinning, and always wore his white smock. I liked his positive, buoyant demeanor and seemingly genuine interest. More than anything, I appreciated his vast knowledge of HIV and other associated medical issues.

It felt like war all over again, being bombarded with new medical terms, treatments, non-conventional protocols, drugs, case studies, group therapies, and illusionary hope. Nobody wanted to admit the truth, that in 1993, countless thousands of people worldwide were dying from this new disease called AIDS. AIDS was brought on by HIV, a self-replicating virus that has no known cure. How was I going to explain all this to Shoppers? Should I even try? Will I still qualify for medical insurance if I do? Will I be able to work in the coolers? Will people be afraid of me? Will I be afraid of having sex again? I had many more questions than answers.

When I returned to work, I was a minute late. That cost me a trip to the general manager's office, a written reprimand, and a two-week unpaid suspension. "You have to set the example, Mr. Pirelli, if you are going to be on our management staff."

"I agree with the presumption of guilt, but sir, I am physically unable to comply. I just learned that I have HIV, which is the cause of my irregular fatigue and illnesses."

"Well then, we can each spend a couple of weeks thinking about the best solutions for your future with Shoppers. Do not to report to work, but be back here in two weeks."

~

Meanwhile, I had nothing to do with my days. The VA entered me into a group therapy program through their HIV Department (a 3-person team dedicated to managing HIV cases at the Veteran's hospital in Buffalo). Carol Caldron, a registered nurse, was in charge of that program. I felt like I didn't fit in. I was not comfortable being the only white man in what appeared to be an all-minority group. I was even less comfortable being the only person who admitted to contracting HIV through homosexual activity, while these other guys all claimed their ill fate from sharing needles. All things considered, I was the minority in that group. Without causing a disturbance, I opted out. Carol, however, put me in contact with the AIDS Network of Western New York, who linked me up with an underground social network of gay men all dying of AIDS. I was networked with a group whose goal was to prepare us for dignified death. It was a morbid approach to a horrid disease, but it was a testament to the times.

I opted to spend my days working at Bernard House, a hospice for AIDS patients who had no home, resources or family support. Bernard House, named for Catholic Priest Father Bernard, who founded and initially funded the project, was walking distance from my apartment. An old phrase kept crawling back into my mind: "Focus on the living." This time, it was easier to focus on the less-fortunate living than on my own disease. It was a way for me to adjust, and be part of the process, while trying to forget about my own plight.

My nights were spent with a new friend I had made from the Kodak School of Music in Rochester. His name was Tze-Liang Chen, an insurance agent by day and student prodigy of keyboards by night. As was practice, I referred to him as "Chen." In his off hours, he would visit me in my tiny efficiency. Short and chubby with a delicate, kindly, and flawless face similar to Thai boys, Chen was a true Malaysian sweetheart. His youthful, tender body and childlike face guaranteed that he would be doomed to stay in the *boy* category all of his days! He was one of the finest, most respectful and, certainly, one of the wealthiest young men I had ever met. He never deliberately flaunted his family money with even a hint of arrogance, but on several occasions he treated me to classy restaurants and lavish nights in one of Hilton's suites. On one occasion, he even offered to fly me as his companion to attend a piano concerto of a friend, taking place in Los Angeles. He was just a kid of twenty-two with a big generous heart, though, and I was a man struggling to keep box dinners on the table. I didn't fit into Chen's world; mine was a force-fit for him. Our relationship lasted only weeks. On his way out, he left an envelope with enough money for rent and food for another month. (Chen, I hope in this age of the Internet that I am able to locate you, to thank you for being there when I had nobody else. You were, I believe, one of God's living angels.)

When I returned to Shoppers, the upper management deemed it appropriate that I be moved from the deli department, because it was ill-advised by their medical nurse and personnel department that I should be permitted to work again with open food. I was cautioned not to inform fellow employees of my HIV status, then moved to the pharmacy department to be trained under one supervisor and two (soon-to-be transferred) employees. It was a glorified stock-boy position, like I had at Pratt Drugs in 1968 before my then-promotion to marketing manager. Only, it was non-stop stocking. It sucked big time!

~

During one of my group sessions, I met a young man I will call Dwayne. He lived with two girls in an apartment complex on Delaware Avenue, where the biggest of the turn-of-the-century mansions are located in Buffalo, now housing mostly not-for-profit agencies. The first girl, Annie, was diminutive, skinny, and dark-haired. I don't think she ever ate. Her partner was Kelli, a Canadian from Hamilton, Ontario. Kelli lived in the U.S. by night and traveled across the border daily to work. Kelli was also slight in stature, with a beautiful face and short, wavy, blonde hair. She was moderately pudgy from liking food, but certainly not fat. While Annie was cute, Kelli was pretty. They accepted me quickly, having emotionally grown with their friend Dwayne's illness. We became instant friends, and I thoroughly enjoyed their company.

Dwayne had his own family to spend the holidays with, a home where he alone was welcomed. So, having no place to go for Christmas, Annie invited me to her parent's home on Hoyt Street, where she and Kelli would spend Christmas with Annie's parents and grandmother, who lived in the upper, converted apartment. It was a memorable occasion, as that was first time I saw any family openly accept, love, and embrace a child *and* their same-sex partner.

Life for Kelli and Annie, however, was anything but stable. Forced to cross the border daily, as she had for four years, Kelli was starting to get harassed by border security. They suspected something ominous about her repetitive travels in and out of the United States. Lately, they had been stopping her to inspect her vehicle, perhaps hoping to find drugs or other contraband, and they started overtly photographing both her and her vehicle. She needed a reason to cross the border without alarming her own family, who knew nothing of Kelli's girlfriend. We decided over Christmas that I could be a reason to cross. Kelli would announce to her family that she was engaged to me. What? You heard me. Fiercely loyal to my friends, I knew the ropes of international marriage, so I proposed to marry Kelli to bring her permanently to Buffalo to start a new life with Annie. Dwayne wanted no part of that arrangement; shortly after Christmas, he packed his clothes, and off he went (to a new boyfriend, no doubt, already waiting in the wings). To make my proposition materialize, we needed to plot and cultivate a long-term plan.

~

I had been taking AZT and DDI intermittently; duo drug protocols showed slower growth of HIV. The first, AZT, though still used in low doses to treat newborns with HIV, was prescribed in horrendous doses. Most of my friends called it the gay cancer chemo. Side effects included elevated back pain, neuropathy in the extremities, and mental confusion. It depleted so much physical and mental energy that it left users in a virtual fog most of the time. DDI caused massive diarrhea and gastric upset that was grossly severe; I ulcerated my esophagus from excessive bile production. The associated indigestion and heartburn was so painful that I proceeded to the hospital once, certain I was undergoing another heart attack. An old back injury from Yorkshire Steak House flared up; when it combined with other side effects, I often found work to be torturous.

Then, in January of 1994, I began suffering burning pain in my right buttock and leg. It was like having hot grease dumped all over me. Brushing the hair of my skin was enough to cause a yelp. When I could endure no more, I reported to my superior, an unsympathetic woman.

"I need to go to the hospital—I am in severe pain".

She said, "I have nobody to cover for you. You need to finish your shift."

"I can't do any more, Mrs. K.; I have to go. I know you can get other help."

"Your work is pathetic, anyway. If you leave, you will need to report to the general manager before I let you back on the floor."

I didn't bother replying. Instead, I punched out (oh yeah, managers also use a time clock at Shoppers) and slid on my coat while walking to the car. I was awfully ill.

It didn't take long for Emergency doctors to determine that my anguish was from shingles, which required both isolation and IV-strength Acyclovir for a minimum of ten days, followed by ten more days of home recuperation. Since shingles is not a common disease for my age group, it was classified as an ARI (AIDS Related Illness), and I was reclassified from HIV infected to full-blown AIDS. The sunburn sensation soon progressed into large lesions extending from my right back, all the way down to my calf. According to the physician on duty, the AZT most likely exacerbated the pain at the nerve endings. Once again, the VA notified Shoppers of my impending now-mandatory hospitalization due to this communicable disease, with a return to work projected in about three weeks.

Shoppers placed me on short-term disability until I could return. When reporting to the general manager three weeks later, I was also greeted by their corporate personnel manager.

"Mr. Pirelli, in lieu of all that has transpired, we have decided that you will not be coming back to work for Shoppers."

"Excuse me? You can't fire me for getting sick."

"We're releasing you for poor performance. It is not for us to determine if it is your illness or inconsistent behavior that contributed to your inability to accomplish your workload."

"I beg your pardon, but we all know the minute you moved me to the pharmacy department, you transferred both of the hourly employees to grocery hard goods. You deliberately set me up for failure, trying to break me down, forcing me to do the work of two people."

"I'm sure your department supervisor will say that is an unsubstantiated claim and has nothing to do with your substandard performance. Each individual is rated independently; nobody wants to work with you."

"Nobody *has* been working with me; you pre-arranged that. You know about my HIV status; being self-insured, you need me off your insurance rolls before my medical policy kicks in, admit it."

"Why should we? You clearly had a pre-existing condition, which is the underlying cause of your many illnesses, and we cannot be held responsible for those medical costs."

"But you will be held accountable for terminating me when you know I've been on legitimate medical absence caused by HIV; I can prove that you now have determined that I have AIDS, not so coincidentally, I might add."

"Do you have AIDS? You didn't tell us you had AIDS. You haven't been truthful; that alone is cause enough to terminate your employment."

"I'm protected by law. Employers are not required to be notified; if you are, you may not terminate me for HIV or AIDS—it is a protected medical class."

"We most assuredly disagree with you, and are terminating you for meager performance and lack of professional dedication and honesty. We expect a lot from our employees, even more from our managers. You have not kept your end of our work agreements."

"You know I will sue."

"We know, but we want you off our employment rolls immediately!"

"What would you like me to do with my uniforms? I have two different sizes."

"Nobody will want to use them again. Keep them as a gift from Shoppers."

"What about severance pay?"

"We will not stop you from claiming short-term disability for an additional three weeks; after that, we will send you a two-week severance check. It is covered in this termination package."

I was handed a skimpy folder of information and asked to leave the building without speaking to any employee or manager. A security guard was called to guarantee my departure.

~

I went home angry, but relieved. Stopping by the postbox, I found a postcard in the mail from Paul Amsterdam, a platonic friend (and school teacher) from Baltimore. It had been forwarded a few times, but managed to find its way to my mailbox after several months. Paul mailed it from the last leg of his 3,200-mile cross-country bicycle ride. I couldn't help thinking aloud, "Oh my God, I wonder if I told Paul that I once lived for biking, and biking once helped me to live." I craved to know everything about his trip, long concluded now. I dropped him a line, asking for further details of what I envisioned to be a bicycle dream. In my letter, I shared my medical status, unemployed situation, inability to keep a boyfriend, and more frequent thoughts of "finding a way out."

To his credit, Paul was on the first flight he could arrange after receiving my letter. To this day, I have a hard time believing that this man, a friend I had met only a few times in Baltimore, would take time out of his busy schedule to visit someone in need, especially when that additionally meant incurring the cost of an airline ticket. Paul was not independently wealthy like Chen. He wanted nothing more than to be a friend. He was also now my hero, someone I personally knew who accomplished the unimaginable—a bicycle journey across America. We laughed and cried. We shared dinner at one of my favorite Chinese spots in North Tonawanda. We toured the frozen Niagara Falls, freezing our balls off in the process. Paul invited me to see Tom Hanks in *Philadelphia*. Ours was an unforgettable visit. If my friend left tired, Paul certainly left me inspired. If this angel could beat the odds against completing his bicycle trip, I could beat the odds against AIDS. All I needed to do was believe.

Paul ignited more than my aspiration to fight this disease; he reignited a near-extinguished flame burning inside me to get back on a bicycle. The seed for an impossible dream of my own had been planted. Even before the frost vanished, I scrimped and saved to buy a new, inexpensive mountain bike from a local bicycle dealer. I started bicycling everywhere, to and from Bernard House, Kelli and Annie's place, and all around the city, thereby becoming more intimately acquainted with Buffalo; I soon found a trail that started at the Erie basin and ran for miles along the Erie Canal. By summer, I would be able to bike as far as Lockport, take a break and return.

After viewing *Philadelphia*, I kept my promise to sue Shoppers. Unable to find an attorney to take my case, I built my own and filed a grievance with the New York State Division of Labor, claiming discrimination against a protected disability. There wasn't an endless cast of characters in my episode, but the determination to fight injustice was equally abundant. Though a ton of money was never at stake, a measure of pride stood ever present. It would be a long fight, one I hoped to live long enough to win.

Once short-term disability ran out, Bernard House offered me a part-time job driving a van donated by one of their benefactors. Under our unwritten agreement, I would continue some volunteer time, but on paid duty I would assist other volunteers in weekly shopping, taking residents to medical appointments, and filling a quantum of errands for the Bernard House Staff, who were ever gracious and kind to me.

~

That was about the same time Annie's grandmother passed away. Her parents offered Annie and Kelli her grandmother's apartment for a very reasonable figure; if I agreed to marry Kelli to help establish her permanent residency in the U.S., I, too, could move in for minimal rent. It seemed like an absolute win-win situation. Kelli and I, while living under one roof and verifying our legal residence together, would get to know each other well enough to pass the rigid examination of kinship required for her to receive permanent residence once we married. We instituted our unconventional engagement and home together, with Kelli & Annie in one bedroom and me (and my boyfriend *du jour*) in another—a very cozy arrangement. Hoyt Street was a pleasant bicycle ride to Bernard House. I was making enough income part-time to be self-sufficient under the current cost structure, which was a most agreeable situation.

Fortunately, after my divorce became final, spousal support was not rolled over into alimony. Coincidental as it was, at the time of the divorce decree, I was between jobs (Newstyle and Pit Stops) and the Little One was making a fair wage at JC Penny's. Child support would have to be cut to fifty dollars per week, arranged with the court by my advocate at AIDS Community Services. In June of 1994, Kelli and I both got cold feet. Our marriage of convenience needed postponement to see if Kelli could first find employment in the U.S.; even then, we had to cautiously approach issues related to medical insurance and legal responsibilities. A marriage could also affect my own benefits from the VA. Married or not, we truly loved each other as friends, living under one roof, Annie and me full time, Kelli whenever she could be with us.

A few other major events occurred in early summer, 1994. First, Shoppers offered a surprisingly rapid out-of-court settlement, small enough to be less than their legal fees might cost, large enough to be reasonably attractive to me. In settlement, however, I had to agree not to tell my story to the media and not to reveal the company name. It should also be noted that their agreement was contingent on my acceptance of an official statement that both cleared them of any wrong doing and made it impossible for them to be held liable for further damages "unto the end of time," even if I should endure further repercussions of their initial termination decision. I agreed, dancing my way to the bank with what seems now to be a foolishly small settlement. Fortunately for Shoppers (not as much for me), their offer arrived in time to save me the embarrassment and hassle of having to hand my license plates over to the DMV for lack of car insurance, apparent proof to me that God answers emergency prayers in the legal nick of time.

Katelyn Marie West was my first granddaughter, born to Melody and Ollie. Everyone knows I love all my grandchildren equally, but let's face it, this grandpa knows more about girls and girls' stuff than he did about boys growing up. Even though Melody's brother is older, she was in our family first; Look-Bon physically arrived after the baby's birth. Always being late in coming around, I didn't get invited to Look-Bon's wedding, nor did I know his first son, also adopted. I was there for Melody on her wedding day, just as I was when she was a spanking newborn whose mother lay close to death many years earlier. There is something gratifying about living to see my baby have a baby.

Another major event was Stonewall Revival, the 25th anniversary of the Stonewall Rebellion. I was relatively unaware of the original happening in 1969, but now that I had some pocket green, nothing could keep me from marching in what would surely be a historic event. I was one of over a million visitors to celebrate the Stonewall victory. On nearly every corner I felt the sting of haters condemning us in the name of God. We marched on, shielded by our own faith, observing the end of an era when "backrooms and closets" presented the only acceptable way to be gay. Like Manhattan and Greenwich Village, Vinny Pirelli was changed forever thanks to heroes beaten while holding their ground after a raid on Stonewall, a bar I never stepped foot in. Unable to squeeze in the front door in 1994, I pledged to have a celebratory drink there someday if I'm lucky enough to ever return to New York City.

I made an announcement in June that I was training for a cross-country bicycle trip to raise awareness for AIDS. Naturally, this was perceived by most folks as an illusionary pipe dream, some form of brainwashing, recreational drugs, dementia due to HIV, or the combination of them all. Very few people regarded me seriously. When I broadcast my intentions, I hadn't entered a planning stage, but the idea sprouted from a seed planted during Paul's visit. It just popped out, like a sapling, with never a thought of the challenges that tree would face to survive. Perhaps, just like I used to pretend to drive a school bus or Mustang when I was on the farm, I biked for hours on end, pretending I was going to somehow be the first person with AIDS to bicycle across the United States. Right, like that will ever happen. Ha! As one nurse at Bernard House put it, "Vinny, we love you, but you're no longer a child, so stop with the juvenile stories and cockeyed notions that you can bicycle across the country, except perhaps in your dreams." There you have it, nothing but *An Impossible Dream Story*.

~

My life would never be the same from that moment on. Even though I had already initiated training, both on the bike and in my mind, and informed Paul of my intentions, I was perhaps the only person in the world that believed such a feat could be possible. There are so many variables to such a huge endeavor that my brain and body were in a flurry of bizarre business for the next eleven months.

I recently read *A Walk in the Woods* by Bill Bryson, which was ablaze with passion, historical facts about the Appalachian Trail and details about his purchased preparations. Surprisingly enough, Bill admitted to little or no physical training for the trip. He was already an acclaimed author, therefore never once gave the reader any indication that he was unable to fund his adventure. None of that takes away from Bryson's personal triumphs, his compelling story of wonderment and intestinal fortitude, his vast knowledge base and research, or his articulate, artistic account of hiking the 2,200-mile Appalachian Trail.

Let there be no mistake, unlike Bryson, I was one of the "without-s". Without a doubt, I needed substantial planning, extensive training, emotional and financial support, and a never-dying determination to make a difference—to my children, friends, co-workers, fellow HIV/AIDS strugglers, and the entire AIDS community. I needed a ton of prayer and luck. "God be with me."

As I read back over the journals kept during my time of preparation, I laugh and cry in amazement as to how many balls could possibly be juggled at one time. This puzzle had so many fricking pieces, involving so many people, that I could never adequately praise those who assisted in any form without offending someone I would have unintentionally overlooked. I convinced myself that this was never to be about me or them, but about our cause—to bring awareness and funding to HIV/AIDS. Still, it was *my* goal, plan, effort, and organizational skills that would be taxed for the next unknown period of time. I chose to focus on what needed to happen far more than who needed to be recognized. With that said, any one of hundreds of people involved in this biking story may take pride in the fact that, like me, they made a difference, big time.

~

Let's start at the beginning of my journey toward cross-country bicycling. After dusting off my salesmanship skills and persuasiveness, some volunteers and clients at Bernard House willingly bought into the idea of a cross-country bicycle trip. We were vaguely aware that several biking and AIDS organizations had already paved the way by holding group bicycling fundraisers of several hundred miles each that involved a lot of money and countless bikers, presumably with and without HIV. How many people with AIDS had done a cross-country trip, though? Our research uncovered none at the time. One volunteer, named Cheri (pronounced Sheeree) suggested I consider a 5,000-mile bicycle trip because that would historically top anything others might be planning. We would call it USAIDS 5,000. It wasn't long before we had plotted out the tentative route, starting in Buffalo, heading to Seattle, then Los Angeles, and back across the desert to El Paso. Tony, a resident of Bernard House, was an artist. He sketched a logo that our small committee agreed upon. It was an outline of the Continental U.S. with stars at the beginning and ending points. The center featured a picture of a stickman on a bicycle, the middle "00s" doubling as the bicycle tires. The clincher was when he turned the last "0" into an AIDS ribbon. Paul K, another resident who had a CAD computer program that could rework Tony's design, came up with a computerized red and blue layout which could be used by any T-shirt company. An all-red version was later adopted for stationary. We needed a starting date; arbitrarily, we selected May 31, 1995.

The staff at Bernard House, of course, didn't put earnest stock into any of this. They cautioned me to not overexcite the residents to the point of causing further medical complications. Perhaps a ploy to limit my meeting time (as I now realize), Bernard House offered me full-time employment that involved more than driving. They offered a resident care-provider position, which needed training and internship work. They put me through seminars and coaching sessions that were comprised of the most updated information available on related infections, medications, HIV protocols, nutrition, emergency procedures, and spiritual and emotional healing. I was equipped with inspirational readings like *The Color of Light* by Perry Tilleraas and *The Promise of a New Day* by Karen Casey and Martha Vanceburg. I dusted off my old copies of the Holy Bible, *The One Minute Manager* by Blanchard and Johnson, and *In Search of Excellence* by Peters and Waterman Jr. to hone my skills in communicating with clergy and corporate executives.

I thought at the time that Bernard House didn't realize how well they were training me to be an ideal HIV/AIDS spokesperson. I would be able to speak as both an informed worker and a person experiencing the disease; in retrospect, perhaps they did. In October, the day we received our first supply of USAIDS 5,000 t-shirts and buttons, Tony died from Meningitis, an AIDS-Related Illness. He never saw the end product of his creation. The first button went with Tony to be cremated. Frequently thereafter, I needed those inspirational books for myself, pledging that, "Tony must live on in my heart."

For the balance of 1994, I occupied a tight, disciplined schedule. I bicycled from 0600 to 0900, ending my rides at Bernard House Monday through Friday. After working until 1700, I'd bike home to Hoyt Street, where I trained vigorously on the good ol' Solo Flex; it had become the centerpiece of our dining room. After a well-deserved shower, meal, and nap, I'd initiate the endless writing tasks. I managed to make local agency connections during work as I transported residents to various HIV/AIDS service providers, including the hospitals, AIDS Community Services, AIDS Family Services, and a host of others. This was before viable, routine Internet connections, so correspondence with possible sponsors and prospective agencies had to be accomplished by snail-mail, which entailed printing and postage costs. Once there were expenditures, I needed an accounting system for recordkeeping. I had no plans to officially file for 501(c) (3) not-for-profit tax status. I believed that my personal integrity and accounting skills would be all that was necessary for people to be willing to help. I noted that trip donations would not be tax-deductible.

Weekends ensued more of the same, except that I bicycled longer hours, visited local businesses in the afternoons, and connected with bars, pubs, and clubs by evening. Sunday afternoons were reserved for library research of AIDS institutions, biking clubs, and terrain and road services for planning the trip. By the time it snowed, I realized a few changes would be necessary in my plans. First, I might be biking alone much or even most of the trip; doing so would require a spirit of non-reliance, meaning that I had to count on myself when I could rely on no others traveling with me. It wasn't long before I concluded that bicycling across the desert to El Paso was sheer madness, even impossible, without a complete support troupe that was never to come to fruition. I altered the route by recalculating distances. If I traveled eastward through Albany first, I might be inspired to head south through the Catskills to Manhattan, New York City, then work my way northwest all the way to Seattle, ending with a coastal leg south to Los Angeles. That plan would leave me short more than a hundred miles. Yes, yes! If I continued on to San Diego, I could tabulate 5,000 miles. Now, all I needed to do was persevere with training, plans, connections, and follow up. In time, I could devise a media strategy as well, in hopes of helping our cause.

~

Then, just as quickly as the winter subzero freeze sets in on Buffalo in December, I was put off the road and off course by another medical emergency. This time, it was both shingles and sinusitis that hospitalized me in the VA hospital for nearly two weeks over the holidays. Everything came to a halt. I was both physically and emotionally drained. Less than a month earlier, I made a presentation to interested persons and VA Staff on World AIDS Day. They promised to be my medical and emotional support system for this dream. Now, Phillip Sorenson was telling me a new rendition: "Mr. Pirelli, I'm not trying to discourage you, but there is a reason nobody with AIDS has done a cross-country bicycle trip; maybe it cannot be done. Perhaps you can help in other ways." If that wasn't bad enough, Sister Nancy McCormick, executive director of Bernard House, decided I was injuring myself by working, so she put me on NY State short-term disability. She encouraged me to file for social security disability. Sister McCormick believed (and her belief was proven by my physical state) that I could no longer keep working if I hoped to keep living. I needed a miracle. I prayed for a miracle. I asked God and myself, "If I give up, what is left to live for?"

The answer came to me in a dream in January of 1995. There were angels all around me. One was encouraging little Vinny to start training again, one was pleading that she needed an older Vinny to bike for her, another was expressing how my family counted on me, while the last said I should, "bike to save your own life, and the lives of others in the process." As was frequent, I woke up in a massive sweat, drenching the mattress. I turned on the light and looked into the mirror. I saw a skinny creature who was now 43 years old with nothing substantial in his life left to call his own: no family, no partner, no job or savings, nothing but a choice of planning his death and immediate cremation, or, "If you fall off the bike, pick yourself up, dust yourself off, and get back on the road; boy show some guts—be a man!"

Then, while stripping the bed sheets, the telephone rang. My sister Marci was unable to sleep and was thinking about me. She wanted to come for a visit. I was so excited, I nearly wet myself. (If I did, who cares; I was already soaked.) "Oh Marci, I do have family left. You're an angel," then I proceeded to tell her about my predicaments. She immediately began making plans to help "pick me up," so to speak.

In the morning, I was informed by phone that one of the residents of Bernard House, Muriel, had asked for me. I had gotten to know her the prior Thanksgiving when I delivered homemade pumpkin pie, scratch-made from fresh pumpkin, to Bernard House residents hospitalized at Erie County Medical Center. (Muriel was able to eat my pie custard while unable to hold anything else down, which offered nutrition she so desperately needed then.) I stopped by to visit her after breakfast. She was a woman with a tragic story that included rape, prostitution, drugs, and now AIDS (all too familiar to me). She was agonized with pain, often to the point of screaming uncontrollably and cursing at care givers. She refused to eat or take her medications, except when she begged for more morphine. She was at her legal limits already. The aid said Muriel had been, "fussing up a storm all morning," but when I entered her room, she immediately quieted.

Ever so weak, she spoke, "Vinny, come hold my hand."

I obliged with a sense of gratitude for being asked, acknowledging dignity for a woman few seemed to care about. I could see her bones through the thin skin of her arms, hands, and face. She was weathered and withered, making her appear closer to ninety-two than her real age of twenty-nine.

"Vinny, I ain't 'fraid of dyin', you know. You think dere's a heaven?"

"Sweetheart, there is room in heaven for all of us, and puppy dogs, too."

Coughing out a laugh until she choked, almost losing her breath, Muriel gasped before she continued, "You know I had a dream, and I wasn't in hell. It was a sweet-n-pretty place. Then I heard a knock on the door." At this point, Muriel reached out with a solitary knuckle-knock on her bed table, and then continued, "When I opened it, I saw you, and I was *soooo* happy. You think that was heaven? Come 'ere; let me feel yer face—Vinny, I can't see so good."

Grateful that she couldn't see my tears, I replied, "Muriel, you will be in heaven for sure, and when I get there, I want you to be the one to open that door to greet me. Will you promise to do that?" Then, I put her hand to my lips for a soft kiss.

"I will Vinny, pinky promise; can I get some morphine? Oh Vinny, I hurt so..." Then, I heard some gurgling. Muriel was vomiting without the heaving I always associated with it.

Wiping away my tears and her excretion, "I'll ask on my way out for you. I love you sweet Angel. Heaven's doors are waiting for you, baby."

That was Sunday. On Monday, I learned that Muriel and another resident named Rex had both passed. "Focus on the living, Vinny." The directive came subconsciously. I then went to an appointment at the VA. Dr. Sorenson was out sick; his right hand man, Patrick Weller, a nurse practitioner, was there to follow up with my care. Pat, though always respectful and responsible to Dr. Sorenson, reassured me, "Mr. Pirelli, don't let anyone tell you what you cannot do. You can seek medical care at any VA, and I will make arrangements to express medications if you are in a lurch." It was another piece of the puzzle coming together.

Late that afternoon, after getting home, I had a phone call from Atlanta, Georgia. A Valerie Barnstorm from the Center for Disease Control (CDC) called in reference to a letter I sent. She was mailing me a list of all the names of AIDS agencies and service providers in every city of every state I planned to bicycle through. She was adding a bonus: local TV affiliates of ABC, NBC, and CBS also in each area. She suggested that I plan media events to challenge local businesses and corporations to donate to their community organizations on a mileage basis. Valerie said, "Average people can pledge a penny a mile or $50.00, while big corporations might be willing to donate $1 per mile. Even poor people might donate $5 toward the cause. Wouldn't that be great?"

"It would indeed, yes it would, Ms. Barnstorm." Like an answer to my prayers, there was one angel after another literally calling to me. This was no dream at all. This was no accident. This was no longer even my plan. It was God's plan, I believed, and it was another spiritual awakening.

~

Back into training I went. No time for pity parties. No time for anything but training, planning, and fundraising. Now that I had a meager, but stable, temporary income with short-term disability, I could focus on the living—every day, all day until May 31st. Marci's visit was a blessing in January. She assisted me with a big fundraiser at The Continental, a nightclub for rockers with live bands every weekend. USAIDS 5,000 night was organized by a fellow volunteer at Bernard House, Chrystal, who was also a Continental employee. She paved the way for future benefits to be held by all the other gay-friendly bars and clubs. Marci was in charge of selling USAIDS 5,000 buttons.

As if it happened last evening, I still recall one sales pitch to a drunken heavy-rocker: "Listen, if you can afford another stinking beer, you can afford a mother-fucking button, and if you don't want to piss me off, I'd suggest you get your ass to that table over there to buy a t-shirt, too! I'll have you know my brother has AIDS, and if he can bicycle 5,000 miles for this cause, you can damn well buy a button and mother-fucking t-shirt to support him. I'm not taking *no* for an answer, Goddamn it. I want twelve dollars for both." There was no way this dude was about to argue with a prison guard. You go, girl!

Marci further led the way for some family to regain interest in me through the bike trip. By spring, I was operating my own "fabulous" network, where friends connected with friends who knew family members or friends that wanted to be involved. For every nine, "thanks, but no thanks" replies, there would be a positive response or pledge to support the trip in one fashion or another. Some corporations like Westwood Squibb Pharmaceuticals and Ingram Micro (a software wholesale giant) turned cash donations into employee motivational tools and publicity gigs. Ingram Micro, whose eastern headquarters was in Cheektowaga, suggested I bicycle through their western headquarters in Anaheim, California. It was plotted out and added.

Super 8 couldn't guarantee that all franchises would honor their request, but all corporate hotels would grant me free stay as I traveled through cities where they were located. The makers of Ensure (the nutrition supplement) offered me coupons for their high-protein, high-energy drinks that I could collect at any retail pharmacy en route. Subway Corporation provided me a letter to show in hopes that franchises would support my bike ride with submarine sandwiches and drinks. Mayor Massielo of Buffalo offered a rally sendoff from city hall, while my state representative, Sam Hoyt, offered to meet me in Albany. Governor Cuomo promised to link up with me as well, but he lost the election to George Pataki. All these plans coupled well with intensive physical fitness; it was all coming together perfectly. Even during bad weather months, I used stationary bicycles at a local gymnasium on Buffalo's Main Street. One by one, I lined up dozens of AIDS-related service organizations that wanted to be part of, contribute toward or benefit from USAIDS 5,000. The biggest of these was the Children's Hospital of Buffalo, PACT Program (Parents and Children Together), and a program for infants, toddlers, and young children with HIV/AIDS.

~

Crash and burn is the best way to describe what happened at the end of March. Every AIDS Agency in Buffalo, except for Children's Hospital, backed out of letting me back them, including Bernard House. Something spooked them; I overheard rumblings that they feared legal repercussions if I were to die while bicycling for their cause. Once Kelli realized there would be no green card for permanent residence, she and Annie were reconsidering having me as part of their family. They came up with this excuse: If I was biking for AIDS, as someone with AIDS, I would get TV coverage that would be viewed in Hamilton, Ontario; Kelli's family would immediately assume I was gay; if Vinny was gay, what would that make Kelli? Annie's parents, the owners of her grandmother's apartment, sent me a letter through their attorney evicting me in order to reclaim "personal use" of their property. I was demoralized, defused, and devastated, never mind soon-to-be homeless in what they called "a sixty-day grace period."

Having long dispensed with my own HIV drugs due to killer side effects, I started getting sick just prior to a reacquainting visit from my son to meet his family. Kelli & Annie were off to Canada for the weekend. With amends so important, I pretended nothing was wrong; though I declined opportunities to do touristy things, I gladly cooked all meals for Look-Bon, Tamera, and my grandsons (three by then). Our uplifting visit ended Sunday afternoon; Look-Bon and Tammy both had to work on Monday. They planned to drive all night back to Indiana. By that evening, I was so ill that I called my case manager at AIDS Community Services to beg a ride to the hospital; I was too sick to drive myself and too broke for a taxi.

Once again, I found myself hospitalized for ten days. This time, it was bleeding sinusitis, a urinary tract infection so bad that it, too, caused bleeding, thrush (a throat fungal infection), some kind of fungal rash all over my privates, and lymph nodes swollen throughout my body to the point of disfigurement. I have no idea how many different medicines I was on that time, but the IV drugs were highly caustic, causing disintegration of veins; the IV lines had to be relocated every second day. My white blood cell counts dipped again to a critical low, while my body temperature was critically high. Moreover, I was advised to stop my activities as Dr. Sorenson sternly warned, "Mr. Pirelli, it is better to live for a cause than to die for it. Perhaps you can do something locally after you recoup."

With that competent advice, I decided two things. First, my doctor was right; biking would likely kill me. Second, it didn't matter; because I'd rather die than break this promise to all those angels counting on me. Boosting my morale like a shot in the belly does for my white blood cells, I watched the Academy Awards. Tom Hanks won Best Actor for *Philadelphia*; in his acceptance speech, he said, "The highways to heaven are crowded." So they were.

My own closet was full of angels: nameless, faceless folks that needed me to set them loose to clutter the highways of heaven while I gave them a voice on the highways of home by peddling the message that HIV/AIDS is indeed a killer, and we need a cure.

Throughout the remainder of spring season, I bicycled with might in preparation for May 31, 1995. I added a bicycle trailer and loaded it with cement blocks to simulate the weight I would haul with needed travel essentials like water, food, camping gear, clothing, maps, medicine, and whatever else was deemed necessary to prove this ride possible. While towing that weight, I learned to start reciting the names of personal friends who died since I began training only eleven months prior.

I kept cadence: "This mile is for Chuck. This mile is for Raphael. This mile is for Big Carlos, Martha's husband. This mile is for Little Carlos. This mile is for Cassandra. This mile is for Paul D...for Richard...for Paul K...for Anthony...for old Al...for Big Allan...for Skinny Allen...for Jim...for Benny...for Robert...for Hank...for Eddie...for Rex...for Tony, my inspiration. And this mile is for Muriel, my angel on the other side of the door." While I was at it, I added, "this mile is for the President," whose grave I found among weeds (before I stopped to clear them away) while bicycling through Forest Dawn Cemetery, including him out of respect for a fallen patriot and for the fun of it. As I would haul the weighted trailer, in between my chants I'd sing my favorite Hollies song, "He Ain't Heavy, He's my Brother."

There was yet another angel to add to my list: a living guy simply named Cal. He learned of USAIDS 5,000 during one of my fundraisers. Cal was addicted to sensationalism, a drama queen for any cause or crisis, even if it meant closing his hair salon. "Cutting Calvin" was the perfect man to be my partner on the bike trip. No, Cal would not bike with his frailty, but he would make one hell of a companion and campaign manager. He knew how to get attention, sell a story, and add accent to emphasis. He knew how to snap his fingers while flicking his wrist! If the adventure promised free food, complimentary camping, massive media, cool beer at night, and a frisky fuck every now and then, he would agree to manage the fun and fame of it all. To his credit, Cal had no shame! He could drive the support vehicle, manage meals, get a leg up on lodging, arrange agency appointments, message the media, massage me, and sell t-shirts and buttons like there was no tomorrow. He could outsell Marci without a single threat.

With only two days before departure, Annie served me final notice to vacate the apartment, or her family would not be responsible for my belongings while I was gallivanting around the country on a bicycle. She and Kelli became fallen angels. Cal sweet-talked his domestic partner (and ex-lover) into storing my few belongings until I was settled at the end of the bike trip. Cal was my fabulous friend, my manager, and vital part of USAIDS 5,000. He was queen of angels!

The one dream not realized was to ride the best bike known to man. It was too late to pick up the bike for 1995 sponsor promotions. If only I could ride a . . . oh, never mind!

I Have a Dream
(Melody & Lyrics: 1975)

V.1
I have a dream
A buried dream
A dream to nourish; watch it grow
A dream love
I swear, I'll never let it go
And it's my dream
Please make it your dream!

V.1
I have a song
A lonely song
A song needing to be heard
A song of love
There can be no greater word
And it's my song
Please make it your song!

V.3
I have a prayer
A simple prayer
A prayer of dreams, a prayer of song
A prayer of love
With love, no prayer can go wrong
And it's my prayer
Please make it your prayer!

Ending
I have a dream

Pride Parade
(2010)

A parade of sorts we call *Pride*
To celebrate our rights denied
Today, we sing; our tears have dried
So to the streets, no longer hide

In pink and black and lavender
The colors worn that we prefer
And freedom's cries, in forms of flags
And jocks on stags, and rags on drags

From closets and hatred and bigots claws
And gnashing teeth with vice-like jaws
Of a vulture's beak, soaring high
Where one might think a dove would fly

Then dropping bombs of lily white
In Jesus's name, the Christian right
Commands we learn the Eleventh truth:
"Thou shalt *not*—convert our youth"

Kids watching wide-eyed, just amazed
It's not the marchers who seem crazed
By spitting taunts with ill intent
Condemning love of ten-percent

Who walk in peace, who march with song
Who often pray they might belong
To a parent lost, to a spouse of choice
To hope that we can all rejoice

In equal rights for one and all
We'll take your taunts, but we'll stand tall
In God we trust; for fairness we've prayed
We're God's children, too, in the Pride Parade

No Boundaries

"No fooling, USAIDS 5,000 is pleased to announce the first known 5,000 mile national bicycle journey in support of AIDS awareness and funding." That was the opening message from the first press release organized by my overburdened little team on April 1, 1995. Life for this dreamer was about to change forever. Not only did the gears on my bike get kicked into high speed, with no less than six hours of bicycle training daily, the campaign went into overdrive, as well. Cal would not assume management until May, but my volunteers were starting to fizzle, juggling work, school, relationships, home life, and this growing project. With nothing but roadblocks being tossed my way by Annie and Kelli, meeting goals rested solely on my ability to function *without* rest. I maneuvered my way onto Buffalo talk-radio stations at un-Godly hours and into every gay-friendly bar that permitted USAIDS 5,000 to sell t-shirts and buttons to help cover travel costs. Morning TV news programs also gave me a few promotional minutes if I promised to stop by the studios closer to my departure date.

Newspapers, however, were a challenge. I couldn't convince a single paper to run a human interest story, small featured article, or anything except for one-liners pertaining to fund raisers. Even the *City Alternative*, the anti-establishment *free* weekly rant found at entrances of nearly every club, restaurant, and Laundromat, wouldn't run a piece. It's one thing to be ignored, but after writing several letters, it ran a centerpiece article on *Vegetable Quiche*, of all things. Now that pissed me off big time; one final note penned to the magazine minced no words:

> "Dear Editor, for being a newspaper that seemingly shows no boundaries in telling city government how many boundaries they overstep, I'm shocked that *City Alternative* would find more relevance in lives enhanced by quiche than lives quitted by AIDS.

USAIDS 5,000 will be peddling more than miles on a bicycle—it will be peddling the message that *AIDS shows no boundaries*. If you ignore AIDS, you ARE the establishment! Eat that! Thank you for your social disinterest. Sincerely, Vincent Pirelli"

That snagged me a phone response from part-time volunteer and editor Joseph Cappalolla.

"Hello, Mr. Pirelli. This is Joe Cappalolla from *City Alternative*. We received your many letters, and the owner asked me to contact you to explain how we operate. First, we're accustomed to folks telling us what to write about, but, that said, quiche certainly is not more important an issue than AIDS. That was our only article on quiche that we can recall, but we have had countless articles covering the AIDS pandemic. The other thing is that your bicycle trip isn't news until it happens. When is the race going to be, anyway?"

"It's not a race, but a 5,000-mile trip to promote AIDS awareness, starting May 31st."

"We can probably give you a free ad, but there are dozens of AIDS charities; what makes yours so special?"

"Sir, I will be biking for AIDS agencies in a dozen states. One thing that makes this trip different is the distance; another is that each agency will handle its own funding. My personal fundraising is to help pay for the bike trip itself."

"You said it was cross-country, right? Call me Joe, okay?"

"Joe, cross country is about 3,200 miles; I will be bicycling 5,000. Please call me Vinny; my friends call me Viper, if you prefer."

"Well Vinny, or Viper, I'm sorry, but I still don't see a breaking story here; we can give you an advertisement if that will help you."

"Joe, I believe I will be the first person with full-blown AIDS to ever attempt anything like this; I have to do something." With an audible sob over the phone, I continued, "Joe, all of my friends are dying; I need to bike for them. This is not a movie with a happy ending. I thought you read my letters."

Pissing me off further, I heard Joe chuckle, almost to a choke. "Vinny, let's meet for coffee somewhere tomorrow. Perhaps we can do a story. By the way, I thought you read *City Alternative*. If you did, how could you miss our many articles on AIDS?"

Clearly understanding the nature of his chuckle, I responded, "It must be a coincidence."

"I'm *sure*," he said in disbelief. "Let's talk tomorrow, about two in the afternoon at The Grind on Elmwood. I will tell you this much; I intended to fart you off, thinking you were some kind of nut job, but you got my attention; I want to hear more—tomorrow."

The meeting went better than expected! Mr. Cappalolla promised to do a story a week before departure, with follow-up articles throughout the summer if I provided them with periodic updates. (We each kept our commitments and stayed in contact.)

~

All our plans were clearly coming together. By May, Cal was full-steam promoting the bike trip, establishing person-to-person communication with my contacts (AIDS agencies, reporters, and local TV networks) and organizing one final round of fundraising activities in Buffalo and Rochester. Cal convinced Cellular One to provide free cell-phones and air time for the support vehicle (my car) and for me during the planned three-month trip. (Back then, cell phones were big and cumbersome, used for basic calling only, with far less reliability and Oh-my-God expensive. This would prove to be no small gift; we consumed over $1,500 in air-time. I expected Cal to run Cellular One out of minutes before they could run him out of breath.) Unable to recruit other cyclists for the summer, Cal's plans incorporated my independence and security beyond the typical first-aid kit. I wasn't keen on hauling the extra pound of weight; when I rebutted, claiming no place to store it on the bike, Cal flexed his authority: "Damn it, Viper. If you want me to be your manager, you have to let me manage. I think you need to carry a cell phone for emergencies. I don't care if you have to shove that thing up your ass; no, you'd probably enjoy that too much. Find a place; the phone goes with you." With the snap of his fingers and wrist, it was settled. I don't like not being in charge, but Cal was right (not about the ass thing, but about being prepared). I had to adjust to his precondition of trusting him to manage me. Life has taught me not to trust others; suddenly I was being asked to trust without boundaries.

Perhaps I was out of my comfort zone, but Cal was certainly not out of bounds; by May 31st, Calvin had enveloped my plans with his own management style. Little by little, he started calling the shots. He didn't want to get bogged down with worrying about who would or would not be biking with me. He was responsible for me and me alone. Whoever wished to tag along for any stretch of road was free to bike: at their own pace, risk, and expense, and with any support they could muster.

Mayor Massielo, a few city council members and representatives of the Children's Hospital, the VA, and Ingram Micro (my largest cash sponsor) pooled a sendoff from the steps of Buffalo City Hall on Wednesday, May 31, 1995. Several cyclists from bicycle groups or supporting organizations joined us on what the team billed as "One Day—Fun Day," our Buffalo to Rochester AIDS Ride. Cheri, Cal, and a friend named Greg planned to alternate biking and riding in the support vehicle. "A.M. Buffalo," a local morning TV entertainment program, broadcast live segments of the ceremony as friends and supporters gathered to wish us all well. My pastor opened with a touching prayer, followed by the Mayor's declaration of USAIDS 5,000 Day, V.I.P. remarks, and a song written for the occasion by local songwriter and folk singer Mike Maffei. Timed for TV, we departed at 0945 with a flashy escort all the way to the city limits offered by Buffalo's Finest. It was an incredible moment for me and my friends.

The first day proved to be the warmest day so far that year, reaching no less than 80 degrees. Cheri alternated biking with Greg every several miles until neither of them could force another stroke of peddle, both surrendering after reaching the town of Pembroke (about 30 miles). Cal tried his best to bike, but just after Batavia he gave up as well. I didn't realize that safe biking routes would be closer to eighty-miles. Ultimately, day one proved to be my second-highest mileage day. We arrived at our predetermined destination on Liberty Pole Way following rush hour, as planned. After a brief welcome party, Cal and I said heartfelt goodbyes to our team, who were returning to Buffalo. There was little time to rest with an early evening fundraiser scheduled at Club Marcella. I had been running on adrenaline for nearly two months, and there was still plenty of steam left for the gala event Cal organized in his hometown.

Swarms of people crowded in to support Cal and his new project. The Imperial Court of Buffalo drove in to put on a drag show, drawing more business and funding for the bike trip. Stripped to my sweaty underwear, exposing my chiseled body, I was dragged onto stage as the gals danced their way into my heart. Each dance grew more seductive, while tips multiplied as the guys stuffed dollars into provocatively private places on the gals and me. After the show, Cal sold (for a buck each) opportunities for folks to sign my t–shirt, which was tacked to a wall, with colorful felt markers. When there was no space left on the tee, Cal attempted to auction off chances to sign my briefs, which were still being worn: $2 on the sides, $5 on the back, and $10 on the front. When I flinched, he snapped his fingers, exerting management authority, "Suck it up, Viper; money trumps modesty. You're lucky I'm not selling your ass; believe me, we've had some juicy offers. Everybody wants a piece of you, Vinny; enjoy it." I did!

~

Day two began with a 0900 Buffalo-like copycat celebration at AIDS Rochester when the deputy mayor and Monroe County officials surprised us with proclamations of their own. With little sleep and food, our biggest reward was liquid energy (hot java) and jelly-filled donuts. After photo ops and an interview for the *Democrat* and the *Chronicle*, the event concluded with another police escort down Central Avenue. Tired as I was, I couldn't help but tease, "I could get used to this," only to be guiltily slapped by my subconscious: "Knock it off Vinny; focus on the cause."

It would be a short, visually beautiful biking day, ending at the Macedon Fire Department, where the on-duty volunteer (a kindly 71-year-old lady named Ruth) provided us a place to set up our first camp. A police officer showed up overnight, waking and shaking us from our tent, demanding hands on our heads while we shivered in our skivvies until we could explain that we had received permission from the fire station to camp on their grounds. He apologized after we showed him a welcome note Ruth left by the coffee pot inviting us to use the bathroom and shower and to eat the snacks in the fridge.

By day three, we settled into our routines of breakfast, biking, breaking, biking, lunch, biking, breaking, biking, dinner, biking, and ending at a donated camp. While I did the biking, Cal arranged the stopping points and finalized accommodations. My appetite seemed to be endless; I was burning so many calories. By day four, I could tell I was trimming the last ounces of fat from this frame, but I was feeling healthy, energetic, happy, and hopeful. Camping with Cal was a blast, as he busied himself each evening setting up what he called our "dream house," a 2-man tent donated by my youngest sister Sandi, who held a combined bake and yard sale in Tennessee and timed the tent to arrive on my birthday. Calvin was one class act, tireless in pampering me and tenacious in our purpose…I know when I am blessed with good management and friends.

~

After being interviewed by Auburn's the *Citizen*, I was deliberately run off the road, in the rain, in a construction zone, by a bad citizen in a black sports car. Even if the teen saw my bike and trailer, he didn't see the cop car only two lengths behind his own. The kid was apprehended a quarter-mile down the road and charged with a hit and run! The bike was damaged with a warped front wheel. I couldn't help shouting to God, "Are you angry that I skipped church, or what?" It was an early Sunday evening, and nothing was open— nothing except Guy's Bike Shop! This guy name Guy worked diligently for two hours, restoring the "dream machine," donating time and parts to get us back on the road before dusk. Was this a coincidence or a miracle?

At one campsite in Morrisville, the owner had acute Alzheimer's and was thoroughly convinced it was August, 1938 in Mexico. He was intending to charge us for our stay, but forgot. We felt sorry for the ol' chap, though not enough to reject a free stay as his charitable donation. *Muchas gracias, Senor*.

It's true that I trained for months on end, but Buffalo didn't have mountains, shocking me with the unforeseen difficulty of seemingly unending inclines. (Perhaps I neglected to mention it, but I had been an avid cigarette junkie since my Burger Boss days—that's twenty-eight years. Quitting was not a priority, remaining somewhat financially and socially acceptable in 1995, even in New York.) On three occasions to Albany and another few to New York City, Cal tethered a rope from the frame of the bike to the back bumper and towed me up the mountainside. I justified it to myself as, "a promise to bike 5,000 miles didn't stipulate peddling each one." It wasn't cheating; miles towed were easily made up in uncounted miles touring towns…Okay, it was cheating, but it wouldn't be long before I was able to master most any hill on my own, stopping every few minutes to catch my breath.

Albany was a thrill when assembly member Sam Hoyt introduced the USAIDS 5,000 team to the full Assembly (in progress at the time), where we received a formal welcome and ovation. Later, Sam steered us around the state capital, spouting tidbits of historical trivia. The Albany stop was co-hosted by the AIDS Council of Northeastern New York, granting our first access to AIDS facilities. We were meeting clients for the first time on tour, savoring a chance to talk with, shake hands with, and deliver hope to a struggling few. Nothing could be more energizing, or rewarding. That connection added passion and credibility to the message I shared with TV and newspaper interviewers before moving on. With each face of love, I etched another name onto my solemn list of Angels chanted in cadence. I thanked God for an opportunity to now bike for the living as well as the dead.

~

The view from U.S. Rte. 20 to Albany, then south through the Catskills (primarily on NY 9W and 9) to New York City was a sight to behold. After Albany, even the baby mountains didn't seem burdensome. I was psyched and ready for the next phase. We had car issues to contend with, weight issues to worry about (I dropped twenty pounds since Buffalo), and wild woods to combat during camp, but nothing could dampen our dreams. We were on a mission, on target with our plans, time, and budget, and on top of the world, even with the ups and downs of hills and issues.

Following a late camp setup in the Catskills, Cal freaked out when he saw a pair of eyes looking at him from a distance. As they got closer, he ran to the tent. Before he could see what it was, he tossed out one of two roasted chickens provided by a nearby diner. Shining a flashlight, I caught a glimpse of a raccoon dragging off what was going to be *Cal's* chicken. Seeing his reaction to the critter was worth the price of sharing mine.

In New York, I could see banners and waves from a crowd gathered at the AIDS Service Center on the corner of 14th Street from a distance while peddling down 5th Avenue with one of New York's Finest escorting us on a motorcycle. There was no tickertape as is often seen on hero welcomes, but our single motorcycle-bicycle-car parade was overwhelmed by the show of support and reception put on by the ASC. After visiting and meeting dozens of their clients, each sharing harrowing stories of infection and rejection, Cal was given a finely printed note that read, "The Royal Family of Malaysia cordially invites bicyclist Vincent Pirelli and his entourage to be our personal guests for the night uptown at New York Palace, overlooking St. Patrick's Cathedral." The note was dated with a seal, but no signature.

New York Palace was originally Leona Helmsley's Palace, but after her many scandals (one of them earning her a jail stint), the property was purchased by the Royal Family of Malaysia. Her Majesty, the Queen, had been visiting when she heard on local news about our impending arrival to Manhattan. A family representative called ASC to confirm our story, and then routed the hand-delivered invitation, appropriately, by bicycle courier. The hotel takes up an entire square block. I deliberately approached the east entrances, opposite the red-carpet side, which looked intimidating to commoners like me. There were many brass & glass doors to enter from, but not a single pole or place to secure my bike. Cal hit the automatic door opener then ran back to the car, double-parked and still running with its flashers on. I eased my way into a door, bringing my bicycle with me, heading through a corridor and another set of doors into the lobby, moving carefully, as not to clank metal and cause damage or undue attention. I must have appeared grungy with my biker shorts, sweaty tee that doubled as a face mop; helmet, biker gloves, and "I don't belong here" look on my face. Two security guards in three-piece suits must have studied that expression as they flanked me from either side, abruptly turning my filthy ass and bike around and urgently escorting me back out the doors before they even spoke.

"Sir, you are in the wrong place."

"I'm sorry, I thought this was the New York Palace, but I didn't want to come in on the red-carpet side. I'm Vinny Pirelli, the biker."

"This is definitely the New York Palace, but our lobby is reserved for *our* guests."

"I was told that you would be expecting us; we were given an invitation by the Royal Family of Malaysia." Now, my hand trembled from intimidation as I pulled out the wrinkled, damp invitation from inside my shorts (I had no pockets), then handing it to the meanest looking, most Secret-Service-like security guard.

"Sir, wait here while we inquire with the front desk to see if they know anything about this."

Several minutes later, out came a full security patrol, the desk manager, and two doormen. One doorman took my bike while the other flagged down Cal and directed him to the front drive, where valet service would be provided.

"Sir, we humbly apologize. You are, indeed, a guest of the Royal Family. We have been instructed to make sure you receive our VIP welcome. We have a suite ready for you. We ask only one thing."

"You would like to put my bicycle in storage, right?"

"Absolutely not, sir, it will go with you to your suite, but we ask that you permit us to take it up the freight elevator to prevent possible injury to other guests. Will you require a second room for your gentleman friend?"

"Thank you for helping with the bike—I'd be lost without it. Calvin is my trip manager, but we are close friends; we generally share a room, if that's okay."

"Perfectly fine. Now kindly follow me, Mr. Pirelli; an attendant will escort Calvin after his automobile is secure."

When I entered the room, I realized New York Palace was beyond anything I could imagine or would ever be able to afford in my lifetime, even as a supervisor. The bed was a double-sized king (like having two king beds butted together) with a 7-foot head stead of gold-plated carved wood. The glass and brass shower was actually a shower room with a sunken Jacuzzi tub on one end, fully enclosed by plate glass. A fruit gift basket large enough to feed a platoon adorned a glass table; fresh-cut yellow flowers graced a side table to match. There, sitting on the all-white short-shag carpeting was my filthy bike, dripping grease from the sprocket.

"Oh my God, I cannot let my bike ruin this carpet. Let's put it in storage."

"Nothing of the sort, sir—your bicycle will stay with you for security, even if we have to replace the carpeting. And sir, you may order from the menu to your content with our compliments; we were instructed not to accept gratuities of any form. We are most pleased to have you as our guest, and, on behalf of the Royal Family, we sincerely hope you enjoy your stay at New York's finest hotel, The New York Palace." (We asked for a price listing upon checkout. Our suite was mid-priced. Clearly printed on the brochure was, "Valid through 9/1/95"; the one-bedroom suite went for $650.)

That night, we experimented with the subways and found our way to the Village and Stonewall Pub. It wasn't what I expected; it was just a bar. It sported both the name and history of Stonewall and a bartender named Terry that was built like a brick wall. When the manager asked us for our drink order, Cal said, "I'll have a Guinness, and Vinny wants a Stonewall T-shirt." With that, the manager yelled over to Terry, "Strip off your shirt and toss it to me." It might have been damp, but for an old boy who biked his way to Stonewall, it was a damn fine gift (both the tee and the view of bare-chested Terry).

During our second day in New York City, we toured most of Manhattan and Central Park by bicycle, shopped in Greenwich Village, walked the pier, and strolled through Times Square. Toward evening we shared stories, hope, and dinner with AIDS residents of the Bailey House on Christopher Street, which was similar to Buffalo's Bernard House. I recall one beautiful Italian boy named Stephan with a broad smile far more infectious than any disease, a smile that made it nearly impossible to reconcile his being outcast from his family and the U.S. Air Force. With a forgiving tongue, he told of horren-dous harassment and insensitive insults, ending in final separation from both of these things. His focus was now on living, a prayer we prayed together, lit-erally touching head to head, "God keep you, Stephan." I cherish the photo of him, his military brush cut, red plaid shirt-jack over tee, and haunting angel-like deep green eyes, crying volumes of love with a smile. I cried when he asked me to please bike for him and his friends at Baily House, which I promised to do. "This mile is for Stephan, and this mile for his friends."

Then, arranged by ASC, we lodged another night at Incentra, a private garden suite on 8th Avenue in the Village. It was a quiet evening to reflect and summon energy to move on. Before heading out, Cal made sure we stopped by the Today Show, knowing he could talk Al Roker into conduct-ing a brief USAIDS 5,000 interview, where I would be able to plug both the AIDS Project and the Baily House before the weather report. Move over Miss Piggy—The Viper has now done Manhattan. Before day's end, I would cross into Pennsylvania.

[I want to expose a little more about the great state of New York. I've been blessed to travel it from one corner to the other by automobile and train; on one occasion, I had a perfect view of the Finger Lakes Region by air. Nothing, however, can compare to absorbing this grand land on a bicy-cle. Sure, the mountains were ass-kickers, but they were some of the most breathtaking ass-kicking moments of my life. They trained me for bigger mountains to endure and paved the way for golden and green pastures, lit-erally, from sea to shining sea. Yet, the people I met in town after city were more beautiful in spirit than this land they occupy. God has already blessed America, because of my adopted state of New York.]

~

During our next leg westward, we camped most of the time. Each destination was an experience, some more adventurous than others. On the fun side, Bucktail Campgrounds in Mansfield, Pennsylvania was for kids at heart, with a mini-train to ride around the park and a full-scale carousel with not just horses, but the entire animal kingdom. The Foote Rest Campground permitted pet rabbits to hop about, keeping everyone company. Some offered primitive sites for tent camping, "no frills" spaces so far off the beaten path and hidden from the rest of the domesticated world that it became easy for boys to be boys, daring each other to get down to real nature, like running in the buff. Cave man Cal couldn't rest until a campfire proclaimed civilization. Though prepared for attacks by mosquitoes and spiders, several locations couldn't hide unique brands of infestations: half-inch black flies (for which no repellant works), silk worms, moths, and oversized ants, to name a few. Nothing will compare with the May flies from hell, however. Each year, these critters hatch by the millions near Lakes Ontario and Huron over a ten-day cycle; there is no escaping their presence. Though they were physically harmless, we witnessed one campsite convert from pleasant environment to plague epidemic in less than an hour. It made Alfred Hitchcock's *The Birds* seem tame. Not only did they crunch under your feet, you had to wipe the two-inch bad boys away to see in mirrors and sit on the pot. Each morning, the overnight onslaught left a thick layer of fresh, but dead, insects that needed to be swept from every campsite article used before it could be stowed. Being freakishly fanatic, I stalled departure once by two hours to make certain no companion bug was onboard me or the support vehicle.

Throughout Pennsylvania, I was blessed with heavenly weather: cool evenings to rest by and sunny, warm days where I found some of my most enjoyable country roads. Winding through rolling hills of forestry and breathtaking valleys, peddling through scattered quaint villages set apart from isolated bungalows, I would (if lucky) bike past a farmer tilling soil, repairing a fence or fetching mail, but always waving hello. I often suggested that Cal meet me in the next larger town or city so that I could enjoy the serenity and solitude of spiritual sightseeing, unobstructed and undistracted by the follow vehicle.

While in cities, we preferred staying in motels to be rested and clean for the media; Erie was no exception. Unable to locate a Super 8, Cal appealed to two popular motel chains, which both went from "vacancy" to "totally booked" within seconds of learning my story. Apart from that, Erie was a friendly place. Dan Luca supplied dinner for us as we met with all the major networks to promote Friends of the Heart, a small, but important all-volunteer AIDS agency caring for immediate needs of PWAs (persons with AIDS, a classification which later became PLWA to include the word *living*).

As planned, Cal returned to Buffalo and Rochester to resupply, including picking up more USAIDS 5,000 tees for sale on the road. Dan followed me forty-seven miles west to our next campsite, crossing the Ohio border. On one of the breaks along the way, Dan (a member of the Seneca Tribe) shared Native American traditions, passing on ancient healing stones. He also blessed a dream catcher made specifically to assure my proper rest, unencumbered by night demons. While resting in grassy shade behind a church, Dan spotted an eagle soaring overhead, swooping above us. He revealed, "This is a sign of great vision, and I believe it is meant for you Vincent." Dan had contracted HIV from tainted blood during surgery following an automobile accident that occurred prior to medical understanding of HIV transmission. Instead of condemning his fate, Dan seized his circumstance as a sign from heaven to devote his life, apart from being a committed husband and father to three teens, to helping his brothers and sisters with AIDS, without personal benefit. Dan exuded great vision and hope—I shared the eagle's flight.

With Cal safely back, the trip continued to Cleveland, almost sixty miles in muggy heat—I was drained. Our friends at Mandy's Burgers in Madison traded fries, Frostcups, and well wishes for an autographed Polaroid of all of us. One student employee about to end shift, a strapping lad named Tom Connors, helped to motivate, if not to rejuvenate me. Tom, a star on Madison's track team, jogged alongside my bike in support of our cause until his athletic legs could endure no further punishment. Tom is among God's greatest miracles and certainly left his footprint on my heart that day. "This mile is for Tom, because you ran one, two, three, and several more for me. "

Cleveland proved uneventful overall. Stopping by the AIDS Task Force of Greater Cleveland as prearranged, I performed a single TV spot for "Dancing in the Streets," their annual funding dance-a-thon, before hitting the road again. Worming my way through the city toward the lakeshore, I was flagged down by a bicycle-riding policeman. At first, I thought we were going to be harassed, but he greeted us, saying, "The family thanks you." I understood the distinction between *my* family and *the* family. I winked.

~

I made good time through Ohio, even with temperatures hovering above ninety degrees. I trekked along, cooled by the lake breeze, enjoying the scenery of northern Ohio and stopping only for routine water bottle refills and meal breaks. I normally drove through on the Interstate; I never realized the beauty now discovered by bicycle. Making it a shorter biking day, we crashed at the Gay and Lesbian Service Center in Lorain, which doubled as an outreach facility for the AIDS Task Force. A retired nurse volunteer named Riccardo had limited resources, but set up cots for our comfort. He gave accounts of young moms and infants with AIDS who were dumped by their families, fearing the disease. He recounted one memory of finding one teen and child living in an abandoned barn. Riccardo distributed medicine, food, and hope, sheltering the desperate. The very facility we stayed in had served as emergency housing on occasion. It was an uncomfortable, restive attempt at sleep I made that night, wanting relief for these forgotten people. Except for praying and conveying their stories, we were helpless. This was not the America of my dreams.

A living home of hope and love, dreamed up by a young man named David, provided a family setting for some astonishing people in Toledo—it was David's House of Compassion, my next stop. Similar to other AIDS homes in many respects, David's House differed by encouraging residents to live precious life to its fullest. While dining with the guys, we learned that Peter wanted to start a Men of Color program, Nerean stayed productive with a car-washing service to help the home; and Chico's poetry came alive with the passing of his dear wife. "These men epitomize the lust for life God wants us to have," was one of the remarks I shared with the *Toledo Blade* and a local news station, "they are what this bicycle journey is about." Challenging corporations to pledge funding, I appealed for compassion: "Help these hardworking men step outside the boundaries of AIDS."

Another sixty miles of ninety-five scorching degrees took us to Harrison Lake State Park, arriving before dusk. After a perfect picnic of sizzling smoked sausage over a crackling campfire and showers to remove road grit, Cal & I were wrapping up the campsite to turn in. Looking down, by our feet we saw a smiling raccoon showing hungry eyes. Cal scrambled so fast that he literally ran out of his flip-flops; he could have been in a sitcom. Nature has its way of getting paybacks; I'm not sure if our friend was digging for potato chips or toe nips, but I woke to the bugger scratching through the tent at my foot. Cal got the last laugh. Before heading out in the morning, we met Wade and Jean, senior citizen camp volunteers from Florida. In trade for their own camp space, they care for the park and guests as if it were a hotel—a creative way to make for a perfect stay. "This mile is for Wade and Jean, and another for raccoons we've seen."

On June 23rd we crossed into my home state of Indiana, stopping to camp at Happy Acres RV Park in Angola. Surviving the worst storm of our trip, we verified that the "dream house" was waterproof, but rest was uncomfortable, at best. Another seventy miles through Amish Country brought us to a Super 8 in Elkhart. Cal managed to lose me. Hey, Viper knew exactly where he was, but my cell phone had insufficient charge—so much for emergency contact. Before the day was out, Cal had the sheriff put an APB (all-points bulletin) and a county-wide truckers' watch out on me. Finally, it dawned on Cal to call the hotel. Duh!

In relief, Cal murmured "Thank God; are you alright? We thought you were lost."

Now I scolded him, "Lost? Me? I showered, took a nap, and I'm patiently waiting for you to take me to dinner—I'm famished. You're lost, pal! Where are *you*?" After listening to some pitiful mumble, I felt guilty. "I'm fine, really! You're about three miles in the wrong direction. Cut across to U.S. 20 Business; you'll see Super 8. Come on; get a shower, and I'll give *you* a massage today. You need it more than me, buddy."

To celebrate finding the missing child, Cal called the Italian Fiesta to ask for a dinner donation. As conveyed to me, some guy name Donald Park said, "If it's the Vinny Pirelli I know, I'll buy you both dinner." It was! Don and I worked together eight years earlier when he first started in management with Yorkshire Steak House in Marion.

Don, now a successful general manager of the Elkhart Italian Fiesta, had to ask, "Mr. Pirelli, are the rumors about you true?"

"Probably, what have you heard? Some of it might even be news to me. By the way, I'm nobody's boss these days, call me Vinny. This is Calvin, my manager."

In the same polite, cautious tone he always used, he started relaying rumors with, "For starters, I heard you raised all kinds of hell in Boston, and then walked out on them to join Italian Fiesta after they pissed you off. Years later, somebody said you were working again for Jim Black and Bill Wolf, and I heard about your earring. I can see that part is true."

"You're leaving out the best part. Didn't you hear I was a flaming queen?"

Now laughing, he responded, "I don't put any stock into rumors; your business is *your* business."

"So, you *did* believe it. Yeah, I'm gay, and," now whispering, "I do have AIDS. But I'm the same guy you always knew; only you know a little more about me. If you liked me before, you still will. If not, you wouldn't have invited me to dinner—you're a good guy, Don, and congratulations on becoming GM—I didn't last that long!"

"I respect you; you taught me success—this thing called Philosophy of Archism. Do you remember it? I could never buy what you taught me, but can I buy one of your t-shirts?"

Cal went to the car for a t-shirt for Don. He didn't have the heart to charge him. I didn't argue; he was my manager. It had been a long time since I heard good things about me from the past. I needed that as much as the

Fettuccini Alfredo. That night, Cal and I both slept sound and long. I was looking forward to biking Indiana.

The media showed no mercy as I biked from Elkhart through South Bend to New Carlisle; they followed my every move. One station taped me doing a nature call. Another attempted to video my comments with a microphone boom dangling from a tree limb, smacking me upside the head and leaving a bulging bruise. Those clips didn't get aired, but oh, the price of stardom! I was finding it difficult at times to strike a balance between being a spokesperson and demanding attention while remaining humble. A part of me needed so badly to be somebody's hero, while another part wanted to hide my hurt inside. Cal helped keep it real, always reminding me, "Vinny, just be you—let me handle them."

Another first was our stay with a family who opened their home to us. Mack and Ruby forged an eclectic life for their sons, wanting them to be reared in a safe country setting and learning to appreciate nature while bringing the world into their home through newspapers, books, music, sports, pets, friends, and now an overnight guest with AIDS. Ruby (a registered nurse) represented AIDS Ministries of South Bend, an outreach for HIV testing and education. By night, she rescued homeless dogs found on country roads; she was a marvelous mom and a confectionary/culinary colossus, mastering morning muffins and heart-pleasing Chicken Heart Attack, a hungry man's dream. Mack was a literary professor (with a creative writing specialty) at St. Mary's College, a sister college to Notre Dame. Mack urged me to write a story of biking adventures, and encouraged as much with a gift copy of *The Writer's Digest Handbook of Short Story Writing* with a preface by Joyce Carol Oates. Only jogging distance from Oprah's Ranch, this splendid countryside home proved a peaceful respite from the vigor of battling vigilante reporters. Thinking about the unlikely possibility of writing a book, I drifted away and napped, sharing the shading oak tree of their front lawn with Casey, one of several family dogs. I love puppy dogs . . .

~

Wrapping up our first month, I biked through steady rain as Cal patiently followed me to my first hometown of Portage by lunch time. As if on cue, the clouds parted to let through warming sunshine as I approached the parking lot of the new Super 8. We were greeted with waves and applause by my children, four grandchildren, sisters Marci and Sandi, hotel employees, the Portage Visitors Bureau and a *Gary Post-Tribune* reporter. In addition to providing us a room, the hotel manager set up an attached conference room with cordial amenities for visiting with my family, some of whom I was meeting for the first time. While Cal busied himself with secretive plans for the morning, I agreed to a press interview. The *Tribune* thought it time to feature AIDS as a theme for an edition, which was tentatively scheduled for June 28th. In addition to USAIDS 5,000, the paper wanted to chronicle the life of Irene, a fellow PLWA whose life had spiraled downward with the onset of AIDS; she was still hospitalized when taking marital vows at her bedside. Overwhelmed by the day, and in need of physical and emotional rest in order to continue biking, I asked Cal and my sisters to visit Irene, passing on my best wishes. They found her still clinging to life in the hospital. With her husband Dean, Cal, and my sisters by her side, Irene (a lovely lady with more courage than strength) called me at the hotel room to say, "Vinny, thank you for biking. You are riding for us all—me too." With that, Irene was added to my chants.

I crawled out of bed early to get my lemon-filled donut and piping hot coffee at the continental breakfast for Super 8 guests. I saw the 8x10 color photo appearing on the newspaper cover page, face up and waiting outside our hotel room door, but I stepped over it and headed to the lobby. I prayed with a smile on my face, "Lord, please let Kurt Klemm at Pit Stops find today's *Gary Post-Tribune* on his desk as usual. Amen!"

"Congratulations, Mr. Pirelli," came from the front desk, "Your children must be very proud of you. Can I get your autograph on my copy?"

"Sure, do you have any extra copies? I've never been on the front page before."

I returned to the room with a small tray of coffee, donuts, and copies of the news.

Cal was barely awake, slowly moaning, "Oh man, I need some of that java."

"Here it is sir, and I brought your morning paper; this will wake you with a smile."

Almost spilling the coffee, Cal grabbed one of the papers from the tray and started reading aloud, "'*An Inspirational Journey*: A native son cycles the country to show there is life after AIDS.' Oh my God, Vinny, I can't wait till your kids see this at breakfast. Oh yeah, I almost forgot. Your family will be at the restaurant waiting for us in 45 minutes. We better get rolling, no pun intended."

Now, with both of us laughing, I retorted, "That's pathetically lame, Cal. You can start by *rolling* your scrawny ass out of bed if you want some of this coffee."

After breakfast and photos with the entire family, even babies, all dressed in USAIDS 5,000 t-shirts, we said temporary goodbyes and headed west on U.S. Route 20 through Gary and Hammond to Calumet City, following the curvature of Lake Michigan en route to Chicago. I had so much to be grateful for, so much more to look forward to. It started raining. "God, let me appreciate this rain. I feel redeemed; it's like a personal baptism. Thank you Lord. Amen."

More rain, but even so, I enjoyed biking the full distance of Lake Shore Drive trail from Calumet Park, Illinois all the way to Belmont in Chicago. Never have I seen Lake Michigan like this before, with the rich, blue-green waves crashing on the stone barriers on the right, picturesque weaves through grassy knolls beyond the sand line on the trail and the ever-beautiful Chicago skyline on the left.

As would prove to be true for most of the trip, I drew far more attention in smaller venues, thereby living the saying, "It's better to be a big fish in a pond than a little fish in the ocean." There would be no invitation from Oprah, and due to President Clinton's overnight stay in Chicago, there was zero media attention. Unfortunately, I was unable to promote the work of two tremendous agencies we hoped to support. The Women's AIDS Project preferred no publicity, wishing to protect the privacy of their clients. We learned their work was similar to Riccardo's in Lorain, Ohio, only on a massive scale.

The Children's Place is a residential home for kids with AIDS, as well as an outreach program for little people infected with and affected by AIDS. The staff had a tough job, but they did it with grace and unending love. I was filled with joy when I got to meet the children on a bus returning from a day trip to *Taste of Chicago*. Cal sucked in his emotions after visiting little Ronisha, struggling for breath, yet he made her smile. Being a twin himself, we could all feel his love radiating toward the unnamed newborn twins still awaiting HIV status. I heard him whisper at their bedside; perhaps he was praying, too.

~

Following time in Toledo, Elkhart, South Bend, Portage, and Gary, I recall an abnormally large number of vehicles flashing their beams or honking their horns while waving in support. No doubt, they had seen TV or newspaper clips of the journey. These little encouragements from strangers were an impetus not to be underestimated. The part that nobody really saw, however, was how many times I was ill from heat, physical exhaustion or occasional contaminated food. Everyday bacteria, found on many foods, which would never affect a healthy being, might cause miserable cramping and deplorable diarrhea when the immune system is compromised or weakened. This was the case when I often fooled the press with silly smiles that really meant, "I seriously got to shit, so hurry up!"

I had become accustomed to, and often (though not always) liked, meeting with the press, including radio, TV, and print media; I have found that each journalist puts their own fingerprint on the stories they produce. If I had editing authority, I'd change much of what was written—especially anything that referred to me or my fellow survivors as *victims*. Perhaps some of the folks I met along the way were innocent, certainly the children and infants, but none of us adults considered ourselves victims. We owned our illness. In some respects, we took pride in our active fight against HIV and AIDS. We focused on our abilities, rather than the weakness brought on by our disease. I think it would be a fair statement to say that other causes learned well from the AIDS movement of the 1990s; we taught them how to compete with us for attention and money.

Equally as fair, though I'm sure many will contest, AIDS (still urgent worldwide) is not as critical in the United States today due to the onset of new and better drugs called protease inhibitors, the combination of which is known as "the AIDS Cocktail." My story obviously ends better than so many stories before me, but it is good to note that USAIDS 5,000 occurred pre-protease! We were part of an astonishing national movement to focus on the living. That's exactly what our USAIDS 5,000 mission was about—to promote *living with* AIDS rather than succumbing to it.

For Cal, so much of our trip had to be focused on our survival. We relied on him to sell t-shirts, buttons, and Polaroid pictures with me to get the cash needed for the support vehicle, campsites when not donated, and emergency medical supplies. Even more emphasis was put on getting FREE stuff. We needed to count on the generosity of local town's folk to feed us at home or in restaurants, which was no small task with my immense appetite. I required five energy meals daily. I was convinced that Cal could get just about anything free if he earnestly applied himself. Often, we were down to piddly crumbs, which was when Viper turned venomous, big time. All I could think was, "I need food NOW"; there would be no peace from this biking peddler until the promotional peddler got the grub by hook, crook or I really don't wanna know how!

Speaking of food and restaurants, there was a special lady I feel compelled to write about. Her name is Isabella Krol, a gray-haired senior citizen with dignified wrinkles who was visiting from Poland (she was in Chicago on the day we met, but she was in the states primarily to visit her daughter in Hammond, Indiana). We met in Nookies Breakfast Café, where she recognized me from her copy of the *Post-Tribune*. In broken English, she described her family struggles during WWII. She said, "We are both survivors," then pulled me to her breast and hugged and loved me for a gifted, generous moment. It was as if we were long-lost siblings. She bought breakfast and gave Cal a donation for our cause. It was then and there that I understood the ever-growing power of a hug. From that point forward, I have signed all my personal correspondence with "Hugs from Vinny." From one survivor to another, "This mile is for you, dear Isabella, with no boundaries to my hugs."

Hand in Hand
(Melody & Lyrics: 1995)

V.1   What has gone wrong?
             To cause a loss of dreams
             When melodies and song begin to fade
             When all hopes of life
             Are shredding at the seams
             Leaving six-foot quilts of strife man has made

V.2   What has gone wrong?
             With hunting for the gold
             As rainbows grow too long, no end in sight
             Bury all that we believe
             Unsung stories never told
             Leaving nothing to achieve, just a fight

Chorus 1   We will fight, we will fight
             Band together with might
             Hand in hand, marching to the light
             Should one fall, we must all . . .
             Hold on ever so tight
             We will fight hand in hand; we will fight

Chorus 2   We will fight, we will fight
             Stand together in plight
             Hand in hand, marching to the light
             To believe, to achieve
             Hold on; never lose sight
             We will fight hand in hand; we will fight

Achieving Mountains

After cycling up the Illinois and Wisconsin lakeshores, Cal and I found ourselves among new friends in Sturtevant where Cecilia, a school teacher working summers, sponsored our stay at Traveler's Inn Campground. Having spent several previous nights in comfort, adjusting to the Midwest sticky-steamy air of Lake Michigan, which was augmented at dusk by mosquitos and crickets, took some effort. Of all the Vincent Pirelli DNA building blocks, one that I could part with flashes signals to insects that invite them to dine on me. Recently refreshed from a shower, I doubled down with gooey repellent to enjoy Cal's campfire while watching lightning bugs dance at a distance. Cal was blessed with the DNA for building a perfect campfire and for attracting attention with his *flaming* personality. Promising beer and tales of the trails, Cal invited two fellow campers to share his wood-fired creation.

(Seldom did a day pass without meeting some sensational individuals with incredible stories of their own. These people may be giants in God's eyes, but often, they are among the most down trodden that we had seen in our travels.) Steven and Joseph were men like these. I sensed they traded cleaning projects for a camping spot, possibly camouflaging homelessness. Visibly disabled and disfigured from some unknown incident, perhaps involving fire, Steven counted his blessings and his friends, not his misfortunes. We didn't get into the details of Steven's catastrophe, only that he faced rejection by most everyone, and that Joseph remained his loyal friend. I didn't get the impression they were gay, but it was evident that these two held unyielding devotion, each to the other, for life. Their friendship transcended sexuality, superficial looks, and materialism.

When was the last time you've been really freaked out by something or someone? I admit now that when I first met Steven, he grossed me out, because, physically speaking, Steven was freakish at best. His face reminded me of a melted wax statue. His right arm was nearly as bad, and the left was replaced with a hook. I could tell one of his legs was also a prosthetic version. I cannot imagine the trials of living like that, or even wanting to live like that. I would be unable to face the horror in other people's eyes when they would meet mine. I wondered if Steven could see my horror. Why did I have to meet this man? What was it I needed to learn? I found the answer over breakfast. There's only one appropriate word for it—*transformation*.

Joseph told me that Steven couldn't sleep, worrying about whether I had proper nutrition for the trip. He thought I looked weary, beat up (now that's the pot calling the kettle black). Steven, therefore, having not much more than love to his name, rummaged through his pockets and went to a local store overnight to purchase a few breakfast items he had not planned to buy for himself. I watched this near-cripple go about his blissful task of making breakfast for me, Steven's VIP guest, at his picnic table. Extra-strong coffee brewed in a percolator outdoors has an invitation of its own. Mix in the aroma of maple-cured bacon, eggs, grits, and toast cooked over an open fire, and who can resist? By the time breakfast was over, I had been transformed from being that freaked-out boy back in Leroy, Indiana, unable to deal with dried blood in the ass-end of an ambulance to a compassionate man of greater tolerance. All I needed to do was enjoy a prayer, breakfast, and morning laughter with friends. Holding back tears was a challenge when it came time to say fare thee well. It's our group hug that I cherished most. "This mile is for Steven & Joseph, his friend."

En route to Madison, bike problems slowed our cavalcade—two broken spokes and a warped rear wheel. We prepared for flats, but did not stock extra rims. Of course, it would be Sunday. This time, I snapped at God: "We prayed this morning; doesn't that count? Good Lord, we're out in the middle of fricking nowhere, so give us a break already!" Bleak were the odds of finding a bicycle store out in these wooded hills. Expecting to find a repair shop *open* was beyond hope...unless the next town happened to be LaGrange. God must have been toying with me, because up pops this biker's haven with cyclists from all over the country, trouncing the trails of Wisconsin Dells. There, in town, was The General Store with repair shop OPEN for business. Nate generously fixed the "dream machine" without charge. Cal thanked him with one of our t-shirts, but Nate had to reciprocate with one promoting his store. "This mile is for Nate, and another for the miracle of answered prayers."

Our next destination was the AIDS Network in Madison, a statewide program with outreach facilities in most Wisconsin cities. With my growing name recognition and fundraising activities in the works, I was asked to put a face on AIDS. In doing so, I could help them keep the issue alive. Showing off my embroidered flag shorts, *The Capitol Times* covered USAIDS 5,000 on the Fourth of July front page. I appealed for corporate life-sustaining funding for AIDS Network based on my mileage. While Cal spent the holiday resting at Super 8, I two-wheel-toured the picturesque parks of Madison, touted in 1995 as being the second most livable city in the country.

It appeared to be a straight shot west to La Crosse, but because of hills, head winds, and rain, the jaunt proved one of my most labored cycling days. I was wearing down physically. No, it was more than that; I was sick to the point of not wanting to continue. A 1730 quit time helped, but Cal called for a bedside physician to the hotel room. After communicating with my VA hospital, the doc gave me two injections: one in the belly (Neupogen, to boost white blood cells) and the other in the hip (an antibiotic to fight an upper respiratory infection and to prevent pneumonia). I prayed myself to sleep, "God, I'm sorry, I just can't do any more. It's too hard!" I slept soundly for twelve hours.

Cal planned a morning news interview to take place in the parking lot, for my convenience, scheduled for 0900 sharp. With eye-opening breakfast waiting for me, it was a new day. The Super 8 whirlpool revived my attitude, but it was little 7-year-old Gary Johns that revived my spirit. (Little Johns was missing his grandfather and namesake. The elder Gary Johns had passed away almost exactly a year prior from AIDS, contracted through hip surgery.) Devone, little Gary's mom and big Gary's daughter, set aside her own loss to show support and strength for me. When the TV cameras arrived, Devone permitted both Johns to be part of the USAIDS 5,000 story. My little buddy did us all proud as he sat (with help) on the "dream machine" and told the world how kids, too, are affected by AIDS.

Little Gary Johns had gone shopping earlier to find a special gift—something he personally picked out. It had to be something I didn't already have. From earlier news coverage, he learned that the "dream machine" was equipped with everything imaginable: comfort-cushion Saddle, dual suspension, dual rear view mirrors, first aid kit, head and tail lights, emergency flashers, bell, odometer with clock, radio, trailer hitch with trailer, Cellular One telephone, and a security alarm system. It didn't have a horn, though, so Gary bought me (with his own savings) a blue Fisher-Price squeak horn for the bike. "To keep you safe on the road," he told me as reporters covered him like paparazzi. I wanted to shout, "Look Mom! Look Dad! Look Gary! Look Jeff! Look world! Vinny's got a horn, *hee-haw, hee-haw!*" Oh, the memories it brought back to me. A half mile down the road, a Wisconsin state sheriff pulled me over. He heard the story on the radio about our bike trip and the horn a boy had given me. Partly as a joke, but partly out of sincerity, he presented us with Citizen's Badges, plastic police badges from Wisconsin, which are no doubt intended for children. The sheriff insisted he honor us with a police escort to the Minnesota border. There's nothing like a parade-type escort with lights flashing to pick up the spirit. It was quite a twist on the ol' "sheriff making sure you leave town." I honked four times while crossing over into Minnesota. "This honk is for Devone, this one for her dad Big Johns, this one for my newest hero, little Gary Johns, and this one for my new horn—*hee haw!*"

~

La Crosse, named for being "The Crossing" from Wisconsin to Minnesota, is where we also traversed over the Mississippi River before heading north. Geography was never my forte, but I had learned some basics. I knew about the mighty Mississippi River (you know, flowing from St. Louis, Missouri to, say, Mississippi). Who knew it streamed from north of Minnesota? Added to all my other experiences, I was getting a first-hand, third-grade education on a bicycle! There is nothing like doing it on a bike! (I strongly suggest you don't take that line out of context.) Like something out of Mark Twain, the fifty-mile ride along the Mississippi River brought to life the kinds of scenes one generally only reads about. There were dams and locks, tugboats and barges, blues and greens, flowers and wild life. Anyone can drive by, but if you really want to breathe it all into your soul, do it on a bike. Each curve, each nuance of trail is a worthwhile experience. I hardly even noticed that the days were getting yet hotter. We heard of, "record-setting temperatures across the Midwest; scores of seniors perished in the squelching heat in Chicago." It must have been pushing 100 degrees Fahrenheit the whole day, but compared to the cold, bone-chilling rain, this was a welcomed reprieve. Today, giving up wasn't an option. Our next major metropolis would be Minneapolis.

Local media and AIDS agencies totally ignored us in Minneapolis. The focus of passing through Minneapolis was visiting my eldest sister, ("Ubangi Lips") Sharon (also a PLWA, as it turns out). After the death of her fourth or fifth husband (I lost count), sis went back to school to become a registered nurse. Her next husband was a member of the Greek Orthodox Church who was doing mission work in Kenya, in which Sharon was invited to participate. She helped open a medical clinic at the base of Mount Kenya, about thirty kilometers from the city of Nyeri. They served disenfranchised mountain folk, some dying of AIDS. She was accidentally pricked with a contaminated syringe, leading to her own infection. Another husband or two later, she settled temporarily in Minnesota; however, she still does mission trips to Kenya. She remains healthy and working. Having been estranged for years over the gay issue, we ultimately decided our ties are predicated on being siblings, both of us having AIDS, being alienated from our parents and living to make a difference. We needed each other. "This mile is for Big Lips and her mission work in Kenya."

~

Due to a family emergency, Cal returned to Rochester on July 10th. I continued on alone, pulling my now-seventy-five-pound trailer. The weight alone wasn't too bad, but when it was combined with 100-plus degree temperatures for three consecutive days, it was too much for me. I collapsed while heaving during a break not far from Glenwood. A passing resident in a pickup truck most likely saved me, hauling me (with bike and trailer) to Glenwood First Care, where I received IV fluids. Only a few hours later, against medical advice, I was back on the road, headed to Fergus Falls. There was no bill for services (I hope), only sketchy journal entries, lacking information perhaps due to disorientation. Heat exhaustion continued to plague my journey for several days, limiting mileage and detracting from the beauty of surrounding lakes and rolling hills. In between heat waves were violent storms, one of which yielded tornadoes that I camped through in terror. I rolled the trailer inside for security and convenience; only a prayer kept the tent from blowing away, with me and the trailer as tenants. Pictures in papers the following day captured the remains of thick trees twisted off, leaving only stumps.

Facing the wild without support prompted me to nearly give up on more than one occasion. Constant thirty-five-mile-per-hour head winds daily seemed more brutal than mountains, yet less than a few violent attitudes I encountered in western Minnesota. After being called a bum twice when asking for meal discounts in one town, I biked on to the next town, only to be physically accosted and tossed from a diner after mentioning the AIDS issue. I still recall the aproned owner pushing me out the screen door with a literal kick in the rump, shouting, "We don't have the AIDS in this part, and we don't need you city queers bringing it here." It wasn't the scuffed arm or bruised rear and shin, but the torn soul that hurt the most. I doubted my ability to continue without Cal. Yes, I had tenacity of the trail, but lacked Cal's gift of gab; being short on cash, I kept meals to precious little. The label *bum* caused me to question in prayer, "God, I need help. Does that make me a bum?" Then, a feeling of defiance cloaked and energized me, as I thought, "Peddle one stroke after the other, Viper, and dream of achieving mountains—dream of doing something nobody else with AIDS has ever done. This mile is for us bums of the world."

Before crossing into Fargo, North Dakota, I met Cindy & Rebecca, two members of a cycling group called Bike Aid going the opposite direction. Traveling from Seattle to Washington D.C., they were biking in support of environmental awareness this summer; however, the group had supported AIDS awareness the prior two years. After sharing snacks, stories, and good wishes, I continued on, rejuvenated by their encouragement.

Who knew that cross-country biking should start on the West Coast, keeping the wind to one's back and pushing you along? Nobody told *me*! It would have been something kind of nice to know, don't ya think? It was a big time reality kick in the gut. If my average MPH without wind on a flat surface and pulling a trailer is twelve, and I've been doing about seven, I'm losing five MPH and forty in a day. In fact, heading east, I could have gained five MPH, which would have made a very respectable seventeen MPH pulling a trailer. I just wanted to turn around and go home! Why did I torture myself like this? *Start peddling, Vinny*; it's a long, long way to Seattle, they say. "This mile is for Cindy and Rebecca today. Another is for reality…and for stupidity, okay?"

In the midst of yet another storm approaching, I pleaded with two farmers for a place to camp. Rejected twice, I continued biking and looking for safe terrain to set up the "dream house." One clearing looked promising, but it proved to be mosquito bed, or, rather, a mosquito haven, where I was ambushed. Before I could jump off the bike, I was under siege by hundreds of the critters. What would normally be a nuisance was now a nightmare and emergency. Dropping the bike and tipping the trailer, I couldn't get away fast enough. They bit through two layers of clothing (my shorts and underwear). Tending to more than a hundred bites, I sat alone in the middle of the gravel intersection that I dragged the bike and trailer to after regaining my senses. It was still ten miles from the nearest village, almost dark, and it started to rain. I openly cried to an audience of one in near defeat, "God, why won't anybody help me? I can't do this alone!" Strangely, the rain soothed my skin, making the tears seem insignificant. As long as it rained, I could peddle on to civilization. "God, please let them be *civil*."

I found no trace of a tower in the town called Tower City, but I did locate a tower of a friend in Carol. She owned the Tower Motel and Campsite. It was after midnight; Carol didn't fear me. Instead, she donated a spacious, grassy site for camping. I was invited to rest in her kitchen until the rain stopped. I watched the next day as she singlehandedly cleaned rooms, crisped linen on a line and picked fresh strawberries from her garden. After I opted to stay over a second night (at Carol's near insistence), she offered me a jar of fresh strawberry jam, saying, "I'm glad we met; I wish I could do more."

Bump, bump, bump, clink, squeal! Oh No! The rumble strips along I-94 took a toll on two more spokes from the rear wheel. They snapped this time, causing the wheel to quickly warp from the trailer weight and ending in an abrupt halt. Not quite to Jamestown yet with three-fourths of North Dakota to travel, my dream of a pleasure-ride bicycle tour of America was relegated to a never-ending series of crises. (It should be noted that through much of North Dakota, Montana, and Idaho, there were insufficient side roads with local town support stops; therefore, cyclists were, at that time, authorized to bike on the Interstate highways.) Perhaps one of the thousand pickup trucks on the highway would stop to help a lone cyclist? No, I was forced to dig out Cellular One to call emergency 911 after a tediously hot two-hour attempt at hitch-biking. The sheriff, whose pretty new car couldn't be used to haul a bike and trailer, called a tow truck. Another two hours and sixty dollars later, Jebb's Service finally taxied me to Jamestown, with a courtesy stop at a local ATM to guarantee payment. Too late for bike repairs, and unable to get donations or discounts, I paid for a crappy room and prayed for some better luck tomorrow.

Early Saturday morning, I walked through town with my wrinkled dream manually in tow. Goodroad Sports Shop had their hands full with a summer sidewalk sale, but after evaluating my calamity, they devoted attention to my ailing transportation. These folks were a gem in the rough, replacing the wheel with a better, stronger (free) version, tuning the bike, and directing me to Riverside Camp, an in-town park whose owners donated a night's stay upon Goodroad's request. I wanted to make up mileage, but needed time to rethink the entire stinking scenario. I opted to stay; camp was pitched before lunch. After devoting an hour to silent meditation and prayer, I intended an early afternoon siesta. As I began to doze off, fellow campers, inquisitive of the bicycle trailer, popped their heads into the tent, alerting me to their presence with a, "Yoo-hoo, hello, anyone home?" Their names were Danny and Jill, his fiancée. They had been doing cross-country with (not on) a Harley, and they, too, pulled a trailer—slightly more elaborate than mine. Danny drove a pickup truck that pulled his Harley on a trailer. They were pleasure riders who drove to vacation destinations, then explored the local scenery on a hog. They were a young, nice-looking couple, cleaner than I might have expected for bikers—you know *real* bikers. Their plans (providing they survived each other during travels) were to be married in October.

Danny made an offer I couldn't pass up: First, they mapped out a bicycle tour of Jamestown, including Pioneer Village (a restoration of life in the 1800s). Upon return some 27 miles later, Danny granted my first ride on a hog, taking me up a nearby shallow mountain that boasts the world's largest buffalo, created from cast iron. Being a Buffalonian, I had to pose with the beast for posterity. Herds of live buffalo grazed the hillside below, giving Jamestown the historic name of Buffalo City. As if that were not a treat enough, Danny offered to help make up the time (if not miles) by hauling me, the "dream machine" and my tipsy trailer to the next larger town heading west early Sunday morning. That would be Sterling, and, "that would be wonderful, so very kind, indeed; thank you!" It was one whopper of a prayer being answered ever so nicely. "God, this mile is for you and the angels you sent to rescue me in Buffalo City."

~

Showing more courage than normal, I avoided rumble strips and biked along the road's edge, rather than the emergency lane. As long as there was daylight, the chance of getting clobbered by some trucker paled to the risk of another single unserviceable spoke or warped wheel. Finally, it seemed that God was not only watching over me, but urging me on, redirecting winds in my favor. I cruised through Bismarck, stopping for water only, to a truck parking lot that doubled as campsite not far from New Salem (home of the largest cow, not willing to be outdone by that big buffalo). It made a respectably distanced ride for the day, but I had my sights set much further west: to Belfield by the next night, then through Beach (a seemingly water-frontless town) the following day, ending 220 miles later in Glendive, Montana by evening. Cal arrived shortly thereafter. Like was true of Western North Dakota, Montana is mostly rolling valleys, rich farmlands, and long distances between towns.

Once united at camp in Glendive with my friend and support, it was like God was saying, "Cal's back, you don't need ME anymore!" It was very late (it often stays light until 2200 in Montana during July.) Far off, we could see what I believed to be heat lightning, which is more distant than thunder can travel; we were not worried. Wrong again! About 0200, Cal was shaking me to wake up, feeling the wind's ever-increasing volatility. Frantically, I tied down the tent with greater reinforcement, but the storm ravaged the camp before everything could be secured. It was another tornado. This time, it took all the strength that we scared creatures could muster up to prevent losing our shelter. I begged Cal to abandon the effort and head to safety in the shower room, or, at a minimum, the car. "No," Cal shrieked. "I'm staying here—we've got to save our home!" He admitted later that it was the cellular phones he fretted about. It would be easier for me to bike without water than Cal to follow without a phone!

Montana is colossally gorgeous, with breathtaking sights like the winding rapids of the Yellowstone River, but it is also gigantic in size, too. With perhaps 525 road miles (a far cry more than a crow's fly) to our next scheduled event on Sunday in Missoula (it was already Wednesday morning, and we were running on insufficient rest) we had to formulate a new plan. Even if we mounted the trailer atop the car trunk, I couldn't feasibly bike 400 miles in four days, let alone 125 more, on a mountain bike heading west, against the wind. Let's face it: the "dream machine" was designed for comfort, not speed. On the other hand, I was immeasurably stronger from two months of touring. Here was our new plan: I bicycled to Miles City on Wednesday (76 miles), to Hysham by Thursday evening (74 miles), to Billings on Friday (78 miles, also where the route switches to I-90) then ending that leg of the trip in Big Timber on Saturday night (83 miles, which would prove to be my furthest-mileage day). Instead of settling in Big Timber, Cal hauled me to Drummond to set up a late-night camp. I started extra early on Sunday, biking the remaining 49 miles to Missoula and thereby tacking on 187 miles to the dreaded "make-up mileage" list. We saw no other choice, if I was to keep a promise to the Missoula AIDS Council to hold an afternoon rally and fundraiser on Sunday. It was agreed that all lost miles would be made up, one way or the other, with that total burgeoning at 225 miles.

Missoula is touted (according to the sign I passed rolling into town, anyway) as being the Biker's Capitol of the World, perhaps because it sits on the foothills of forest-filled mountains that grace the horizon from western Montana to Washington. I surmised that it would make an awe-inspiring bike tour, but as a cyclist passing through, I didn't find a single biking trail in Missoula. Maybe they were promoting bicycle lanes throughout the city; I did use them. First, we located the Outpost, a countryside campground west of the city, where Cal wasted no time putting us both to work. While making contact with the Missoula AIDS Council, I was asked to co-host an outdoor benefit concert organized by Rock Slide, a local pop group giving their farewell concert to Missoula. The gifted music artists were heading to Seattle to promote their first CD. Getting me on live TV was a simple task for Cal; a host of media gave us an opportunity to promote the concert beforehand from the donated campsite. Our host family struggled to make ends meet, yet Marj (the owner) seemed pleased to be able to help. I plugged Outpost big time.

We were told that the concert was an enormous success, with revenues nearly tripling expectations; our team was credited in part for that success. One guest speaker was Shanna, a lovely twenty-four-year old girl who told her account of having been intentionally infected with HIV after having very carefully selected her date. It served as a wakeup call for many in attendance. I had much to talk about on the Sunday Evening News at the local NBC affiliate, where I was granted a live, five-minute interview.

Later, adjacent campers came to Cal's bonfire to ask about USAIDS 5,000 t-shirts, insisting they heard about my quest on a TV news clip not in Missoula, but in their hometown of Bonn, Germany. Franz, Rita, and their son Andrej visited until wee hours, bonding like long-lost friends. I tried to convince them it wasn't me on their news, but Franz claimed to recognize me. He served up a German-American breakfast the next morning, complete with bacon, Kaiser Rolls and an assortment of cheese spreads. In addition to purchasing t-shirts for themselves, the team's first foreign family made a substantial donation to our own coffers. We wished many good days to our Missoula friends, *und viele gute tag um unserem deutschland fruende*. Looking forward to the mountainous six-day ride to Seattle, I needed to start chanting to help my soon-to-be-burning tired legs.

[It wasn't until I was Internet savvy that I learned the significance of Missoula being the "Biker's Capital of the World." Headquartered there (then and now) is the Adventure Cycling Association (which is an advocacy group that publishes *Adventure Cyclist* magazine), founded by the same folks that created Bikecentennial. These pioneers were the first-known persons to bicycle what was coined as Hemistour in 1974, an incredible 18,000-mile trek from Anchorage, Alaska to the southern tip of Argentina. It was on that trip, in Chocolate, Mexico, where the concept of Bikecentennial was created. If that doesn't qualify them to claim the title "Bike Capital Pioneers", nothing will. Hoping to return there now that I am far more informed, I request that they forgive my early ignorance.]

~

There are mountains, and then there are serious mountains. These were seriously steep slopes! Let me put it to you plain: it is near impossible for a healthy, athletic, highly-trained young adult on an aluminum or titanium speed bike to climb through the winding mountain wilderness, some 575 road miles from Missoula to Seattle, in six days. Now consider Grandpa Vinny, an avid smoker for twenty-eight-years who was riding a loaded, steel-frame mountain bike. Consider grandpa Vinny, who couldn't even get through the Adirondacks and Catskills without a tow due to lack of training. Now, add to it the fact that this guy has AIDS and sometimes gets sick as a dog. Oh, but I tried and tried—peddle, peddle, huff and puff, peddle, peddle, huff, huff and puff...to no avail.

Forget high gears; don't even consider middle gears. Go for the low gears, lowest of the low; that pretty much also expresses how I felt going up—very low indeed. At first, I could peddle about four minutes before having to stop, catch my breath, and slow down the ol' heart rate, which was pumping in excess of 150 beats per minute. Downhill, on the other hand, was a breeze—in some cases, it was more wind than I cared to get. Going down in a car or motorcycle is one thing, but doing 30-plus MPH downhill on a bicycle is insanely dangerous. Fearing that my breaks would give out, I manually governed the speed to keep from registering over thirty-one killer miles per hour. Road signs warned on some downward slopes to use low gears and reduce speed to 20 MPH. At the base, a stop would be required to shift my gut and catch up a heartbeat, but starting again on an incline would be worse, knocking me down to three minutes between stops. A half hour into the mountain, I was at or below two minutes between breathers. The climb slowed to a crawl. This was beyond impossible; who knew it would be this difficult? Within an hour, I had consumed a full day's worth of energy. I needed a miracle—no, I needed a tow! As he was getting out the items needed to tow my bike and trailer, Cal reminded me that, "It's the ride that counts, not peddled strokes, because a mile is a mile regardless of pushing, pulling or peddling your ass on a bike. The rope might break; let's dig out a chain. Seattle, here we come!"

The first fifteen or twenty minutes were tricky. Cal could easily tow at a respectable twenty-plus MPH, but he needed to anticipate a safe speed going downward as not to have too much slack on the chain. Nothing would be worse than biking over a dragging chain, tumbling, and being tugged, bike, skin, and all, to pavement. Cal said I earned every one of those miles by sheer risk and gumption alone. Every so often, I would signal to stop, unchain the bike, and peddle a spell. It was hard work, but doable.

Somewhere near the town of Superior, we set up camp for the night. It would be another seventy-plus miles to Kellogg, Idaho. Being aware of Kellogg, Michigan, I knew that's not where corn flakes came from; I wondered what product this place was known for. We arrived earlier than expected thanks to the chains. While on a break and considering a possible place to camp, Cal spotted the Silver Mountain Gondola Ride. Cal never asked much for his own desires, so I wanted to treat my friend to this special entertainment, which was a twenty-minute upward excursion by cable car for a panoramic view of the historic Bunker Hill Silver Mines. Five thousand, six hundred feet and several ear poppings later, visitors arrived at a welcome center and ski slopes overlooking mountain ranges and the city of Kellogg. Cal's face was almost green from the ever-rocking and swaying ride. Also visible only to God and gondola travelers, I could see trails winding downward. What? Ah! Bike trails—Kellogg produces fun!

"Oh Cal, I've gotta do it! I'll never get this chance again in my life; please, oh please?"

Kellogg residents see their ski slopes transform during summer months to become ultra-adventurous bike trails—*for extreme cyclists only*!! That would be me, right? What we couldn't see going up was an outdoor amphitheater used for a summer concert series. As we exited the gondola, I picked up a concert brochure from the stand. "Look Cal, my favorite rock group of all time! Iron Butterfly—they're playing here this summer. I like the drummer the best though—man can he play some skins! Oh, if only . . . ah, forget it. It's an *old* story about a teenage friendship."

Cal was already gabbing and making friends with visitors. Steve, from the McGrowland family, suggested that he ask Lulu's Ski Shop to send up a bike for me to rent going down. After telling our story, Lulu's supervisor (Bruce) agreed to supply a rugged mountain bike free of charge if I would sign a release. While I was drumming up the courage to play a new version of high-roller, Cal was busy asking to see the Silver Mountain general manager, probably to ask for a donation. It seemed like everything was put into slow motion. Why was it taking so long to get the bike and helmet up the hill? When it finally arrived, it was accompanied by the Silver Mountain marketing supervisor, who wanted to meet and wish me a good ride down.

"Thanks a lot for loaning me a bike, I really appreciate it. By the way, just out of curiosity, when is Iron Butterfly scheduled to rock this mountain?"

"Oh, did I forget to mention that they are in town? They will be on stage tonight, and we're all wondering if we could talk you into staying over to be our guests at the concert."

"Are you shitting me? Sorry for the expression, but that would be unreal!"

"Good, then we'll be looking forward to seeing you tonight. Cal, come with me; let's get you those tickets and gondola passes you'll need. By the way, the owners of the local Super 8 have invited you to stay at their hotel. I heard it was booked up; you must have friends in high places. Do you know what? I think Iron Butterfly is staying there, too. Who knows, maybe you'll run into them."

With the misty-eyed giggle of a child, I replied, "Now we're dreaming, but thank you for everything you and all your crew members are doing for us. This is unbelievable."

"Take the ride first; you can thank us at the bottom—good luck!"

I chuckled, thinking, "Shit, I'm already lucky; I don't need luck doing a twelve-mile zigzag. After all, I just biked from New York, *and* got a ticket to see Iron Butterfly. Is there any luck left?" I felt cocky and giddy all at the same time.

Showing off, I ripped down the track, flying by several cyclists, including four girls from Oregon I tease-challenged a race with. Well ahead of average time, I was having the joyride of my life, laughing my guts out and thinking, "I've got to be nuts, because I'm laughing all by myself, and there's no comedian!" Keeping a strong pace, about three-quarters down the trail appeared a splendid clearing overlooking the city of Kellogg, nestled in a backdrop of mountain greenery. "Wow, what a spectacular view," I thought to myself. Then I realized that seeing that much could only mean one thing—*it's a cliff!!* The trail cut sharp right, leaving a Dead Man's Curve, complete with an unguarded 600-foot drop off. Slamming both breaks, I knew there was only one method of stopping what was going to be a short distance plunge to death. I had to drop the bike *now* to the right, and tumble. I did exactly that, skidding on my right side some fifteen feet over earth and cutting stones, the result of which was shredded clothing and skin. In shock and stunned by blunt force, I was stumbling around assessing the damage when the Oregon gals arrived. One girl noticed a good-sized stick that had penetrated, and was still protruding from, my right shin. She said, "We've got to take care of that right away." Working as a team, two of them administered extensive first aid and comfort while the others worked to straighten handle bars and reconnect the chain. Offering water and encouragement, they insisted on staying with me until my nerves were calm enough to again mount the bike. When I asked their names, one of them said, "We're your guardian angels from Oregon, now *bike safe*!" Luck took on a new dimension after that.

Shaky and hesitant at first, I cautiously finished what had become the trail from hell, still beating average ride time by five minutes. I landed at the rental office covered in dirt, blood, and bandages. Along with wrenching my right shoulder, I suffered a badly bruised bottom. But I did it! Greeting me with a worried hug, Cal insisted, "I don't care what you say, that trip knocked off a chunk of those miles on your "make-up" list." Finally noticing my bloody leg, he went on, "and it looks like a chunk of your leg is gone, too, from the way it's bleeding. Oh my God, let's get you to the hotel; we've got to get you cleaned up. I'll get a doctor if you need one…oh my God!"

It would take more than a gaping hole in my leg to keep me from the concert. It was beyond anything I could imagine—it was the great Iron Butterfly. Who told them about my bike trip? I just had to ask Cal.

"You dog, did you know they were going to introduce me to the crowd and give our bike trip a plug?"

With the cutest smart-ass twang of voice and snap of his limp wrist, Cal belted out, "I knew it was coming, and I know a lot more! After the show, we've been invited to hang out with the guys in the conference center at the hotel. Now, aren't you glad I'm your manager?" A hug was in order, but not too tight, as I was bruised from my afternoon adventure. "Oh, that hurt," I yelped in pain.

It proved to be a short, but exuberant, meeting with Iron Butterfly, where I collected autographs from the entire group. It seemed they also headed to bed early those days. That's right, they're older than me, and 1967 was a long, long time ago.

About 0300, there was a knock on the hotel room door. I opened the door to a huge surprise. "Cal, get your ass up—Ron Bushy, the drummer, is here. Come on in guy! WOW, what a surprise."

"Sorry if I bothered you, but I was wondering if there was any way you would be willing to trade t-shirts. Here, I brought you one of ours; it's got our newest design on it. I really want one of your t-shirts. The guys and I were talking; you're our hero man, honest to God. So, will you trade? And, we're doing a gig in Santa Barbara a week from Saturday; we want you on stage with us. Didn't you say you were biking down the coast anyway?"

Ron and I traded addresses, phone numbers, t-shirts, and hugs. It's unlikely we will be to Santa Barbara in time, but this time, there would be no chanting on the road—only singing, "In-A-Godda-Da-Vida, baby, don't you know I'll always be true. In-A-Godda-Da-Vida, honey, Guardian Angels are here for you," after which I'd mouth a drum solo.

~

Cal and I arrived at Seattle's Volunteer Park, a day late, in support of the Northwest AIDS Coalition, which was holding its annual International Croquet Tournament and Fundraiser. My leg was still bleeding under the bandages, and though it was partly camouflaged with a bandana, I couldn't hide that it was hurting like hell. We doctored the injury as best we could, but I had yet to be seen by a physician. With our booth all set up, the Coalition was counting on me to be one of the stars of the day—to help bring in money. Cal sold autographed Polaroid photos of anyone wanting to be seen with the crazy biker. For extra big bucks, I took kiddies on a short ride around the park in the trailer behind the "dream machine." All of the money went to the Coalition, not just the proceeds, because we didn't get reimbursed for our huge film expense. Unpleasant officials came by to greet us, mostly to collect money. I returned their snotty attitudes.

My thinking was that I had just biked in from Kellogg, Idaho, crossing insane mountains with a fresh hole in my leg, thank you. I was hot and tired and sick to start with. Furthermore, I had become spoiled. Never before had an agency we supported not made some effort toward provisions for our team. We arrived by noon on Sunday, worked until 1830 non-stop and earned them a lot of cash. Yes, we were a day late for the two-day event, but if someone was delayed at an airport, all would be forgiven...but not us! They had all kinds of support for their own teams, but we outsiders were not included, even when Cal asked. We were not offered a sandwich, soda, bottle of water, or anything. We were not even offered a mother-humping cup of coffee for my pounding caffeine-withdrawal headache. And I was hoping for a place to stay?

Then, to add insult to injury (literally), they sent us an impersonal note by messenger, which read, "USAIDS 5,000, you are expected on stage at 8:40 p.m. this evening to appeal to corporations for pledges based on your mileage. It will be a live TV spot. We suggest you clean up before your appearance—*NWA Coalition.*" I was scheduled last on stage. I cried, mostly because I was so sick, but also because I had a broken heart. Even the Minnesota AIDS Project, who wanted no association with us, rounded up a complimentary room. This agency hadn't even asked for a campsite. When Cal approached the officials to ask for a volunteer family to take us in for the night, he was bluntly told, "No family wants a bleeding man with AIDS to stay in their home, get real." (It should be noted that my late arrival probably caused embarrassment for the person designating booth space, thereby setting into motion a series of disappointments. By and large, the people of Seattle were friendly and generous, especially to the AIDS cause. In retrospect, I remain pleased to have helped a little, but I had to get real: I needed to get to a doctor more than I needed to be on stage.)

We headed to the Seattle VA hospital instead of heading to the stage. We left a farewell note by messenger, of course. Infection had already set in. My temperature was above 101° Fahrenheit; my whole white blood cell count was depleted, as was my humor and strength. Intravenous antibiotics and a Neupogen injection were required overnight. Cal slept by my bedside in the Emergency Room. The morning attending physician cleared me for release, with instructions to be grounded for three days—like that was going to happen. Folks at the VA hospital in Seattle were courteous, compassionate, and caring, like my home VA in Buffalo.

Cal was unable to find an affordable room due to the croquet tourney. He recalled seeing some campsites before entering Seattle, so we headed eastward. We were offered a discounted campsite that we gladly claimed. Sick as a dog and with a badly bruised behind, I begged for a bed. Sleeping bags would have to do. There was a ban on campfires, eliminating all hopes of cooking. Mountains blocked reception, reducing radio and Cellular One to nothing but static.

At least there were hot showers only a short drive or long walk away. Not only could you shower under spurting water (like it was being hand-pumped) for four minutes per quarter, but the restroom lights were controlled by a motion detector. Thirty seconds after entering the shower stall, the lights would go out, leaving us terrified in total darkness. Clumsily, we slip-slid from the stall into the open, and the detector sensed motion; we ran like hell back to the shower to get that precious water we paid for. Back and forth, in and out, on and off; showering became a marathon race, made even more difficult for limpers like me. Naturally, the water flow ended just before getting all the soap suds off. What? No more quarters? Well, there's always the sink. It didn't have a plug, so we cupped with our hands. The sink did, however, have its own motion-detection feature, making water available when putting your hands in front of the sensor. Water spurts were so forceful that they ricocheted from our palms. Rinsing our hair and bodies was all but impossible. Then the lights went out again, only this time for no reason. There we were, naked, all but sitting in the sinks and trying to rinse with water streaming down our legs to puddles on the floor, when in walks a fellow camper, igniting the motion detector. With an embarrassing grin, Cal mumbled toward him, "You'll never believe this!" Cal was right—he didn't! Out walked the fellow camper with who-knows-what image indelibly imprinted on his brain. As for us, our dignity was left in nasty, sudsy pools on the floor.

By Wednesday morning, August 2nd, one day ahead of advice, we packed up. Cal plotted me onto a road south of Tacoma, halfway to Olympia, where I could bike across to highway 101, which would take us south along the seashore to our next destination—Oregon. I took the liberty of counting about a hundred miles extra there, to pay me back for Sunday's peddling pains.

~

It was only two easy biking days to Seaside, and what a treat it was to cross into Oregon, the only state I had never stepped foot on. With few exceptions, one doesn't normally go through Oregon to get anywhere, but Oregon is an unimaginable destination all by itself. It's the next best thing to heaven. Cloud-spattered blue skies, mountainous scenery, spacious campsites *with* campfires, the ocean, rivers, and endless timber forests are just a few reasons that everyone there seemed to be in their glory. They all had friendly faces with flourishing smiles, celebrating freedom at its finest. I had never seen sights like this before. There were narrow roadways on the very edge of cliffs, hanging over the ocean hundreds of feet below. Biking was a thrill, and certainly, by now, a skill. Highway 101 is both a biker's and photographer's dream. Every curve promised new excitement, with mountains of lava rocks and caverns speckling the mossy green coastline under the bluest of skies. At one point we stopped to see the Sea Lion Caves, holding hundreds of the creatures nesting and playing in the sun and coves. Each day in Oregon was a new adventure, only to be trumped each night by new friends and campsites, like those we met at Silt Coos Resort, where Cal held a "cut-a-thon" (cutting hair for fund raising) to ensure our bike trip could continue down the coast. We were scraping by one prayer at a time.

With a planned detour one night in Portland, crashing with some of Cal's relatives, our schedule included a visit to the Cascade AIDS Project. We met a highly motivated crew, organized and dedicated to servicing more than 1,500 clients each year. They documented amazing outreach programs in education and prevention and strived to ensure that no programs are duplicated to protect resources. With pride, they boasted that their limited funds were allocated where they were most needed—for their clients. Like several places we visited, there was little we could do for them, except call for corporate challenges, and, of course, thank them for all the hard work and love they obviously put into our cause. I wish you could have seen the bright faces of these devoted workers huddled in one small room for a chance to meet me—what an honor! "This day, Cascade, I am peddling for you and you and you and you."

Some days were long. One might think that a visit to Cascade would be enough, but we headed back several hours to the Pacific Coast. We were pleased with an article, drawn from an on-the-road interview the prior day, appearing in the *Oregonian*, a state-wide newspaper. That feature determined how incredibly well we were treated throughout Oregon. By dusk, we settled at Coyote Rock Camp and had already struck up friendships with residents Josh and his fiancée, Courtney. Josh worked for his father in construction, but the enterprising lad also cut firewood on the side to help secure his plans for marriage. After reading about the bike trip in the daily paper, he provided an unlimited free supply of firewood for Calvin to burn to his heart's delight.

Hilltop Inn in Lincoln City contributed dinner; Sadie was a first-day waitress. Sadie shared a story of love about her 14-year-old nephew barely clinging to life when she visited him earlier that same day. Paulo contracted HIV at age five during a transfusion. Sadie asked nothing for herself, not even accepting a tip, but she asked me to please autograph a copy of the *Oregonian* for the extraordinary boy who had shown great courage in facing dismal odds. Writing a prayer of hope, I penned, "To one of our treasured sons, Paulo: God willing, I will bike the distance, and you will hang in there—new drugs are coming soon. I'm praying for you and an answer for us all—hugs from Vinny Pirelli." The campfire was intense, but we fell quiet. "This mile is for Paulo, one of our precious children—God, give us both strength. Amen."

With only a day to the California border, I resolved that it was time to put Cal on a bike—he had not peddled since giving up on day one from Buffalo to Rochester. My intentions were to climb the hills, then let Cal journey down for fun. After several miles of ascent, I spotted a downward trend—it was time! However, after Cal headed out, the downhill proved to be a dip, leading to three more miles of upward slopes. Then, without warning, there appeared a grand bridge, and I remembered Cal's dirty little secret: his fear of heights. There was absolutely no spot to pull over until the opposite end of the passage. Cal had to brave this one alone. Driving over it, I estimated the depth of Cal's crisis; this was *not* just any bridge. It was about a half-mile long and dreadfully high. I pulled into a clearing on the south end, anxiously and vocally monitoring: "Oh my God, Cal's biking down the middle. Oh my God, there's a logging semi right on his ass. Oh my God, there's no place for him to go—truckers are honking horns. Jesus, now drivers are shouting obscenities, OH MY GOD!" After an eternity of about four minutes, Cal cleared the span. There was a chill in the air, but Cal's sweat attested that his trembling was not from the cold. That evening, we ascertained that Cal had bicycled across Thomas Creek Bridge, the tallest bridge in Oregon. How tall? We didn't know actual dimensions, and Cal didn't look down. I did, and due to fog, I couldn't see the bottom! When I spit out that truth with my newest biking hero, Cal shrieked. Not hearing the word *fog*, he reiterated, "You couldn't see bottom? OH MY GOD!"

~

On August 9, 1995 at 1200 we crossed the state line, entering our (no longer imaginary) final state of California. It was a great photo opportunity, posing with other tourists who were equally enthusiastic. I snapped a shot of Cal simply hugging the *California Coast* post. What is it about that California mystique?

Both of us were suffering with colds, and I had yet to recover from the pain of Idaho. Still, I eagerly tasted the final-state challenge. The ocean exhibited white waves, and the west wind whipped wildly across (what I found to be) the wickedly-winding roadway. This was not the California of my dreams, though—I couldn't get warm. Thankfully, the road headed inland, directly into the Redwood National Forest. A plethora of trees shielded me from the bellowing breeze, but where were the *big* redwoods I heard about all my life? The lyrics of Vanessa Williams's "Colors of the Wind" sawed into my heart: "How tall can a sycamore grow? If we cut them down, we'll never know!" Among the plentiful pines were stumps—massive stumps. There were volumes of great tree stumps. The next thing that blasted into my mind was the judge's chambers I witnessed when Look-Bon was adopted. I could answer the question of, "Where have all the redwoods gone?" At least in some chambers, the beauty lives on. It occurred to me that such vast waste was ironically opposite of this disease. I couldn't help but think that, "When the beautiful people I met have vanished, ugly AIDS will, in fact, dwell and swell." I prayed, "May the beauty of passing angels also live on—at least in the chambers of our hearts. Amen."

DRUM ROLL . . . after many miles, the cut stumps stopped. Around the bend, there it stood, unannounced—the TREE. One unlike any other I had witnessed, here was the tree I daydreamed about so often on a bicycle, the one I studied about in the second grade of our three-room school house in

Leroy, Indiana. Without remotely considering we might stumble across it even one time, here it rested: *The Tree You Can Drive Through*. For the modest price of eight dollars, Cal steered through it. But wait, would I get charged on my bike? NO! I maneuvered through the carved piece of history, stopping to pose, biking back around and through it time and again, halting to pray and, pausing to laugh, to scream, to rejoice, to dance on my bike, and, finally, to cry out in what others must have imagined to be my total insanity, "Cal, it's the tree I dreamed about all my life—*this* is the TREE!" Only God dared create such joy; it was a dream-come-true from when I was a boy. In-A-Godda-Da-Vida, baby—I get it!

~

Arcata and its neighboring city Eureka were this team's first large Californian cities en route. Badly beaten by recent weather fluctuations, we were, at best, sick. We required rest from the raw, rainy road. It could be found at the super, Super 8 in Arcata. Arriving mid-afternoon, we relaxed in comfort. So many times, the Super 8 had been our home away from home and our partners in this lengthy endeavor; sponsoring more than a place to rest and recoil, they had become a communication depot, allowing us to both make and receive urgent phone calls and faxes and permitting express drop-shipments of medical supplies from the Buffalo VA hospital. They served as a conference center for TV and print media blitzes, and generally advocated on our behalf to procure guest meals from local eateries. This day, we feasted at the four-star Abruzzi Italian Restaurant, a place so elegant, dinner jackets were expected. Having been exempted, we were seated and superbly catered to in the center dining room, wearing our biker shorts and tees among elegant ladies and gents. Our presence was announced, and the restaurant urged guests to greet us and perhaps make a donation.

Heading out the next morning later than usual, Cal planned a rendezvous with another corporate sponsor, Subway, where the local manager had pre-arranged a formal press conference—right in front of Subway's Sub Shop, of course. Eager to eat up the attention, I slipped on my "Viper-Star" attitude as I approached a barrage of cameras and reporters on the "dream machine." California was taking notice, *big time*, of USAIDS 5,000. I felt oddly grateful for any coverage they could contrive for the current HIV and AIDS catastrophe. As never before, I played the role perfectly. I realized I had become a celebrity spokesman for something as serious as AIDS, but I felt as silly as a six-year-old cyclist squeaking a horn. A Luther Vandross rendition of Leigh & Darion's "The Impossible Dream" (now "Viper's Theme Song") was playing to further set the stage. I eyed Cal standing far to the rear, as he always did. It was my story, therefore my glory.

While wrapping up questions from the curious crowd, one citizen asked me to, "Tell us how it feels to be a hero for your cause." My response was to bring Cal to the podium, telling them, "This is our cause—yours and mine. I am not the only spokesman, but one spoke in the wheel of hope. My friends, this is Calvin. Without him as my primary support, this dream would have died long ago. We need a second theme song to play: 'Wind beneath My Wings.'" Then, giving Cal a hug, I waved goodbye with a, "Thank you and God bless you all for helping our cause." Then came one final question, "What do you want to do when this is all over?" Like it had been rehearsed a hundred times, we shouted in unison, *"We want to go to Disney Land,"* and the crowd roared with laughter and applause, followed by more intense scrambling of journalists to get a last word and photographers jostling to get one more picture. It was all good.

August 12th was our last official campsite, located in a small town called Jenner. With over two weeks remaining in the project, this marked the beginning of the end. The final stretch would be the shortest in distance, yet logistically and emotionally most difficult, holding many preplanned stops and events. I was in the public eye daily. Funds dwindled to empty pockets, and the stress of day-to-day survival fell solely upon Cal's shoulders. It was a responsibility that was never intended to be his alone.

It was a time of modest celebration, when we first started feeling accomplished. There was something sad about rolling up the tent for the last time. While grateful for spectacular accommodations to come, we overgrown boys would indeed miss our little "dream house," for it represented an unbelievable, if not impossible, era. It was time to pause, to rest and recuperate, to reassess our needs, and to capture on paper and in prayer all the wonders we had witnessed. Warmer weather, magnificent miles, resort hamlets, and quaint accommodations made it possible for us to rid ourselves of our colds while Cal could catch some well-deserved rest.

~

Rice-A-Roni is certainly not the only San Francisco treat! Prohibited from crossing the Golden Gate Bridge by bicycle, I hooked a ride with Cal to the city. Imagine staying in a place named after this grand, historic city! We were staying at The San Francisco Cottage, a one-of-a-kind refuge for the world's elite. Normally, such spots are strictly reserved for the rich and famous. There was a single-day opening donated to us in honor of USAIDS 5,000 coming to San Francisco. It lacked nothing one could imagine wanting during a respite, including a well-stocked, full-size refrigerator. A spiral staircase led to a loft bedroom that had a glass wall that overlooked secluded weaved gardens that can only be compared to King Ludwig's in Southern

Bavaria. French doors on opposite ends of the cottage opened to select gardens on one side and an enclosed patio on the other side that was so private that one could barbeque in the nude if inclined—not that I would recommend it. The guest book was a global who's who of aristocracy, each page carefully dated with hand-scripted notes from people like Bill & Hillary Clinton, Bill Gates, Placido Domingo, Elton John and, yes, there was one line simply signed as *Diana*; is there any other?

Tour day included complimentary breakfast at The Black Stallion (a famous gay bed and breakfast on Castro Street), visits to The Sausage Factory, Castro Theatre in the district, a subway ride downtown to catch a cable car to Frisco Bay, and Fisherman's Wharf, with none other than San Quentin as a backdrop for the perfect photo op. It was a lot to absorb in those precious few hours.

Were there sacrifices along the way? Perhaps, but when we thought of how much we were blessed with gracious, unexpected generosities of personal comfort and joy, I realized we had gained far more than we gave. It was time to go to work for the cause and devote some real labor at Project Open Hand. One would expect me to be devoted; after all, Vinny has AIDS. Not so with Ruth Brinker, though, who was one of the most inspiring senior citizens I will ever hope to meet. After working all her life and suffering the loss of her partner and husband, this kindly lady at a young sixty-nine years old might easily have justified retirement in 1985, a full decade earlier. No, she had heard of a neighbor suffering from this new thing called AIDS. Upon visiting him, partly to reduce her own loneliness, she found a young man who stole her heart. "He was so skinny, he looked wilted. What he needed was a good hot meal," Ruth told me, regurgitating the incident. Accustomed to cooking for more than one, she began delivering him dinner almost daily. Soon, through this adopted son of sorts, she learned of another, then another.

It didn't take long before Ruth required food from outside sources, accepting help from friends, neighbors, and businesses with whom she had lifetime credibility. By the time her project expanded to forty meals daily, it outgrew her kitchen, and an alternative location was in order. "A church, thank God," said Ruth, "generously offered the use of their facilities to meet growing demand." With seemingly no end to the honest need in sight, there were countless times when Ruth didn't know from one day to the next where the food would come from, but it would come, she said, "like a miracle." Inspired by her love, hope, and persistence, volunteers recruited volunteers and food outlets established regular contributions. "San Francisco was caring for its own," said one worker, "thanks to Mom Ruth."

When I toured, Project Open Hand was operating from an industrial food processing center which was headed by a small, highly professional (yet less than highly paid) staff and run by hundreds of volunteers. Still without government funding, they prepared and delivered over two thousand hot, delicious meals daily. At age seventy-nine, Ruth's job was to oversee and inspire the crew, not because she retired, but because she took on yet another challenge—to not only feed, but to create employment opportunities for the homeless of San Francisco.

Meanwhile, twenty five other cities have been inspired to adopt similar feeding programs, though they fall under different names; Project Open Hand is recognized as a premier and national leader of the Meals-on-Wheels-type programs. As Ruth turned a bright eighty-years-old, she not only gave life a better plan, but also gave continued life to countless thousands of grateful citizens. Unlike most of those people, I had the honor of meeting this incredible American. It was a privilege to work the assembly line morning shift and to assist with delivery of meals to Tenderloin District residents. (I remain haunted by the sights of Tenderloin: tattered buildings with shattered windows inhabited by AIDS-beaten bodies with broken dreams. By 1990, San Francisco was known as the Gay Mecca of the world; by 1995, a quarter of its gay population had expired due to AIDS.) After each meal delivered, I prayed, "Lord, please give some extra miles to my brothers and sisters perishing—but for Grace, I could be one of them. Amen."

~

Santa Cruz AIDS Project, like so many others, struggled to stay ahead of demand. They serviced all people, but admitted to a large HIV population in the Hispanic community. They wanted so much to put a face on AIDS locally, wanting to draw media attention and, hopefully, social interest and the funding desperately needed, that Cal diligently organized a press conference directly in front of the Santa Cruz AIDS Project. It was a touchy situation that opened the possibility of client privacy being compromised. Some communities build walls around groups not to protect them, but to block them from sight. I understood the necessity of respecting privacy, but there comes a time when we need to set an example, to show others how to step up and be counted; that was the time. Everywhere we went, I met men, women, and children infected with and affected by HIV and AIDS; until arriving in Santa Cruz, very few persons of color have been among those faces. I almost preached, "These are warm-blooded, live human beings, all with names, faces, families, troubles, needs, goals, hopes, and dreams just like your own; who will tell their stories?" I invited agency spokespersons to join me in the news, but they were largely ignored, and in some cases rudely pushed aside, by the white correspondents and broadcasters wanting the perfect photo of me.

That evening, we accepted an invitation to stay with a humble gay family: George, Sean, and their pup Riddle. We held hands when the late news came on, hoping for some positive press. I couldn't understand why reporters excluded everything except my own story. We watched white-washed TV (appealing to white audiences) in this beautiful home and city of color. Somewhere, lost, was the message that my story had become the culmination of each and every act of mercy, each organized agency reaching out with empathy, and each inflicted person finding his or her own way to live with AIDS.

With tears of embarrassment gathered in my eyes, there fell a pause and one final revelation from the journalist—this one made a difference. While showing the picture of a beautiful young man of color, the reporter articulated, "Santa Cruz suffered a great loss today when the intelligence, wit, and talents of this 24-year-old son joined the countless, faceless numbers in becoming part of our lost future." The volume went silent for about ten seconds, featuring the picture of a Latino boy, titled "Angel, 1971-1995." We knew the impact of such sensationalism; there was hope. Perhaps a couple corporations will now sponsor this agency of angels for angels. "This mile is for the brave, sole journalist who dared make a difference, and God bless Santa Cruz."

Having missed Iron Butterfly's concert by several days, we went right to work when rolling into Santa Barbara. We met Ron and Michael, real people living at Sarah House, a 2nd residential home for persons living with AIDS. Their slogan, "Once a *lot*, now a whole lot more," speaks volumes to the needs of this community being met. In addition to standard fare (private rooms with combined living areas), Sarah House highlighted several apartment complexes for mates and families wanting more independent living arrangements within a protected and supportive environment. This was where we met Ron and Michael, two of the sweetest, loving young men you'd ever hope to find in a couple. Ron suffered with HIV; Michael had full blown AIDS. Both lost their careers, futures, financial security and, worse, their family support systems due to the disease. To keep active, Michael helped make his own piece of the national AIDS quilt. In a huddle, we prayed for Michael's comfort and Ron's strength. (By the time we returned to New York two weeks later, I was informed of Michael's passing. In mourning, Ron had taken a turn for the worse.) Profound is the only way to describe the loss I witnessed all across America.

~

Ten Days & Counting was how my journal read. After biking until early afternoon, U.S. Highway 1 converted into a major expressway that prohibited bicycles. I hitched a ride with Cal into Los Angeles. He got me to the nearest exit and gave me directions to San Vincente Inn. Me being a Vincent, too, this had to be my kind of transitory abode! Offering suites, a swimming pool, and hot tub, it advertised "everything you would expect of a luxury resort and much, much more." It was the second *much* that caught my attention; it seemed customary to lose one's inhibitions, as well as trunks, before poolside lounging.

Nine days out, I biked to APLA (AIDS Project Los Angeles) and we toured this one-of-a-kind service agency. Enormous in size, it housed all the standard services you would expect to find, like testing and education, as well as individual advocacy through case management. Further, it hosted a safe meeting place for clients, as well as a recreation area, kitchenette, library, and food pantry. They even held a medical clinic for many uninsured clients on the premises and boasted a dental clinic. I knew the perils of HIV on oral health, but this program was a first to me.

After interviewing for APLA's *Positive Living* Magazine, Cal treated me to a tour of Hollywood; the famous Hollywood sign appeared just as it does on TV. We walked with the stars down Hollywood Boulevard and touched famous handprints at the Chinese Theatre. We window shopped down on Rodeo Drive, unable to afford anything. That evening, a popular night club, Rage, invited me to judge their local singing contest finals. I expected lip sync, not the Star-Search (now, American Idol) quality I discovered, with each act surpassing the last. The talented lad who won by a hair belted a believable version of "Impossible Dream." His winning was purely coincidental.

With eight days to go, we accepted an APLA invitation to be among a select group of volunteer coordinators to promote the APLA Aids Walk. Hosted by Warner Brothers Studios, the APLA director pumped up the crowd during his motivational speech: "Before bringing up the star of our show, I want to introduce you to a man some call Viper. He is bicycling 5,000 miles for our cause. He has AIDS, and he biked here to challenge all of you to walk with us this year, to make a difference. Vinny Pirelli, stand up; folks, give him a big welcome." After a round of cheering applause, he continued, "Thank you, Viper. Now help me welcome your favorite actress, who plays Lois Lane on the now-popular Lois & Clark series. Ladies and Gentlemen, it's my pleasure to introduce you to Miss Terri Hatcher." Terri was about to take time from her busy schedule to make a commercial for the 1995 APLA AIDS Walk. Cal, never shy when it comes to celebrities, wormed his way to the front both to get her autograph and to convince Hatcher to meet me.

Gracious as she was, Terri reportedly told Cal, "I wouldn't dream of leaving here without meeting that remarkable man. Where is he? Let's get a picture together. I think he's scheduled to make a TV promotional spot with me." Although our scenes were to be filmed separately, I was asked to bike in a short segment of that very same APLA commercial. Now, that is just cool!

(Terri Hatcher was already famous at the time I was lucky enough to meet her, but who knew her stardom would explode with another series which lasted several seasons and is still running today? It, of course, is known as Desperate Housewives. When I tell the story of meeting her, people say, "No Way!") Although we would not meet again while shooting our segments of the APLA commercial, I did stumble across three gals known as the Venice Angels on Venice Beach, where they were promoting their new cassette. They played harp, flute and, my favorite instrument of all, autoharp. The Venice Angels have been contracted in the past to tour with Yanni as part of his string orchestra. They kindly autographed a cassette for me. Someday, I will pass it on to an angel, but whom?

With only a planned week left for my excursion, Venice Beach (aka Muscle Beach) was the setting for my bicycle stint on the APLA commercial. We anticipated an all-day event, but the camera crew knew precisely what they wanted, so the shoot took just over an hour and wrapped up after take seven. I bicycled up and down the same segment of pavement over and over. It was not quite like going around the redwood tree, but it was exciting, none the less. Since there was so much budgeted time left, we resolved to try out roller blading. Cal was a wiz, but I didn't find balance long enough to hit the strip. Wouldn't you expect more from a biker? Embarrassed, I opted instead to cruise the full length of the paved beach trail on the "dream machine": twelve miles north to Malibu, back to Venice Beach, then seven miles south and returning again, of course. Added to commercial miles, I could knock off fifty additional miles from the "make-up" list. There were volleyball tournaments, roller blading championships, joggers (one of which I swear was Jason Priestley of 90210), jugglers, jet skiers, wind and board surfers, and magicians and musicians of every variety, most showing a serious amount of beautifully bronzed skin! There was also an endless array of shops, vendors, eateries, games, and odd-ball rides with thousands of explorers walking, biking or swimming. It was a sandy beach, carnival, gymnasium, concert, and three-ring circus all rolled into one. There's nothing like it elsewhere in the world. While cycling Venice Beach, I lapped up endless salty drops of Pacific sights and sun, a kaleidoscope of colors and shades with perfumed and aromatic smells against a backdrop of royal blue, surfers, jet skis, sail boats, and yachts—I was in biker's heaven.

With plans to spend the night with James & Rudolph from the Imperial Court of Los Angeles, we found ourselves in the former home of actress Mae West. While looking for their residence, Cal decided to pay tribute to Nicole Brown Simpson and Ron Goldman by going by the murder site on Bundy Drive. We were saddened by the flowers and trash accumulated outside the gate. Wanting to follow the story more, we stopped by the Mezzaluna Restaurant made famous by the famously murdered pair, but opted not to partake after hearing that a single cup of coffee was outrageously priced at seven dollars. Cal's final goal before resting was to locate the OJ Simpson mansion on Brentwood.

What's this? Not only was the main access route (Rockingham Drive) closed off with permanent barriers, but all street signs had been removed. There was no fooling this team, though, so we maneuvered bike and car, street after street, looking for a remote entrance. When I spotted street work barriers and a sign announcing "Local Traffic Only," I knew it really meant "this way to OJ." I nailed it with that call, because only a few streets back was the corner of Ashford & Rockingham, the final destination of the now infamous OJ Runaway blitz. Both gates had been covered with molded plywood to offer privacy. That was merely an invitation to "climb the fence if you want a photo, buddy," another offer I couldn't refuse. Not much was visible, but I now have great photos of the white Ford Bronco and covered Bentley.

The chief financial goal of the Imperial Court of LA was to assist PLWAs needing temporary help with medicine costs and utility bills. They also supplied food baskets twice yearly to all hospices in LA County, which was quite an ambitious undertaking for a small group. To further their cause, they contract for a beer kiosk at the annual Sunset Junction Street Fair near one of the stages. While I volunteered time selling buckets of brew for the Court, Cal managed to get on stage to promote the bike trip, sell t-shirts for us, and invite the crowd to meet me at the beer tent three doors down. A double-win, for sure—the Court never sold so much beer before then. By day's end, all the kegs were dry. Any wet celebration had to be back at Mae West's place later that evening. Reeking of stale brew, the only wet celebration I wanted was in Mae's room-sized shower.

Onward to Anaheim was the plan, with five days remaining. Not the longest ride for sure, but certainly the hottest. It spiked to 108 degrees; by the time we reached Super 8 in the evening, Cal and I opted to chill and rest for the huge day to follow.

One reporter after another asked, "What do you want to do when your trip is over?" We replied, "Disney Land, of course," and why not? Isn't that what you hear on all the commercials? Disney Land it was, thanks to the combined efforts of Cal, the Children's and VA Hospitals of Buffalo, and

Disney, Incorporated, who invited our team to dream the Disney dream. In excess of hundred-degree heat, I played kid, dragging Cal to the Bobsleds, Space Mountain, Small World, Lion King Parade, and monorail. The trip wouldn't be complete without a photo shoot with none other than Mickey Mouse. Being fried (literally and figuratively) by afternoon, we headed back to the hotel to crash and rest up for round two that evening. As the evening opened with the Parade of Lights by GE, we marveled at floats and characters from many films, all in millions of miniature lights, including illuminated costumes. I was enchanted and amazed at how the music score was synchronized from float to float. Independently unique, but equally impressive, was the grand fireworks display at Peter Pan's Castle in the Magic Kingdom. (It was a distant interpretation of my Peter Pan role back in Leroy, Indiana.) Not even that could compete with Fantasmic, an outdoor spectacle of such grand scale that only Disney could create it.

The plot stars Mickey with his own quest to dream. The Evil Queen from Snow White fights for control of Mickey's dreams, thereby turning them into nightmares. Prior to the show, a cute two-year-old toddler named Christian entertained us with antics involving his flashlight, which was equipped with fiberglass light streams. Cal kept getting stabbed in the ribs, while I endured bops over the head. When finally worn out, the lad plopped down in the most comfortable spot he saw—*my lap*. Once the show began, Christian stood, clinging to Cal's neck for the full twenty-five-minute extravaganza. That speaks well for the production, which includes live musical performances, animated characters, strobe and laser light shows, cartoon visuals on water screens, fountains and fireworks, live and taped sound effects, a real pirate ship (complete with Captain Hook and his acrobatic sword fights), and the Mark Twain Steamboat hosting all the Disney characters. Orchestrated to perfection, this creation remains the most elaborate production I have ever witnessed. It was truly magic, and proof that we're never too old to be a kid!

~

You've heard of getting up on the wrong side of bed? How about starting the day out bicycling ten miles in the wrong direction? I'll blame it on a late night, but that's what I did. Since my Boy Scout days, I've always prided myself on having a natural ability to go in the right direction, as well as knowing what direction that is. With a major corporate sponsor waiting patiently, I chose this day to lose my bearings—Murphy's Law at its purest. Cal dug out the map and convinced me "the other way is correct." I kicked things into high speed, rolling into Ingram Micro's western headquarters parking lot in Santa Ana in the late morning. Most of the welcoming team had dissipated and gone back to work, a big time oops!

Not surprisingly, we learned how this company had grown to become an international software leader and industry force, then marketing the newly unveiled Windows 95. (That seems like eons ago.) Our tour started with a warm reception organized by the philanthropic committee. One by one, I shook their hands while being introduced to a number of staff that that have been motivated by USAIDS 5,000, enough to participate in the April San Francisco to Los Angeles AIDS Ride, which benefited those two cities. A computer analyst guided us through the complex sales, marketing, purchasing, and warehouse operations of just one facility; there were several. Shipping departments were so highly automated that fork lifts had been designed to ride the aisles dead center.

I was only scantily dressed to begin with, so I couldn't understand why I couldn't pass quietly through the metal detector to get out. Cal saved the day by suggesting that my cycling shoes must contain some steel reinforcements. He was right. Our visit ended with a kick-ass lunch in Ingram Micro's Hard Disc Café. They had one final gift for me—a complimentary night at the posh Windsor Suites, complete with glass elevators and indoor gardens and pools, with suites large enough for a good-sized family. "This mile is for Ingram Micro and a dozen or so more for their bicycling team for AIDS."

To stay on the already-revised schedule, I had to rack the bike half the distance to Oceanside, our next planned stop, which was a Marine base where my son-in-law Ollie was stationed. Visiting was in order, so that's exactly what Cal did while Dad (me) crashed on the sofa. After a scrumptious dinner prepared by Melody, my granddaughter Katelyn, then about 14 months old, fully entertained us by playfully posing for many pictures. It was a good night's rest; it must have been, because I slept longer than I had in three months. With only one full biking day remaining, I was being prodded by media and family, all wanting to know, "now what?" I didn't know the answer. I didn't even have a place to live. I didn't want to think about those challenges yet.

[I doubted that anyone would be aware of my mountains; throughout my time in California, I kept getting questions about some young man named Pedro Zamora: Had we met? Did I know him? What did I think of his story? Pedro had a positive effect on my bike trip, even though we never met. In fact, until asked, I had not heard of MTV's *Real World*, let alone the cast in the production of the San Francisco season. It wasn't until 1997, when I watched an MTV marathon of *Real World*, that I grasped the impact of this character. Pedro was the first openly gay man with AIDS to star on TV in what I believe was the first reality-type programming. He was an adorable young man of twenty-four, in love, and he chose to be an activist for our cause. Millions of viewers felt love for and attachment to Pedro, bringing great credit upon himself and MTV. As it turns out, on the day the final episode was aired in November, 1994, Pedro succumbed to his disease. The short, powerful legacy of Pedro Zamora paved the way for my personal positive reception in California. (The story of Pedro was made into a movie, which aired in 2009 on MTV and is available on DVD.) I would like to have met you, amigo.]

With one day to go, I dug out the "make-up miles" list and knocked another measure off while touring Camp Pendleton. I returned to find that San Diego's *North County News* was on base for a final interview preceding my highly-anticipated arrival. The story was a gimmie, but I was asked to bike up and down the street countless times to give the photographer a chance to snap a perfect picture for the article. After all that effort, the editor selected a posed, stationary photo. Still, my smile was genuine, as was the Iron Butterfly t-shirt I proudly sported. It was one of those rare "I made it" smiles that sometimes make it to the history books, but then, Vinny is no Pedro. After making final hotel arrangements at the Super 8, our team left the base for my final biking day to the planned destination city of San Diego. Melody and Katelyn rode with Cal; they spent the final Super 8 night with us, to be available for the last mile in the support vehicle. While they played Rummy, I slipped off into introspective contemplation, then slumber.

~

Thursday, 0859, August 31, 1995. T-Minus 1 Minute & Counting: I've been able to see America in a unique way, both at its best and worst, with its majestic size and beauty, its vast resources and terrain, and its blessed people who enrich this soil by bringing the many cultures of the world to one land we call these United States of America. The end was literally around the bend. The AIDS Foundation of San Diego had pre-arranged a grand rally and reception for 0900 sharp. The difficult part for me was to not arrive too early; it needed to be timed exactly right for some live TV coverage. I circled around several city blocks in a bicycle version of pacing until receiving the thumbs up from Cal. Appropriately clad in stars and stripes, I turned the final corner of approach, not knowing for sure what to expect. It was time for a new chant: "This last mile is for you and me, God. We did this together— we beat the odds and achieved mountains."

Followed by the escort vehicle, one daughter and granddaughter, and, of course, Cal, chills ran up my spine as I heard the crowd begin to rumble, and then roar in thunderous applause and cheers. I could see the red ribbon across the road, tied with huge AIDS ribbons on both sides—the official end. Camera men scrambled down the street, wanting to photograph this piece of history, this oddity, this feat that no person with AIDS had ever accomplished. Flags, banners, cheers, and tears, they were all present. There would be representatives from Being Alive, the AIDS Foundation of San Diego, and the city and county of San Diego, well-wishers, and a host of TV, radio, and newspaper reporters to document this moment and to welcome me with proclamations, gifts, flowers, and love. This moment was theirs as much as mine, yet they may never know the feeling they etched on one man's heart. Pumping my fist into the air, I was shouting, "We did it" and, "I love you" and, "Thank you friends!" Yes, most of all, thank you to my friends who cared–many friends, hundreds of friends; some who had traveled long distances to see, greet, meet, and hear from me, Vinny Pirelli, the Viper, one man who dared to live out his impossible dream.

For My Hero
(1995)

When first we met, a lifetime ago
Eight months of calendar time
I couldn't know then how my heart would grow
And culminate into this rhyme
That you *believed* in me

Then off we were; exploring this land
While receiving much more than we gave
From hills and woods to ocean's sand
Hearts filled with treasures to save
And *you* believed in me

Yet many were days, through those we met
When our hearts reaching out couldn't feel
The pain and fear of each who regret
Broken lives and wounds that won't heal
Still, you believed in me

With weary heart and withered feet
With major doubts in my mind
As to whether or not this man could complete
A journey and task of such kind
But, you believed in *me*

Now looking back through tremendous trials
Seeing clearly and without remorse
It was God pushing you over all of those miles
Thereby making me stay on course
Yes, *I believe in you*

Grace

Stardom is a fleeting thing; sometimes the difference between being a local hero or not is having sufficient cash for a cup of coffee at your favorite hangout, where perhaps one person will recognize you. On a good day, someone will stop to say hello, or ask what you've been up to lately. Beyond that, the old saying, "out of sight, out of mind" is a more applicable truth. One's history is just that, tidbits of information about their personal life that are pertinent to few others, tucked away deep—unless it somehow benefits them.

There are exceptions, of course, like when I was a permanent fixture at the VA Hospital in Buffalo. On one of my visits, this time to sneak a shower, Carol Caldron from the HIV Team passed me a note from the Children's Hospital. It seems they had been unable to locate me, and hoped I'd consider setting up a USAIDS 5,000 display in October in conjunction with the grand opening of their new hospital wing. Since most of the memorabilia was still packed away in the trunk of my rugged (gone ragged) Pontiac Grand Am (the same vehicle that I once used for Newstyle Family Buffet, that had hauled me to Las Vegas and back, followed my bicycle trek, and still cranked with 163,000 miles), it was doable, providing I could hunt enough returnable bottles to buy fuel to get me across town. I asked Carol to assist with arrangements, and all was set for a Friday in late October, 1995.

Finally, I had a project to occupy my mind, something other than finding a safe place to sleep or standing in line at the soup kitchen near Pennsylvania Avenue. I never imagined how difficult it would be to locate a toilet that wasn't reserved for paying customers, let alone a bunk and hot meal. I was grateful to Cal for all he had done, as well as for the fact that he was still storing my few belongings in the home he shared with his ex-partner, who really didn't want me around), but Cal had a life and business needing his full attention. *My* adopted home was Buffalo—my heart was planted here, even if I had no address. Sure, I could go to City Mansion, a shelter for homeless men, and I tried that. I rejected the notion that attending church service was mandatory if I wanted to eat, however, in some twisted version of, "the way to a man's heart is through his belly." Then I was warned to, "Make sure you sleep with your shoes on; otherwise, you could find yourself barefoot tomorrow"; well, that plain scared the hell out of me. Too ashamed to let my sis and children know my condition, I decided not to burden them. It was my version of, "Vinny is responsible for having no bed; therefore, Vinny can't sleep in it."

Autumn can get damn cold in Buffalo, and I was finding myself more often than not hiking the suburbs and stopping by grocery or department stores to get warm and use the crapper, before calling it a night in the reclined front seat of my car. On one occasion, I found my minister from a tiny Lutheran Church in Tonawanda cleaning the bathroom at Hills Department Store. Times, obviously, were also lean for this aging man of the cloth who had almost reached retirement age. I hadn't been there and able to help financially support the church in a long while; he was only present on Sundays to preach. There was no more pay available, only the run-down parsonage next to the church as remuneration. He showed much grace by praising Hills and God for giving him a job at his age, but was looking forward to returning to his native South Dakota with his ailing wife in a few weeks, having been offered a small parish there. We hugged, but I couldn't tell him my own predicament. Perhaps he guessed, since he extended an invitation to lunch or dinner if I could come for a visit before he packed. I promised to ride my bike there on a sunny day, knowing I couldn't afford gasoline to drive.

The atrium of the Children's Hospital served my display well; along with TV and newspaper journalists, the grand opening was flocked by state and municipal dignitaries, business leaders, and wannabe heroes of every make and model. It was a great *aha* moment, as I was requested by agency after service provider to make appearances on World AIDS Day, December 1st. I'd already committed to plans for a motivational speech at the VA, but I promised everyone else that I'd consider their proposals.

As I was wrapping up, I noticed a familiar face. This guy honestly looked (then) like an older, fatter version of me. It was Joseph Cappalolla, from *City Alternative*, who ran consecutive stories of my bike trip all summer. It was our first reunion, and I thanked him for not "farting me off." We each sparred with jokes and pokes, Joe finally asking, "What do you say, if I help you haul this stuff to your place, would you be willing to give me a followup interview for our paper? A number of people have called, written, or asked us about you, and this display is the first sign of you since your return."

"Joe, if you help me get this to my car, I'll clear out the passenger seat for you; we can chat there."

"Vinny, it's really not a problem. I can help you get it home, unless, of course, I'm not welcome there."

"Give me a break, Joe; of course you are welcome in my home. Why do you think I said 'I'll clear out the seat for you'?"

"You're kidding me right? I thought you were living over on Hoyt Street?"

"I was evicted right before the bike trip. Do you remember meeting Calvin from Rochester in May? He and his partner had room to store my things in their garage, but having me there for more than a couple of days was awkward. I'm doing okay on my own."

"That's bullshit, Viper; it gets cold at night. Listen, I live right down on North Street; though it's an efficiency pad, I can put you up for a couple of days until we can figure something out."

"No, Joe, I honestly don't want to be a burden. You asked for a story, not a roommate."

"I didn't ask you to fricking marry me, I said, 'I can put you up for a couple of days.' Like it or not, you are a local hero, and I don't think people will want you freezing your balls off in a car. Now, let's get going, but yes, you'll have to leave this stuff in your trunk; I don't have the space, okay? Do you have any income? How have you been getting by? We've got a lot to talk about."

"I was on short-term disability from Bernard House, but it *also* ran out right before the bike trip. I lived on the generosity of others for three months during that affair, but being a traveler, nobody except me and Cal knew I was homeless. I was supposed to apply for Social Security Disability, but I had no time."

"Hell, you have no address. You can't even get Welfare without an address, and who knows how long SSDI will take? I've heard horrific stories over the years." Now, with a glassy look in his eyes, he continued, "Vinny, how much money did you generate for AIDS? I reported $600,000 approximately, is that right?"

"Who really knows, Joe; the agencies won't disclose that information. All I know is that we handed over about $3,500 in cash. We used every penny intended for our survival and trip; everything else went directly to the agencies—you knew that."

"So, even if it was a quarter-mil, it's not right that you end up homeless; I'm telling you, *it's not right*." Then he turned to wipe away his own emotion.

Within two days, Joe linked me up with AIDS Community Services, who had been carrying me as an inactive client (is that like dead weight?); he was

willing to put up a rent deposit for me if I could find an affordable apartment, providing ACS would pay the first month's rent. Still, I needed to convince a landlord of my good character in order to let me slide until I could
get approved for Welfare. Piece by piece, it puzzled into place; AIDS Family Services (a church-based organization associated with Bernard House) set
me up with Catholic Charities of Buffalo, who helped me out with cleaning
supplies, dishes, and a few bucks extra to hold me over until I had my own
footing again. When Welfare kicked in, I was blessed with an additional
rental allowance for persons with HIV to make sure that housing conditions
weren't substandard health wise. Because my car insurance was about to
expire, I opted to pass the vehicle on to my youngest daughter (Miranda) if
her boyfriend could give her a ride to Buffalo. It was all good, and Joe made
this happen, taking no credit while putting up cash for a near stranger. I was
receiving first-hand lessons of goodness and grace from the most unlikely of
sources.

~

By World AIDS Day, I stood in front of a supportive group at the VA
with my newest idea: Since dozens of agencies were now competing for news
coverage on World AIDS Day, I thought it was high time we organized a
Buffalo United World AIDS Day program. If the VA was willing to give me
meeting space, I would be willing to organize this venture for December 1,
1996—giving myself a full year to make it a reality. Naturally, my hero and
friend (and now brother-of-sorts), Joe Cappalolla, was by my side to generate interest through articles. It seems that success breeds success, because,
unlike a year earlier, when I promised to bicycle 5,000 miles, people rallied
behind me, rather than dismissing me as some lunatic and relegating me to
the butts of their jokes behind my back, and even to my face.

Billed as United World AIDS Day—Buffalo and Erie County (with Niagara Falls contingent), I turned my own efficiency apartment in Allentown
(Buffalo's artsy-fartsy Bohemian district) into headquarters. With the willing
cooperation of a myriad of local artists, more than thirty AIDS service agencies (both stand-alone and departments of other social and medical support
services), media, merchants, and dozens of sponsors, we pulled off a program
so phenomenal, it paved the way for similar efforts across the nation. We did,
however, borrow ideas from others. (During my tour of the AIDS Foundation of San Diego, I learned just how much can be done for a community on
so little. To keep themselves focused, they dedicated one hallway to honor
those loved ones who had passed and to serve as a reminder of the mission
ever-present. The hallway seemed endless, with tributes to more lives than
can be counted—all lost to AIDS and all from San Diego. Even the names

quilt, a national project, doesn't express the enormity of AIDS as well as this single hallway in but one city.) It was fitting to share San Diego's idea, only in the form of community involvement, by allowing persons throughout the region to place a picture or note on a wall for everyone to view during the all-day program. It was like the Vietnam Memorial on a smaller scale. It reminded me of the room we dedicated to military veterans at Yorkshire Steak House in Marion, Indiana and the Tree of Hope from Southlake. It was a way for people to be vested in the program, as well as the efforts of all these service agencies trying to make life a better place for PLWAs. (Whatever caused that program to be successful, I am pleased to acknowledge that it continues annually, as it had for the last fifteen years.)

Fortunately, the VA hospital kept every single promise made, including organizational meeting facilities. Several times throughout 1996, I played patient and World AIDS Day chairman. Though I can testify that bicycling raised my T4-cells from 63 to 273 without antiretroviral therapy, the stress of homelessness and current projects took a toll, landing my scrawny ass in the Emergency Room and hospital too many times. I feared new therapies, because by slowing the progression of HIV/AIDS, so many of my friends died from heart, liver, kidney, and pancreas failures associated with medication side-effects. Because everyone assumed it wouldn't be long before my own number was up, I easily qualified for Social Security Disability early on.

Many times since, I've tried holding real employment, always ending in critical care. The most difficult part of that is a lagging, gnawing *worthless* feeling, a feeling of always needing to justify medical care, and even my own existence at times. Latching onto one short-term project after another, I could find a glimmer of hope and always land success. (I even contended for Mr. Buffalo Leather in 1998, beating out some of the most likeable, and *lickable*, lads in the Buffalo gay leather community. The next oldest contestant was only half my age. My public projects couldn't lose.) I landed one bad relationship after another as I looked for a glimmer of love and never found it. How could I be so demonstrative and outgoing, while at the same time living an insular life, detached and isolated from anything that resembled a family? With my pastor gone, I gave up church. With my car gone, I gave up much independence. At least I still had the "Dream machine," until it was stolen, that is (from a subway station bike rack while locked with a security bar). Somehow, the thieves broke the rack (in plain sight) and took the bike, lock an all. It was my most prized possession; its loss left me depressed, angry, and turning bitter inside. It represented all of my life's struggles—for naught.

~

Just as success brings about success, waste attracts waste. I was wasting emotionally and physically when I fell head over heels for a drug-addicted alcoholic, fresh from the wastebaskets of this hellish life. I was going to save him, to help him recover, to make him love me like no other. The more love I poured out, the viler his antics. He was turning our relationship into a living version of LSD (my dreams and his toxicity). When I cried over the passing of my mother (reporting that I didn't recognize her, so many years having passed), he laughed and taunted me, "Why do you care if the whore is dead? She didn't love you, anyway—*nobody* loves you—what's to love?" I withdrew even further and started gaining weight, adding to my depression, which thus added to my eating. He responded with, "You're old and ugly— I can't love you anymore." I didn't want to believe him; it was easier to believe it was the drugs. Then one day in 2003 I walked in to find my partner being screwed by a stranger. . .

. . . It all came flashing back in a flood of uncontrollable emotion: the Little One crying on the park bench over my own infidelities...my rabbits being given away...endless beatings...being a tubercular outcast...my dog Cupid that I missed so much...the "dream machine" stolen from me...being brutally raped as a teenager...my buddies Scotty and Jeff and David...my children I missed so much...my grandchildren growing up without me...relationship after broken relationship...body after broken body...my cousin Clip...my newest brother Joe...my little red bicycle...my pretend black Mustang...Aunt Ruthe...Mrs. Header...The Tree...Iron Butterfly...Marci...Clark...Lenny while wrestling...Joe the Pharmacist...The Beatles...all my music destroyed...Pete the Bartender...Gloria Gianetti and her sons...Trendstyle Department Stores...Newstyle Family Buffet...Yorkshire and Jim Black...Italian Fiesta and Shoppers Supermarkets...Jack Ass and Judge Waxer...Annie and Kelli...Bernard House...Paul Amsterdam biking across America...Bikecentennial...Cal and raccoons and cell phones...being assaulted at Unicorn...my mom, who didn't love me...being called a bum over and over...Jimmy Carter...President Kennedy...Dan Luca from the Seneca Tribe...Mack and Ruby and all their dogs...Isabel Krol from Poland...Paulo and Michael and Muriel and Tony and Pedro and name after name of friends who've abandoned me... Robert in Vietnam...the boy in the box...and Bobby Sox...and Bobby Sox, and my Bobby Sox . . .

. . . And . . . "Who are you? Where in hell am I? Why am I tied down? What's wrong with my arm? Damn, it hurts!"

"Mr. Pirelli, are you with us?"

"What do you mean? Of course I'm with you—whoever you are!"

"I'm Reverend Grace, Shelly Grace, from Buffalo United Church of Christ. I happened to stop by this ward, and was told that you were a general Protestant; however, the nurse on duty—Kathy, I think—said you have been delirious for two days. Somebody has to stay by your side. She needed to use the restroom. I offered to be here, and told her to feel free to take a break. I'm not sure of the rules, but I can call someone immediately if you would prefer."

"I'm in Hell, right?"

Shelly laughed her reply, "Well, right now you look like hell, and probably feel like hell, but let me assure you, this the tenth floor of the VA Hospital, not Hell, and not yet high enough for Heaven. Do you know what happened to your arm?"

I couldn't help but smile as I replied, "Not a clue...Reverend Grace, is it? Tenth floor, that's the Psych Ward, the nut house. I *am* in hell, and I need a cigarette!"

"It's okay to call me Shelly, or Pastor Shelly, or just Grace if you like. Are you sure you didn't attempt suicide? It certainly looks that way. By the way, who is Bobby Sox? You kept calling out to him or her or it. Was he your dog? By the way, there is no smoking in here."

"Oh, it hurts so much to laugh, but it sure hurts in a kind-of-good-way. Have I been crying? I feel like I've been crying a lot. And no, Bobby Sox is *not* a dog, but someone from my past. He sure was cute as a pup, though."

"Do you have a church, Mr. Pirelli? If not, may I leave one of my business cards with you?"

"Yeah, I know church is a business. I can't imagine you wanting mine, and please call me Vinny, Pastor Grace. I'm *gay*, you know; from what I recall, churches hate us faggots."

"Please don't call yourself that. I didn't know you were gay, but I assure you, we are an open and accepting place of worship, and not just in name. We actually are."

I started crying again, "But why do you care? Nobody loves me. I'm old and worthless. I have very little money, and a partner that would prefer seeing me dead."

"Vinny, God loves you. I promise you that. So do I, and we're only getting acquainted. You have so much to give yet. I bet you have a lot of people who love and care about you. I'm certain you'll find a lot of love in our church, but you have to get well before we can prove it. Will you do that? Will you get well for yourself? Please?"

"Yes Madam, I will." Before I could continue, the nurse came in.

"Kathy, look who's come to life!"

"Mr. Pirelli! It's nice to have you back, sir. I'll let the doctor know you're awake."

~

As it was reported to me, the little fucker doing my soon-to-be-ex boyfriend tripped over my bloody mess heading to his car. They said I had gotten drunk and slit my left wrist before passing out. I was touched by all that Grace imparted in her few minutes with me. "Oh, God, I want to live. I mean, really live! Please help me out."

I convinced the medical staff that it was a setup, that though I had been drunk from being hurt; I only passed out, not being accustomed to drinking. Though I couldn't prove it, I believed that *bastard* staged a suicide attempt, probably hoping I'd die. That was my story, and I was sticking to it! What were they going to do? I'd already been held the required seventy-two hours; they had to release me without further indication that I might harm myself again. That part was certainly true—never again!

~

After attending church service on Palm Sunday at Buffalo United Church of Christ, I was invited to gather with members in the fellowship hall for coffee and donuts. I was slurping down a lemon-filled version, dusting my hands, face and shirt in powdered sugar, when Pastor Grace appeared, tugging at my sleeve. "Vinny, let me introduce you to some of our members," she said by way of greeting, and with that, Shelly handed me a picture-directory, "here, this will help you match faces to names later, but let's get going. There are people here who will love you to pieces."

One by one, I was introduced to seniors and children, couples and singles, even some folks who made no bones about being gay. It was a great feeling to perhaps have a friendly and safe place to share my faith and prayers. And oh, the music! What great voices they have in that wonderful church. On my way out, one last fellow stopped to introduce himself. He seemed to talk a lot, and he threw around the *effing* word easily, way too easily, it seemed; it's not something one should do in a solemn environment.

"Hi, I'm Bob. Did I hear someone call you Vinny? Don't worry about knowing all these people; I don't, and I've been coming here for a year. But you'll love this effing place, I swear."

"Yes, you do swear! You sure have a mouth on you. You remind me of someone back in my Army days, a long time ago. Funny thing, his name was Bob, too, but I called him Bobby Sox. Man, he was even about your size."

With that, his jaw dropped open. I could have caught a baseball in it...like I could catch a baseball! He also seemed to turn a bit pale. "Oh, I'm sorry, did I say something wrong? Maybe you should reconsider your effing language, just a thought."

"Sergeant Pirelli? Is that you, Viper? I'm Bob Soloux, *Bobby Sox*, don't you recognize me? What the heck are you doing here? Where are Lek and the kids?"

"Oh my God, Sox boy, how are you, guy? Man, you got old, but I still recognize your big mouth! What a sight for sore eyes! I missed you so much. You left without saying goodbye, you *asshole*!"

"*Me* an asshole? You went around telling everyone we were having an affair, didn't you, ya jerk? And if you think *I'm* old, look in the mirror, pops!"

"No, I'd never say that, but I heard the same rumors. Listen, it was what it was, and I loved you like a brother. No, that's not true." Now I hesitated a bit, but went on, "I was in love with you, but never told anyone—not even you. So, *you're* the asshole! But I can't believe you're here—in church, none the less. You whined like a brat every Sunday morning when I'd make you go with me and the kids to church."

"Yeah, I know, but over the years, every time I'd think about our friendship and time together, I'd find my way to a chapel on base, wishing your effing ass was sitting next to me. I really missed you, Viper. They asked me to be a Deacon here; can you effing believe that? Are you still preaching your Archism thing? It was pretty cool, but I don't think it's in the Bible...Did you say you loved me? Wow, nice time to find out!"

"I'm guilty of love, and you're still guilty of chatting like there is no tomorrow."

"So, I was right, you *are* gay," then he started singing, "Sergeant P. is a queer."

"Yeah, I'm gay, and Lek divorced me a long time ago. The kids are all grown and married now. Gee, I've got eight grandkids already."

"Told ya you were old; what the hay man. And if you're wondering, I'm gay, too!"

Now I mocked him with, "NO, you're *kidding* me! I thought all those nights were nothing more than, hmm, dreams! Well anyway, great to see you man, what you been up to?"

"I retired after twenty-three years, and I'm getting little more than half-pay for that. But, I am halfway through nursing school, can you believe it? I went from cyber communications repair to sticking people in the ass! What about you, Viper?"

Now almost rolling with laughter, I told him, "I'm sort of retired, but I've had a very full life." I whispered to him, "And yes, I believe you like sticking people in the ass, you little twerp."

"Yeah, bet *you'd* like that you—" I cut him off short.

"We've got to stop this—we're in church, Sox. Why did you settle here in Buffalo, anyway?"

"Well, technically, we're in the fellowship hall, but I need a cigarette, so let's get outta here. Wanna go for coffee somewhere?" As we walked outside, he continued, "I guess you only knew that I was an Army brat. Dad was an Army lifer, originally from the Seneca Nation in Lewiston. He met my mom during WWII—you know a war bride. They had me kind of late in life. I thought you knew that, but at your age, you're allowed to forget."

While we shared smokes, I responded, "So, *that's* why you were always late for my formations, you little turd. But why nursing?"

"I don't know; it just hit me as something I wanted to do. Why, do you need a nurse? I'm getting VA education benefits at the U.B. South Campus, and I'll probably get some. . ." he stopped to make a sexual grunting noise, ". . . *hands-on* training at the VA hospital across the street. Who knows, maybe they'll even offer me a job."

"No way, that's where I get my medical care. They're a great bunch of people there; the only job you'll get is—oh, never mind." After a laugh I continued, "Honestly, you'll *never* find a better place to work."

"Now, you're setting me up. You always do this, Viper. Whether I agree with you or not, I'm screwed; am I right *Sergeant* Pirelli?"

"I don't have a car, but yeah—on getting some coffee, that is. Ever been to that place on Elmwood, The Grind? My friend Joe usually stops by there in the afternoon. Wanna go? I was headed there anyway—you can save me a bus ride. I have a cassette I wanted to give him. And, we've got to quit smoking, you know that? You're going to be a nurse—go figure!"

"Is he your partner or something? Come on, you can tell me some of your bullshit on the way; really, I wanna know *everything*."

"You wouldn't know bullshit if it were served in the mess hall, and NO, Joe's just a good friend—one with more grace than you will ever have, Sox. Let's go; I'll tell you my life if you do the same, but I doubt you'll believe me. What about you, somebody special in your life?"

"Nobody; you know it was 'Don't Ask, Don't Tell,' and *hands off*—one of the biggest reasons I wanted out. I've fooled around some since getting home, but not much. Why, are you interested? You know I kind of had the hots for you, too. We were buds, kind of love buds, eh? Start talking, I wanna know all the dirty details."

"Well Bobby, let's just say my life's been . . .

   . . . **A**n
      Impossible
      Dream
      Story . . .

 . . . So yes, I'm looking for a nurse. I also still like biking; we should plan a trip, but I need a new bike. Will ya marry me? We can *do it* in Canada! We can get *married* there, too! You know, gay marriage just became legal in Ontario this month, and it's recognized here in New York."

"You keep talking; I'll drive, and let's start with a cup of coffee, okay? Geez, Viper, you haven't changed an effing bit; you want everything done NOW! Well, you haven't changed much, except for being older...and fatter...and bald...and—"

"Down boy! That's enough, you twerp, I still have a bigger—", and he cut me off.

"*Mouth*, so up yours, Pirelli." Then, Bobby started wrestling on our way to his car, jumping onto my back with a bear hug and deliberately brushing his head against mine. God, it felt good. I couldn't remember when a touch felt better.

"Nice wheels, freckle face." I complimented him. As we crawled into his shiny, new black Mustang, I continued, with a double tongue-click, "Nice ass, too; and I like how your nose wiggles—reminds me of rabbits. Hey, what's up doc? Ha, ha, I mean, what's up nurse?"

~

I prayed that night, "God, United Church of Christ likes to say, '*God is still speaking*,' but who would have guessed you'd answer me, especially after I gave up on you...on us? I guess Reverend Grace was right; oh, what grace you have shown unto me. Thanks for letting me live—I mean, really live! And thanks for giving back Bobby Sox, that little twerp with a big mouth. I'm so happy; I'm so in love. Amen."

An Innocent Boy
(1994)

An innocent boy in the hands of men
Submitting from his deepest fears
Beyond all hell, he knew not then
His chains, his pains, his body used
Would leave him more than past abused
But scared and scarred all his years

A constant struggle to be free
With will to live, but wish to die
While searching for lost dignity
This boy of faith raped of his trust
His zest for life had turned to lust
Both living his truth and living a lie

Then finding in the midst of war
A shred of hope, a buddy and friend
Someone to trust like none before
Should give this boy a chance to live
By giving all he had to give
Some love, a cap, his bitter end

This gift of life, his guilt, his pain
His hope, his dream, his drive within
This friend shall not have died in vain
He aimed to learn; then learned to teach
Rising far beyond his reach
Just bury the pain, and strive to win

And win he shall at any cost
His family, friends, his home and all
Because nothing ventured is nothing lost
So winning became a game to destroy
The man emerging from this boy
No trust, no love, only freedom to fall

And fall he does before he dies
Into the grave within his chest
Tormented by unrelenting lies
Cries boy in man, from dust to dirt
From sex and games to lovers hurt
Now feels the pain to gain his rest

With courage new, the boy inside
Submits his trust to God above
While facing AIDS, and pain, and pride
Trying now to share the truth
His rise and fall stemmed from his youth
An innocent boy to man of love

A Personal Thanksgiving
(1994)

Each morn I wake in search of what
Thou have given me with care
That I might know within my gut
Belong to you, though mine to share

A place to rest and be secure
A healthy meal to keep me strong
That I might work and long endure
All of these to Thee belong

A friend to hold, a place to pray
Family near and far to love
Faith that I might never stray
From giving thanks to Thee above

My God, I long to give you more
Than simple thanks for all my stead
You only ask that I adore
And trust in Thee with heart and head

And this I do, though flawed at times
A humble soul enriched by Thee
I pray that I might learn to share
All that Thou has given me

So, as I lay to rest these eyes
I know your hand had guided me
And guarded me, that I might rise
Its life, this life which came from Thee

In Our Quiet Time
(Melody & Lyrics: 2010)

V.1 Dear Lord, when I was captive
You heard me call
Dear Lord, when I prayed for strength
You stood me tall
When I begged for water on barren soil
The rain would fall
What is believed can be achieved
By asking all
In our quiet time
In our quiet time

Chorus In our quiet time when I would pray
You heard every word I had to say
In an empty space, my God and me
When no one saw my bended knee
I knew my God would find a way
To give me hope and help today
Nothing seems too great a task
No miracle too big to ask
In our quiet time
In our quiet time

V.2 Dear Lord, when I was hurt
You heard me cry
When I asked for help to keep going
You made me try
When I was dying, I prayed to live
And didn't die
No life's demand is too grand
For You and I
In our quiet time
In our quiet time

Repeat Chorus

Repeat In our quiet time
In our quiet time

Appreciations

Though I've been putting pen to paper in some fashion or other since age twelve, this is my first attempt at authoring a book. *Writing* is something I'm good at; *writing well* isn't! Listening to my critics is normally something I deplore; listening to the honest critique of the initial manuscript by genuine friends was welcomed. The end-product is vastly improved thanks to their input. I attribute any success of *An Impossible Dream Story* to my mentors in various parts of the country and one international benefactor.

Indiana:
Mr. Norman (Tribute)—my high school English and drama teacher; thank for you planting the seed of writing by once telling me, "James, I fully expect to be reading a book or play that you will have written someday."
Max and Robyn Westler—you inspire me with your love, goodness, justice and compassion, but mostly with your support, no matter what it is I attempt. Thank you for encouraging this book since 1995. You epitomize friendship—I love you dearly.

Washington:
Donn Dale—thanks for helping me fix some atrocious spelling, for attesting to my character's accounts of Vietnam as being believable, and for marketing cautions. I added the *R* rating to one of my chapters, and friend, I will not market this to minors!

Massachusetts:
Joey Yau—you are the only friend listed here that I haven't actually met in person. You supported our work in Kenya and encouraged the first manuscript. Because of you, I further developed some story lines pertaining to the

lead character's Army career. Thank you and I hope we meet on a joint venture or adventure soon.

New York:

Jennifer Michels—my cycling buddy; thank you for your generous on-the-road bicycling expressions. They helped open my mind to developing artistic expressions of my own; you are brilliant and insightful. That you think my work could reach some teens needing this message of hope was not taken lightly, considering your longtime volunteer work with adolescents in a church setting. I admire you so much.

Bob Hunter—you are a consummate professional and a friend. Your suggestion that my work had potential, but "was not the best written," was both an understatement and an incentive to me to rethink my vocabulary. Thank you for being gut honest. You've helped this project much more than you realize.

Betty Cloen—never could I have imagined that you were editing the manuscript, not just reading it. Friend, I've adopted most of your dozens of word and punctuation corrections—thank you for making me a better writer. I sincerely appreciate you!

Jim Mack—friend, I'll forever "remember" what you did for this body of work in one short email, but more than that, for giving a homeless guy a chance to start over.

Joseph Lolla—you make me laugh more than anyone else ever could! Thanks for believing in me from the start, and thanks for being my big brother!

Lorena Garmezy and *Kathy Schaefer*—ladies, I've learned that you two often clash on viewpoints of books discussed in book club. You each provided me in-depth storyline feedback and ideas to try. For sure, some of what Lorena liked most, Kathy liked least, and vice versa. Both of you encouraged me to take the time to make it better. I listened, and believe that each of you had quality input worth adopting. Because of you two, the bicycle journey was de-journalized and shortened, dialogue throughout was enhanced, storylines were further developed and a new ending chapter ("Grace") was added. I could never thank you enough for your time and guidance. I appreciate the friendship and encouragement you always show to me and others. Thanks, Lorena, for the now woven spiritual thread we discussed. Thanks, Kathy for labeling me the *Semi-colon King*; it brought a smile to my face.

Feng Shi—Perhaps you were the most significant of all in making this book happen. Your everyday love, encouragement and kicks in the ass made a difference, both in getting this book done and loving me more than any person in this world could. Thank you for not giving up on me, and for sharing a life with our pups.

Beijing, China:
LI Xuenan—you've achieved great success, but while still searching out your own dream possibilities, you did not refrain from giving me a myriad of support to meet this next dream of mine—to witness the publication of *An Impossible Dream Story*. I love you dear friend, and I hope your dreams will all come true.

To all of you—if I had one final wish beyond getting this published and marketed on the first bicycle book tour, it would be for each of you to meet the others. You'd know for sure how lucky I am to have such quality friends; I love you all. If there is a Heaven, I will see you angels there. Until then, thank you for bringing some Heaven to my life over the years.

Partnerships:
An Impossible Dream Story highlights the 1995 USAIDS 5,000 bicycle journey. It was made possible by hundreds of generous individuals and a few major corporate sponsors. You all Rock!

Appendix: Lyrics and Poems

About the Author

J.V. Petretta is a graduate of the University of Maryland, European Division. He is a ten-year U.S. Army Veteran with three overseas tours, including Vietnam. After his honorable discharge, he received a Meritorious Service Medal for distinguished service as 1st Armored Division's Nuclear Control Chief. In addition to earning numerous business accolades, he organized and conducted a 5,000-mile bicycle tour in 1995, bringing critical awareness and funding for AIDS.

"Throughout my life, I took pride in being a sucker for every worthy cause that crossed my path. Moreover, I was deeply moved by the AIDS Pandemic of the 1990s, having lost both employees and friends to the disease. I have also been troubled of late with reports of so many of our children giving up on life as the result of bullying and abuse. Some of them were gay, making their own paths even more difficult. Until there is a cure for AIDS, until our children are at peace, until my country recognizes that human rights must start at home by embracing the dignity and equal rights of all Americans, I will remain an activist.

You may be wondering, 'how much of this book is based on the author's own life?' This much is true: I am a native Hoosier who planted roots in western New York many years ago. I have had some military experience, and I have endured more than my fair share of restaurant work over the years. I am indeed happily married, but to my longtime sweetheart, a native of People's Republic of China, and I have a special passion for my children, grandchildren, bicycles and puppy dogs. USAIDS 5,000 was a bicycle journey I dreamed up; orchestrated and accomplished (however, real events differ from those of this book). The actual statistics (including routes and benefactors) are quite lengthy and will be made available during the An Impossible Dream Story (Bicycle-Book Tour). (That part is also true, at least in my dreams.) Plans are underway to organize 25 independent cycling tours of 100 miles, each in (or around) a different city, to promote biking in that market, as well as the book, of course. (Bike and Book Club organizers: feel free to contact me directly if you are interested in helping with this project.)

Being a Veteran, I hold great appreciation for our men and women serving and sacrificing in the U.S. Armed Forces. Being a Lymphoma survivor, I do have inti-

mate knowledge of the VA Healthcare System of Buffalo, and I am eternally grateful to the dedicated men and women serving our Veterans.

In recent years, I've been blessed with travels to Kenya to visit and support (in a small way) the Makarios Children's Home (an orphanage and primary school at the base of Mount Kenya, founded by my sister Cheryl Karanja, for children afflicted with and/or affected by HIV). I fell in love with and help support a pair of orphaned brothers, one with, the other without HIV. Cheryl's latest project, New Day Children's Rescue, took me to Nakuru."

Author's proceeds from the sale of this book will be divided among selected cycling and LGBT advocate groups, and his own future work in Africa. Contact: archismo1@yahoo.com

CPSIA information can be obtained at www.ICGtesting.com
Printed in the USA
LVOW122325021111

253274LV00001B/10/P